My Daily Eucharist II

Compiled & Edited by

Joan Carter McHugh
Lake Forest, Illinois

Nihil Obstat
   James P. Campbell, D.MIN.
   Censor Deputatus
   June 20, 1997

Imprimatur
   Most Reverend Raymond E. Goedert, MA, STL, JCL
   Vicar General
   Archdiocese of Chicago
   July 11, 1997

The *Nihil Obstat* and *Imprimatur* are official declarations that a book is free of doctrinal and moral error. No implication is contained therein that those who have granted the *Nihil Obstat* and *Imprimatur* agree with the content, opinions, or statements expressed.

Publisher:
   Witness Ministries
   825 S. Waukegan Rd., A8-200
   Lake Forest, IL 60045

   Phone: 847-735-0556 • 800-484-5350, ext. 5255
   Fax: 847-735-0911
   Email: WitnessM@aol.com

Dedication

My Daily Eucharist II is lovingly dedicated to Pope John Paul II in thanksgiving for his teaching, by word and example, the meaning of the Eucharist as Presence, Sacrifice and Communion.

"The priest has a mysterious, awesome power over the Eucharistic Body of Christ. By reason of this power he becomes the steward of the greatest treasure of the Redemption, for he gives people the Redeemer in person. Celebrating the Eucharist is the most sublime and most sacred function of every priest. As for me, from the very first years of my priesthood, the celebration of the Eucharist has been not only my most sacred duty, but above all my soul's deepest need."

Pope John Paul II
Gift and Mystery:
On the Fiftieth Anniversary of My Priestly Ordination

Foreword

I can think of no better way to introduce the prospective reader to the spirit of Joan McHugh's *My Daily Eucharist II* than to tender the gift of the lovely line from one of the Holy Thursday sermons of St. Thomas Aquinas: "*Here, Lord Jesus, you are both Shepherd and Green Pasture.*" Brevity is best whenever we try to limn the inexpressible mystery of the Eucharist and, in a very real sense, these words of Thomas "say it all." In the Eucharist Jesus is indeed both Shepherd and Green Pasture.

You who are privileged to "take and read" from the spiritual cornucopia you hold in your hands will immediately recognize the reference to the twenty-third Psalm:

> The Lord is my shepherd; I shall not want.
> In verdant pastures he gives me repose.
> . . . .
> You spread the table before me . . .
>   my cup overflows.

At every Eucharist we are guests at the banquet table of the Lord. The Lord is the host (portrayed under the figure of the solicitous shepherd) who not only provides the feast, but *is* the Feast! "Here, Lord Jesus, you are both Shepherd and Green Pasture."

And we? We are "the people of his pasture, the flock he tends" (Ps 95:7).

> Jesu! Shepherd of the sheep!
> Thou Thy flock in safety keep.
> Living Bread! Thy life supply;
> Strengthen us, or else we die . . .

The reader will find rich food for thought in this *vade mecum* so carefully collected and prepared. With this little book the table has been set, a feast is laid before you. Come then to the banquet all you who hunger for the Living Bread!

Most Reverend James S. Sullivan
Bishop of Fargo

Author's Preface

Our Holy Father, Pope John Paul II, describes the life of faith as the road all must take on their journey to God. He said that "the awesome mystery of the Eucharist introduces us to the plan of God, Creator and Redeemer. He has given us the Eucharist in order to nourish and sustain us on our arduous journey toward eternal life."

How privileged we are who have been gifted with faith that gives us the desire to make the journey! And I do believe that our faith and hunger for God is His gift to us, His call to us to respond to His love for us. Our loving Father God gave us Jesus to accompany us on the journey of faith. He walked the walk in order to show us the way to the Father. *He is the way to the Father!*

After Jesus multiplied the loaves and fishes, people followed Him because they saw Him as a wonder-worker who could fill their hunger. He told them that they should not be working for perishable food, but for the eternal food that He would give them—Himself in the Holy Eucharist. Over and over He repeated His message—that He is the Living Bread come down from heaven, He is the One sent to nourish the people on the journey. "He who feeds on My flesh and drinks My blood has life eternal. . . ." (Jn 6:54) His statement, "My flesh is real food, My blood is real drink, " caused quite a controversy. "Does it shake your faith?" Jesus asked the crowd beginning to disperse. Despite their hunger and need, many walked away because His saying required too much faith.

His teaching on His Real Presence in the Eucharist divided the Christian community then as it does now. There is widespread confusion today over this central teaching of the Catholic Church—that during the Mass the bread and wine become the Body and Blood of Christ. A recent survey of eight parishes in the Rochester, New York, diocese in which parishioners filled out evaluation forms that included a question on the Real Presence of Christ in the Eucharist, resulted in very disturbing findings: 60 to 65 percent of the people indicated they did not believe in the Real Presence. (Those results were consistent from parish to parish and between age groups). Those results parallel that of a poll conducted by the *New York Times*/CBS News in April 1994. Of Catholics surveyed, 34 percent said they believe the bread and wine become the Body and Blood of Christ, while 63 percent said they are just symbolic reminders of Jesus.

I think the people of today are similar to the people of first century Palestine. Many Catholics do not go to church, let alone understand the meaning and value of the Mass and the Eucharist. Perhaps they, too, don't want the demands that faith will place on them. So often people want Jesus to fill their hunger, but they don't want to acknowledge Him as their food. They want to experience the joy of His kingdom without facing their own darkness. Sin and the need for forgiveness produce fear and guilt, many say, which serves no purpose. They want new life without laying down their old life at the foot of the Cross. Sacrifice isn't necessary, certain Scripture scholars say, because Christ brings us new life through His resurrection, not through His death. Modernists want to celebrate Easter without experiencing Good Friday.

"There is nothing in all of Scripture which stands on stronger ground than the Real Presence of Christ in the Eucharist," Bishop James Timlin of Scranton, Pennsylvania, said recently at a Eucharistic conference. "Why," he asked the participants, "have our people lost sight of the great gift they have in the Eucharist?" and "What can we do to help our people understand this great gift?"

I believe the answers to the first question are many and complex, extending back to the time of Christ. The answer to the latter question, Bishop Timlin said, is to "teach by example." In a letter to his priests, he writes that we need an habitual, ongoing effort to bring back to our churches a manner of acting befitting sacred places. He wants to build reverence back into our worship—reverence owed the Real Presence of Christ in the Most Blessed Sacrament.

It seems to me that we share the burden of response to Bishop Timlin's questions. We must not only "talk the talk" but we must also "walk the walk" by living and loving in such a way that our separated brothers and sisters will be drawn to the love of Christ in us—and so come to believe in His Real Presence. The more we become like Jesus, the better able we will be to sacrifice ourselves to bring Jesus' risen presence to others. May each person and story in this book lead you to a place of deeper awareness and trust in the transforming power of Christ's love for you in the Mass and the Eucharist.

"All the answers are in the tabernacle," God the Father said to Australian visionary Matthew Kelly. Although Jesus died for us two thousand years ago, we, in the twentieth century, have the awesome privilege of standing at the foot of the Cross at Mass with Mary, our Mother, where we can unite our lives, our loved ones and all of our intentions with Christ's suffering and death, pleading with Him to transform us into His glory. "We adore You, Oh Christ, and we praise You, because by Your holy Cross, You have redeemed the world." Calvary is the reservoir of all the graces and blessings and mercies that God has destined for all people. The Mass and the Eucharist is the channel through which those graces flow upon this, our age.

Joan Carter McHugh
Lake Forest, Illinois
September 1997

Acknowledgements

Where would I be without the friends and angels God sends at just the right times to share the workload for this labor of love?

My husband, Tom McHugh, walks with me through every step of production, supporting me spiritually and emotionally, assuring perfection in every way. Judy Kozak types and types and types; her enjoyment of the entries encourages me and confirms the selections.

The Conventual Franciscan Friars of Marytown in Libertyville, Illinois, have been like a support team, with guardian Fr. Pat Greenough, OFM CONV., in the lead, putting Marytown's resources at my disposal. Also, I have been blessed with the help of Daniel Gallio, editor of *Immaculata* magazine, who proofread, edited the copy, did the layout and polished the pages with TLC; Peter Ptak put his heart and soul (and his computer expertise) into the design and color graphics for the cover; Michael Wick offered insights, ideas and practical suggestions just when I needed them. Fr. Howard Ralenkotter, CP, whom I had never met, phoned one day when I was in the doldrums and affirmed the need for this book with great enthusiasm. He has been a Passionist priest for fifty-nine years and his continued support energizes me. Fr. Bob DeGrandis, SSJ, is the number one supportive angel for this book and for our apostolate.

To each of you, thank you for your help and your love of Our Lord in the Blessed Sacrament. May He reward you a hundredfold for your commitment and dedication to His Real Presence.

I recall the words from a hymn that in Poland often accompanies Eucharistic adoration and processions. I repeat them because they contain the truth that, together with praising Christ present in the mystery of the Eucharist, almost of necessity we recall the memory of the Mother of God.

It is thanks to her generous *fiat* that the Word of God was made flesh by the work of the Holy Spirit. She offered her own body to the Word so that He might take it upon himself and the miracle of the divine Incarnation would be accomplished. In her virginal womb Mary bore the incarnate Word, awaiting *with love beyond all telling* the birth of the Savior. . . .

Every Holy Mass makes present in an unbloody manner the unique and perfect sacrifice, offered by Christ on the tree of the cross, in which Mary participated, joined in spirit with her suffering Son, lovingly consenting to His sacrifice and offering her own sorrow to the Father (c.f. *Lumen Gentium*, no. 58).

Therefore, when we celebrate the Eucharist, the memorial of Christ's passover, the memory of His Mother's suffering is also made alive and present, this Mother, who, as an unsurpassable model, teaches the faithful to unite themselves more intimately to the sacrifice of her Son, the one Redeemer.

Through spiritual communion with the sorrowful Mother of God, believers share in a special way in the paschal mystery and are opened to this extraordinary action of the Holy Spirit that produces a supernatural joy because of communion with the glorious Christ, on the example of the joy granted to Mary in the glory of heaven, as the first person to share in the fruits of redemption.

Pope John Paul II
To the 19th International Marian Congress, August 15, 1996

If we love the Blessed Sacrament, and if we delight to spend our time in adoration of this tremendous mystery of love, we cannot help finding out more and more about the charity of Christ. We cannot help gaining an intimate and personal knowledge of Jesus Who is hidden under the sacramental veils. But in proportion as we grow in knowledge and love for Him, we will necessarily grow in the knowledge of His will for us. We will come to understand more and more how seriously He means us to take His "new commandment" that we love one another as He has loved us.

Indeed, if we fail to take this commandment seriously and if we find our devotional life concentrated upon a selfish desire for pious feelings that enclose us within ourselves and narrow our hearts, making us insensible to others or even contemptuous of them, we can be sure that our devotion is an illusion. We do not know Christ because we do not keep His word. For he only manifests Himself to those who do His will. And He wills to come to us in this Sacrament of His love not only in order to console us as individuals, but in order that we may give Him our hearts and let Him dwell in them, that through us He may love our brothers and sisters with our own love.

Thomas Merton
The Living Bread

Coming to this earth, Christ brought us the knowledge of God. Becoming food for each one of us, Christ carries into us the revelation of the things of Heaven.

Feeding upon Christ, I enter the "Invisible," I enter Heaven, I begin an immense process of development within myself, I receive the knowledge of God which must lead me to the maturity of "sonship."

The Eucharist brings me knowledge of God: feeding upon Christ as food of eternal life makes me become co-heir with Him, like Him, as intimate with the Father as He is. Naturally for this to happen fully, we must reply to the Eucharist. This reply is prayer, which is the dynamics of living faith. He comes to us, but we must go to Him; He comes to us in food, but we must make a gift of ourselves.

The Eucharist is dead without prayer, just as faith is dead without works.

You cannot make love by yourself. Love by yourself remains sterile and empty: it has no reply to welcome and to fertilize it. We cannot listen to God's "yes" without offering Him our "yes." God's "yes" is the sacrament of the Eucharist; our "yes" is prayer.

Carlo Caretto
The God Who Comes

Feast of St. Elizabeth Ann Seton
1774-1821

Yet we can only realize it by His conviction. That He is there—oh, heavenly theme!—is as entirely true as that bread naturally taken removes my hunger, so this Bread of Angels removes my pain, my cares; warms, cheers, soothes, contents, and renews my whole being. Merciful God, and I do possess You! Kindest, tenderest, dearest friend, every affection of my nature absorbed in You, still is active, nay, perfected in its operations through Your refining love. Hush, my soul, we cannot speak it. Tongues of angels could not express our treasure of peace and contentment in Him. Let us always whisper His name of love as an antidote to all the discord that surrounds us. We cannot say the rest. The harmony of heaven begins for us, while, silent from all the world, we again and again repeat, "Jesus, Jesus, Jesus!" And how many say the adored name, looking beyond Him: while looking for Him, they deny Him on His altar.

Fr. Charles I. White
Mother Seton: Mother of Many Daughters

Feast of St. John Neumann
1811-1860

On his visitations he carried along a portable altar to be ready to say Mass in their homes and gladden them with the blessings of the sacrament. Not every place he visited was a parish with a church. For groups like this he selected a residence and named someone to gather the people, read the Gospel and other spiritual readings and recite the Rosary. It was a taxing and exhausting schedule.

The Eucharistic fast was different in those days. Often it was one o'clock before he had breakfast. Despite the rigors of the work, Neumann loved these visits. He felt at home with the poor and the simple country people. Kenrick could well tell Rome that "he travels throughout the diocese like a shining light and with indefatigable labor promotes the piety of the people.". . .

In 1853 Neumann began the Forty Hours Devotion on the feast of Corpus Christi in the Church of St. Philip Neri. The Forty Hours Devotion was known three centuries before Neumann's time. It had been held occasionally in Philadelphia before 1853. What Neumann did was to inaugurate it on a diocesan level. A schedule was made calling for the devotion to be held in designated churches so as to cover the entire year. Neumann gave great edification by the way he joined in these devotions whenever possible. To Neumann the Forty Hours was not merely the pious practice of making visits. To him it was the way of seeing that Catholic life in Philadelphia was rooted in the Eucharist.

Alfred C. Rush, CSSR, Trans.
The Autobiography of St. John Neumann, CSSR

After Communion, my soul was filled with such peace that I could not help saying: "O Jesus, I know Thou are here; I am certain of it . . ." Before I had finished whispering the words, He stood before me. His hands were extended, His face expressed the most loving tenderness, His Heart was escaping from His breast, and His whole Person shone with resplendent light. It was as if a fire were burning within Him.

"Yes, Josefa, I am here. . . ."

I was beside myself . . . But regained sufficient hold on myself to beg His pardon, and to bewail my failings, miseries, and fears.

"If you are an abyss of miseries, I am an abyss of mercy and goodness."

Then, stretching out His arms towards me, He said: "My Heart is your refuge."

Sr. Josefa Menendez
The Way of Divine Love

"The Mass is ended, go in peace." The significance of these familiar words is often missed. They are not simply a signal that it is time to leave church and go home. They include a statement and a *command*. The dismissal rite sends us forth from the Liturgy to continue Christ's mission in the world. The formula indicates a transition from worship and contemplation of the sacred mysteries to *acting* on them. It echoes Jesus' last words to His disciples before His ascension: "Go, therefore, and make disciples of all nations . . ." (Mt 28:19).

In the Eucharist we are nourished and strengthened by the Word of God and Christ's Body and Blood. The Mass gives us the grace we need to live faithfully as His disciples. What we have witnessed in the Sacrifice of the Mass, we are to proclaim to others. . . . We share responsibility for carrying out the Church's mission—that is, Christ's mission—in the world. We meet this responsibility in many ways; for example, by treating everyone with due respect, telling the truth, living chaste lives. We also continue Christ's mission by feeding the hungry, caring for the sick and elderly, defending the rights of the most vulnerable—including the unborn, the dying, the chronically ill, the disabled. Most profoundly, we carry out Christ's mission by proclaiming Him as Lord of the living and the dead, and inviting others to become Eucharistic people.

In other words, when we are dismissed from Mass, we are mandated to carry Christ with us and make Him visible in our neighborhood, the marketplace, the public arena. What a privilege! What a responsibility! What a joy!

Archbishop Francis E. George, OMI
From his Letters

The origin of the word "Eucharist" is from two Greek words, *Eu Charis*. The direct translation is good gift. What an understatement! The Eucharist is the greatest gift that God has given to us. It is the good gift of thanksgiving. The gift of Christ Himself, which comes from God, Our Father, and it is ours for the taking. I cannot understand why our churches are not packed every time there is a Mass. Christ is there. The Eucharist is there. It is real to us if we allow it to be. Jesus is real to us if we allow Him to be.

Thousands of people travel the world over visiting apparition sites of Our Lady. They go to look at a statue of Jesus bleeding, or a statue of Our Lady weeping or exuding oil. People travel to Fatima, Lourdes, Guadalupe, Medjugorie, Scottsdale, and many other holy places hoping for a miracle. What they sometimes forget is that the holiest of all places is where the Lord is present in His Blessed Sacrament. The real miracle happens every day, on every altar, in every Catholic church. Each time Mass is celebrated Jesus Christ comes to us in the Eucharist. I question the spirituality of people who travel from apparition site to apparition site and never go to church for daily Mass. It is a disservice to Our Lady to seek her throughout the globe and to ignore her Son in the Eucharist, to ignore her requests to return to church. The Eucharist is the miracle of all miracles. Why travel around the world looking for apparitions when, on the altar the most glorious of all miracles happens, the Lord appears daily? We are so blessed to have this gift from God. Why our churches are not packed every day is a mystery to me.

Fr. Jack Spaulding
Hope for the Journey

L inda Callaghan reluctantly joined Paul, her husband, for Mass at Marytown on August 1, 1996. She felt the presence of Our Lord and Our Lady in a way she had not experienced since childhood. She made Paul bring her back the next day. And the next. Four days in a row she attended Mass at Marytown, and now she found herself unable to remain separated from the Eucharist.

On Saturday, August 4, 1996, Linda prayed, "Please hear me God. I'm so sorry for not having gone to confession. But I'm going to go up for Holy Communion anyway. Please forgive me. I want you so badly.". . . "I had such a burning desire that I was actually sweating. I had no thoughts except my desire for that Eucharist." Her eyes closed and her smile widened as she remembered the crucial event.

"And I inched to the end of the pew and headed up the aisle. I was near the altar as I realized that I had left my walker in the pew. And I was walking!"

Linda's body froze upon discovering what was happening. "I just stopped, feeling trapped. I can still see myself glancing back over my shoulder. I was looking back at the pew, thinking about whether or not to head back for my walker. But I had to trust God, and I just kept walking towards that priest and that Eucharist, which I received. And I haven't stopped walking since."

Carrie Swearingen
Immaculata, March/April 1997

The second ineffaceable memory is my morning at St. Peter's, the following Wednesday, April 22. I set out alone for St. Peter's, and after going to Confession to a French-speaking priest, I went to Communion in the chapel of the Blessed Sacrament. Those moments were completely and supernaturally happy.

I felt in myself the living presence of the blessed Christ, of God Himself, bringing me an ineffable love; this incomparable Soul spoke to mine, and all the infinite tenderness of the Savior passed for an instant into me. Never will this divine trace be effaced. The triumphant Christ, the eternal Word, He who as man has suffered and loved, the one living God, took possession of my soul for all eternity in that unforgettable moment. I felt myself renewed to my very depths by Him, ready for a new life, for duty, for the work intended by His Providence. I gave myself without reserve, and I gave Him the future.

I then heard Mass in another chapel in profound joy and peace. I prayed again, and then I knelt close to the Confession ["confession" here refers to a place in St. Peter's where the relics of the saint were venerated], in a last intimate and solemn consecration.

On my return I found myself in an atmosphere of irony, criticism, and indifference. But nothing mattered; the flame of Christ was still burning within me.

Elizabeth Leseur
My Spirit Rejoices

Our longing is to be true to ourselves, our deepest selves. To do this we must die, die to the false self with which we have so sadly and so strongly come to identify. The false self must die—with Christ on the Cross: that is the meaning of our participation in the Mass. Then the true inner self, the self animated by the renewing Spirit, can emerge with Christ from the tomb. This is the Paschal mystery that is at the heart of all that is Christian and truly human.

It is not enough to remain the same self, the same individual ego, taking on a new set of activities and a lot of religious practices, no matter how good. As Father Louis wrote in *New Seeds of Contemplation,* "The obstacle is in our 'self,' that is to say, in the tenacious need to maintain our separate, external egotistic will." We must be reborn of the Spirit who is free, and who reaches to the very depths of everything. He wants to reach to the inmost depths of our heart and take our heart to Himself by making Himself one with our heart, creating for us a new identify, by being Himself our identity. When we are completely freed from our old self by a true death to self in Christ, then we will be able to live totally in the spontaneity of the Spirit. And, no matter how we might seem to be to others, we will be fully integrated. It will be the final integration, that integration into complete oneness with God—and in Him with all others—in Christ Jesus our Lord.

M. Basil Pennington, OCSO
Thomas Merton, Brother Monk

It was as if I was standing beside Jesus and he let me look out over the city of Jerusalem. The city was filled with bishops and priests. Suddenly Jesus began to weep. He said to me, "Briege, these are the men I have chosen to shepherd My people, to feed My people, to encourage My people, to lead My people. They are losing faith in Me. They are seeking the wisdom of the world. They are denying My power and choosing earthly power." He revealed to me there would be a great crisis in the priesthood. Priests would lose faith in Jesus and fail to acknowledge His power working through them in holy orders.

I sensed God asking me to go into the world and remind bishops and priests with this word. "It is not humility to deny the power of the priesthood, but it is humility to acknowledge that I have chosen them. I have chosen them not because they are holy, not because they are better than others, but I've chosen them because of My mercy, love, and compassion for humanity. It is because of this mercy, love, and compassion, that I use them to make Myself present. But how I long to do it more effectively through them! Go out and tell them to believe in Me."

As I got up to leave the chapel, after nearly four hours, my attitude had changed. God, in the twentieth century, is still giving us the gift of priesthood.

My attitude changed toward the humanity of the priest. I became much more aware of the need to pray for priests, that they are truly men of faith.

Sr. Briege McKenna, osc
Miracles Do Happen

The rest of us received the Eucharstic Body and Blood of Christ, but in Julia's [Kim] mouth the Eucharistic species of the Host, the wafer, and the species of the wine in the chalice, changed to the species of flesh and blood. The rest of us savoured the taste of wafer and wine as we received Holy Communion. We knew with divine faith that these were the very Body and Blood of Christ in the Eucharist. We were joined to the living and glorified Christ, renewing His mystical and real oblation, offering Himself as the Divine Victim and His Mystical Body to the Father.

As Julia experienced the commingling of blood and flesh, the flesh expanding and moving in her mouth and the strong odor of blood, Father Finn observed the white of the Host disappearing and changing into the dark red of living flesh. Only later, as we examined the photos, did we begin to apprehend the full magnitude of the miracle. The Host had changed into a living and vibrant Heart. For the first time, human eyes saw the living Heart of Our Lord and Saviour, the Heart that had so loved the world that It offered Itself in holocaust that we might live and not be lost. All those present at this memorable evening shared the same sentiments. We were one in mind and heart.

It was two months later, in November, that I finally received and read the text of the message of Jesus to Julia during her communion. As I read this message from Our Lord during that time of communion, I became aware that the words of Jesus confirmed our conjecture. "My Mother is now showing and revealing My heart to a bishop. . . ." What we had viewed that September evening was the very Heart of Jesus.

Bishop Roman Danylak
Heart of the Harvest

"**M**y children, come before my Son, who is truly present in the Most Blessed Sacrament. There, before Him, in hours of adoration you will receive the graces needed to be true followers of Christ. There, before this Sacrament of Love, you will be refreshed and you will find peace amidst the confusion of your lives.

My children, I urge you to pray and to make hours of adoration and reparation before my Son, in the Most Holy Sacrament of the Altar. Come to Jesus, who wishes so much to transform your lives. Come, my little ones, before the Light of the World." (Words of Our Lady, January 14, 1994)

Michael McColgan
Open Your Hearts:
Messages from Our Lord Jesus and His Blessed Mother

I t is true that they did not in general celebrate the Eucharist daily—for technical reasons this was scarcely practicable—but the Eucharist could be taken home after the Sunday celebration. There is evidence of a widespread custom of receiving daily the holy bread, "before any other food." The practice was taken for granted to such an extent that the prayer for daily bread in the Our Father was understood, in the earliest patristic exegesis, to refer primarily to the bread of the Eucharist.

There was no precept of the Church imposing Sunday celebration. But participation seems to have been so general that, as Justin reports, all came together on Sunday, townspeople and country folk; deacons bore the Eucharist to those who were prevented from coming. Further, there was great reluctance to forego the Sunday liturgy when persecution broke out again and participation spelled mortal danger. For what caused the Christians to be persecuted and threatened with death was not their faith—anyone could believe what he liked—but their particular form of divine worship, so early on Sunday morning, and so independent of the official pagan cult. Persecution was directed against the form of worship. Yet the Christians held firmly to their Eucharistic meetings. And when we read in the *Acts of the Martyrs* the defense of those who were accused during the Diocletian persecution, it expresses the feeling of many others: without the *dominicum* we could not exist. One can perhaps say that the majority of the martyrs of that period died because they held fast to the Eucharist. (Josef A. Jungman, SJ)

Raymond A. Tartre, SSS
The Eucharist Today

"And so then, you must go before the tabernacle to gather the fruit of the prayer and of the communion of life with Jesus which develops and matures *into your holiness.* Beloved sons, the more your life revolves wholly and entirely at the foot of the tabernacle, in intimate union with Jesus in the Eucharist, the more you will increase in holiness. The Eucharistic Jesus becomes the model and the form of your holiness. He brings you to purity of heart, to humility which is sought and desired, to a lived-out confidence, to loving and filial abandonment.

The Eucharistic Jesus becomes the new form of your priestly holiness which you attain by means of a daily and hidden immolation, of a continual presence of love toward your brothers, of a capacity to welcome in your own person the sufferings and the crosses of all, of a possibility to transform evil into good and to act profoundly that souls, who have been entrusted to you, may be led by you to salvation.

For this reason I say to you: The times have come when I want you all before the tabernacle and above all I want you priests who are the beloved sons of a Mother who is ever in an act of perpetual adoration and of unceasing reparation. Through you, I desire that the cult of the Eucharist again flourish in all the Church in an ever more powerful way.

As for now there must be an end to this profound crisis in regard to devotion to the Eucharist, a crisis which has contaminated the entire Church and which has been at the root of so much infidelity and of the diffusion of such a widespread apostasy." (Words of Our Lady, August 21, 1987)

Fr. Stefano Gobbi
To the Priests: Our Lady's Beloved Sons

It is the noon hour. We come home exhausted, shattered. New vexations possibly await there. Now where is the soul's morning freshness? The soul would like to seethe and storm again: indignation, chagrin, regret. And there is still so much to do until evening. Should we not go immediately to it? No, not before calm sets in at least for a moment. Each one must know, or get to know, where and how she can find peace. The best way, when it is possible, is to shed all cares again for a short time before the tabernacle. Whoever cannot do that, whoever also possibly requires bodily rest, should take a breathing space in her own room. And when no outer rest whatever is attainable, when there is no place in which to retreat, if pressing duties prohibit a quiet hour, then at least she must for a moment seal off herself inwardly against all other things and take refuge in the Lord. He is indeed there and can give us in a single moment what we need.

Bl. Edith Stein
Essays on Women

"Go in peace to love and serve the Lord" has replaced the ending, "Go the Mass is ended," because the Mass and its healing continues as we bring Christ into our homes and community. Healing happens not just around an altar but in a community whenever people meet Christ's love in each other. In our workshops, participants' painful memories get healed not only through prayer and Eucharist but also through meeting a loving person who frequently resembles a parent, teacher, or someone who has hurt them. Just as we have power to hurt a person, making it difficult for him to love people like us, so too we have Christ's power to love unconditionally a wounded person and free him from fearing people who resemble us. If we hear, "I wish my friend had been more like you," our friendship has usually healed some wounds from the other friend.

But to continually heal wounded people in this way, we need help in laying down our lives as totally as Jesus did on the cross and continues to do in the Eucharist. For instance, if a family came to us without food, clothing or education, and needed a home, health care, and a job, could we meet all their needs? No matter what a person needs, we need a community because none of us alone has all the resources to care for someone as lovingly as Christ cares. As we in a loving community take care of each other's needs, we begin to heal our painful memories and live out the Eucharist.

Matthew Linn, SJ, and Dennis Linn
Healing Life's Hurts:
Healing Memories through the Five Stages of Forgiveness

"My beloved priest-companion, tell My people how I long for them to come to Me in the Eucharist. The Eucharist is the great Sacrament of My love for My people. So many are indifferent to My Eucharistic presence. So many have no real desire to receive Me in the Eucharist. So many have no desire to visit Me in the Blessed Sacrament. How I long for My people to come before the tabernacle and to talk with Me!

"I am offended, many times seriously, by all the outrages, sacrileges, and indifferences committed against My Eucharistic presence. I ask My people to make reparation for all this. I especially ask that they often say the prayer of Eucharistic reparation given by the angel to the three Fatima visionaries.

"I am Lord and Master. Please do as I request. My Eucharistic Heart is beating with unfathomable love for My people! Let them come to My Sacred Heart. How I long to take My people to My Heart and shower them with Its abundant graces! I love My people with a tremendous love, and I give them this message with the greatest love!" (Words of Our Lord)

Fr. Edward Carter, SJ
Tell My People: Messages from Jesus and Mary

This was the conviction for which Karl Leisner lived and for which he ultimately died. His whole life long he sought intimacy with Christ in prayer, in the daily reading of Scripture, and in meditation. And he ultimately found this intimacy in a special way in the Eucharistic encounter with the Lord. The Eucharistic sacrifice, which Karl Leisner was able to celebrate as a priest after his ordination in the concentration camp of Dachau, was for him not only an encounter with the Lord and source of strength for his life: Karl Leisner also knew that whoever lives with Christ shares the Lord's destiny.

Karl Leisner and Bernhard Lichtenberg are witnesses not of death, but of life: a life that extends beyond death. They are witnesses to Christ, who is the life, and who came so that we may have life and have it abundantly (cf. Jn 10:10). In a culture of death, they both bore witness to life.

Like the two blesseds, we are all called to bear witness to life. Therefore, hold fast to the life which is Christ. Resist the culture of hatred and death, regardless of the guise which it may assume. Do not grow tired of dedicating yourselves to those whose life and dignity is threatened: the unborn, the terminally ill, the elderly and the many needy people of our world. By their death Bernhard Lichtenberg and Karl Leisner made visible the life that is Christ, and which Christ gives. The Church will always honor them and their witness.

Pope John Paul II
Homily, June 23, 1996, for the beatification of two German priests, Karl Leisner and Bernhard Lichtenberg

The author of *The Imitation of Christ*, Thomas a Kempis . . . lived to the age of ninety-two. Of the sixty-three years he lived as a monk, fifty-eight of these were spent as an ordained priest. In his *Chronicle of Mount St. Agnes* he relates two miracles of the Holy Eucharist. Regarding the first of these he tells us:

"One of our brethren commenced to say Holy Mass at the altar of St. Agnes. For a long time he had been obliged to make use of two crutches in order to go there. After having said Mass he found himself, through the power of Jesus Christ and the intercession of St. Agnes, so much strengthened that he was enabled to leave his crutches behind, returning to us in choir with a joyful heart. One of the brethren asked him of what he had done and thought during Holy Mass; he replied, 'I considered the words of the Evangelist St. Luke, who himself relates of Jesus, "And all the people sought to touch Him, for there went virtue out of Him and he healed them all."' Therefore the Most Holy Sacrament, in union with the prayers of the saints, is able even now to heal the sick in soul and in body."

Joan Carroll Cruz
Eucharistic Miracles

"When I pronounced these words: 'Do this in memory of Me,' I was not addressing Myself only to priests. Of course, they alone have the power to change the substance of bread into My most holy Body and the substance of wine into My Blood. But the power to unite in one single oblation all oblations belongs to all Christians. It belongs to all Christians, members of one single Body, to become one with the Victim on the altar by faith and works, offering Me as Host in propriation to My eternal Father" (*Diary*, June 7, 1916).

This twofold participation in Christ's Priesthood constitutes the *structure of the Church of the Cross*, of the Church of Christ Priest and Victim.

"I cannot separate Myself from this sacred heavenly bond, for it is through it I came into the world. My universal Priesthood is naught else but My infinite charity to save man. The Father, I might say, found no other adequate way to save the world than the priesthood, which forms the body of the Church and of which the center or the heart is the Trinity itself. That is why the Word was made flesh, most particularly to be a priest and to spread His Priesthood in souls.

"For thence proceeds the spiritual and mystical priesthood. Religious and laity in the world form part of the mystical Priesthood to the measure of their more or less close union with Me" (*Diary*, Nov. 29, 1928).

M. M. Philipon, OP, and Aloysius J. Owen, SJ
Conchita: A Mother's Spiritual Diary

I write these lines in Chicago's O'Hare Airport waiting for the next flight to a preaching assignment. In a quiet corner of this extremely busy airport there is a spacious interfaith chapel, which contains a tabernacle, vigil light, and the reserved Eucharist. I had a long wait at the airport and was delighted to find Him here. I am joined during my holy hour of adoration by a Latino workman in overalls who prays very devoutly. On the other side of the chapel two Muslims genuflect as they make their midday prayer. A few people quietly come and go, mostly acknowledging the mysterious presence of Christ in the tabernacle in traditional Catholic ways.

Today I am tired, concerned about obligations, and I am late. But as I come into the presence of Christ, all these considerations fade away and become silent, like the constant flow of traffic I can see but cannot hear as it encircles the airport. I try to observe the admonition of the Cherubic Hymn of the Eastern liturgy—to put aside all earthly cares as the King of Kings approaches. But He does not come to me as the great King—He comes as my oldest and dearest Friend. ". . . I have called you friends. . . "—"Come to me, all who labor and are heavy laden . . . " (Jn 15:15, Mt 11:28). I have always been aware of His presence in many different places, in the mountains and on the subways, in the stars and in the garbage-strewn streets, with the sick and the dying, with the poor and the suffering. I have even caught a glimpse of Him in my enemies when I remembered that He loves them too. But nothing—nothing—can duplicate or come near to His presence in the Holy Eucharist.

Fr. Benedict J. Groeschel, CFR, and James Monti
In the Presence of Our Lord:
The History, Theology, & Psychology of Eucharistic Devotion

Feast of St. Francis de Sales
1567-1622

S t. Francis de Sales had special devotion toward the holy angels charged with the guardianship of the tabernacles. His veneration for these angelic guardians was increased by an instance which showed that these pure spirits revere not only the Sacred Species, but also the ministers who consecrate and handle them.

After having conferred Holy Orders on a pious young man, St. Francis noticed that the newly ordained priest hesitated before a door as if to let someone pass before him. "Why do you pause?" asked the saint. "God favors me with the sight of my Guardian Angel," replied the priest. "Before I was ordained to the holy priesthood, my angel always remained at my right and preceded me. Now he walks at the left and refuses to go before me." Such is the great veneration which the angelic spirits show even to God's ministers because of their reverence for the Blessed Sacrament.

Tan Books & Publishers
The Guardian Angels: Our Heavenly Companions

A t Johnny's First Communion, I asked him whom he loved most in the whole world. "My dog!" he replied. "How much do you love your dog? Could you show me?" Johnny stretched out his arms in the shape of the cross. "That much."

I asked Johnny to look at the large crucifix behind the altar. Jesus had his arms outstretched too.

"Do you love your dog that much, Johnny?" I pointed to the crucifix. Johnny looked up at Jesus above his head and nodded, his arms still outstretched.

"If you really do love your dog that much, I can tell you how to prove it. Why don't you give up that party after Mass, the hamburgers and the hot dogs and the ice cream. Give up your nice clean bed, your friends, your football. Give up being a little boy. I'll wave a magic wand and you can become a dog. You can live in a kennel and eat bones and dog biscuits."

Johnny shook his head, "No, I don't love him that much!" Johnny lowered his arms.

"But Jesus loves you that much. He loves you enough to become a boy, to talk like a boy, to eat like a boy, to play like a boy—and to die like a man. 'Greater love hath no man than to lay down his life for a friend.' That cross is the greatest sign of Jesus' love for you as a man. But Jesus is also God, and he can show even greater love than that. If a boy doesn't love his dog enough to become a dog, he certainly doesn't love him enough to become a dog biscuit. That greatest sign of God's love for us as God is Jesus, who becomes our food."

Fr. Ken Roberts
You Better Believe It

God does not like unfinished symphonies, or unfurled flags. In His mercy He will finish the temple we have left unfinished and clean and polish that which has remained unadorned. What we may regard as an evil may be actually a hidden good like the surgeon's use of a scalpel. He does not ask us if we will accept the finishing of the work His Father sent Him to do. He drafts us into His service as Simon the Cyrene that we might not be unripe and unplucked wheat in His Eucharistic sanctuary.

Since I would not take up the Cross, the Lord would lay it on my back as He laid it on Simon of Cyrene, who later came to love it. The cross took two forms: trials *inside* the Church and *outside* the Church. Eventually I came to se that the Lord was teaching me not only to be a priest, but also to be a victim.

I can remember when, after four months in the hospital, I began to recover; I was reading Mass on an altar constructed over the bed before a few priests and friends. I spontaneously gave a sermon, which I remember so well. I said that I was glad that I had open-heart surgery because when the Lord comes to take us all, He will look to see if we have any marks of the Cross upon ourselves. He will look at our hands to see if they are crucified from sacrificial giving; He will look at our feet to see if they have been thorn-bruised and nail-pierced searching for lost sheep; He will look at our heart to see if that has been opened to receive His Divine Heart. Oh what joy is mine just to have endured the minuscule imitation of His suffering on the Cross by having a wounded side. Maybe He will recognize me from that scar and receive me into His Kingdom.

Archbishop Fulton J. Sheen
Treasure in Clay

F ather Eymard's sermons were quite of a new kind; they filled his hearers with admiration. People had never heard anyone speak about the Eucharist as he did. They would have listened to him for hours. In less time than it takes to tell, his reputation covered Toulon, and the priests of the city vied with one another in inviting him to come and preach in their churches on the days of weekly adoration which they were quick to sponsor. People, of course, looked upon him as a saint, whose words seemed to be inspired.

One evening he preached such a wonderful sermon in the Cathedral of Toulon that some of those present could not help telling him so. Somewhat surprised, he said: "Do you really think I said fine things? An hour before preaching, I was not yet prepared. But that hour I spent before the tabernacle. There I said to Our Lord, 'Let us go preach.' It was Our Lord who preached."

Fr. Martin Dempsey
Champion of the Blessed Sacrament:
Saint Peter Julian Eymard

Feast of St. Thomas Aquinas
1225-1274

S uch progress did he make in learning, that he was but thirty-two when he was appointed to assist Albertus in teaching at Cologne. All the while his prime consideration was his preparation for Holy Orders. His greatest love was the Blessed Sacrament, of which he was to be the world's greatest witness. He would spend hours at a time, day and night, before the altar in adoration and meditation. Here was his great school. The Eucharistic Lord Himself was his Master. When he celebrated Mass, he was in raptures and often in tears. After saying his own Mass he would serve another—or at least hear one.

In December 1273, when he was but forty-seven, he laid down his pen, determined to study and write no more, so that he might given himself to God entirely in meditation and prayer. He was ordered by Pope Gregory X to go to Lyons to assist at the General Council. Taken ill on the way, he was obliged to stop at the Cistercial Abbey of Fossa-Nuova. His first visit was to the Blessed Sacrament. At Fossa Nuova he lay seriously ill for a month. He made his general confession. While Viaticum was being brought to him, he had himself taken from the bed and laid upon ashes on the floor. The tears came to his eyes as he beheld the Host in the hand of the priest. He made his profession of faith: "I firmly believe that Jesus Christ, true God and true man, is present in this august Sacrament. I adore You, my God and my Redemption, the Viaticum of my pilgrimage, for whose honor I have studied, labored, preached and taught."

He died a little after midnight, March 7, 1274.

Fr. Hugh F. Blunt, LLD
Witnesses to the Eucharist

O nce Matt had knelt stiffly before the Blessed Sacrament, unable to listen to or speak to God. But gradually, prayer had penetrated the surface of his flesh and seeped into his soul. The drudgery disappeared and Matt realized that he had received from Jesus the gift of prayer. As Matt had cried for deliverance from the cravings of his body, he had also asked: "Lord, in Your mercy, give me the gift of prayer." Even though he felt he could not pray, he had asked over and over for that gift. The man who had once served the god of alcohol was wise enough to realize that he needed a substitute. That substitute would be love for and conversation with Jesus, Mary and the saints.

Matt's basic program of spirituality was positive and concrete: friendship with Jesus in the Eucharist, reception of the sacraments, prayer, self-discipline and spiritual reading. Following this program of spiritual wealth, Matt prayed that he would be led to love and sacrifice for his neighbor and would grow in his dedication to daily work. How different his thoughts were now! If Matt walked down the street smiling to himself, it was no wonder. What a wonderful feeling to have spiritual topics in his mind and imagination instead of "the drink." He would whistle a tune softly as he walked along.

Susan Helen Wallace
Matt Talbot: His Struggle and His Victory Over Alcoholism

I can clearly recall the first time I experienced a sense of gratitude for being entrusted with the service of the Eucharist. While I was a student-deacon at the Church of the Canadian Martyrs in Rome I was asked by a priest to preach the homily at the Mass he was celebrating at a nearby convent. The Gospel was on the use of the Talents. I remember my fresh enthusiasm and also the glow of satisfaction I felt—not only because I sensed I had made a decent job of communicating (in Italian, to boot!), but also because I had "preached the Eucharist." The theme of my homily was about how the Eucharist is our best Talent, our Lord's greatest Gift to us.

The natural pride I felt was, however, soon deflated. For as I was assisting in distributing Holy Communion I became struck by an indescribable sense of awe and wonder at the humility of God himself who communicates his treasure in the silence of the Blessed Sacrament. What we cannot express for all our way with words or even the best of our art, God says so simply in this manner of revealing the grace and truth of his Real Presence! Furthermore, his "simultaneous translation," as it were, of the Word of Life into the people's loving response of adoring faith awakened in me immense gratitude. It seemed that I was the recipient—rather than being the communicator—of the deepest lesson of Love's truth: the humility of God both in the great silence of the Blessed Eucharist and also in the silent endeavor of his people to respond to his Gospel in their lives. In that instant I knew what gratitude is. I experienced *Eucharist*, that is, the inner worth of being full of thanksgiving.

Michael L. Gaudoin-Parker
Heart in Pilgrimage

Feast of St. John Bosco
1815-1888

I n 1882, on the third Sunday after Easter, at Rome, in the sacristy of the Church of the Sacred Heart, the [deceased] youth appeared to him as a man who was drawing water from an inexhaustible well, a clear symbol of the infinite graces to be obtained from devotion to the Sacred Heart. In 1883, at Hyeres, and again during Mass, Don Bosco saw Louis Colle showing him a region of South America still awaiting the Salesian missionaries, and heard the lad say to him: "Make the children receive Communion frequently, and admit them early to the Holy Table. From the age of four or five, show them the Sacred Host, and make them adore it in order to prepare them for their first Communion."

In April 1883, at Paris, in the church of Our Lady of Victories, where he was celebrating Mass, Don Bosco, at the moment of Communion, saw young Colle before him. The Beatus stopped administering the Sacrament, being lost in the vision, and the assistant priest thought he was ill, and finished giving Holy Communion in his place. On May 14, 1884, Don Bosco had to wait four hours for his train, and had a long talk with his young friend, who promised him a notable improvement in his health, which actually took place next day. Lastly, during the night of May 10, 1885, he saw the youth for the last time, but of this vision he thought well not to speak.

A. Auffray, sc
Blessed John Bosco

Of all the great gifts that God has given us, there is none so wonderful and so filled with grace as the gift of the Eucharist which we celebrate at Holy Mass.

In my own life it is an enormous grace and strength, and I am so very much aware of the consolation and the blessing that it brings into the lives of our Catholic people. If it were not for the Eucharist, if it were not for this marvelous manifestation of God's love, if it were not for this opportunity to place ourselves in the very real presence of God, if it were not for the sacrament that reminds us of His love, His suffering and His triumph, which indeed perpetuates for us His saving sacrifice on the cross, I am sure that I could never face the challenges of my life, my own weakness and sinfulness and my own need to reach out to the Living God.

Archbishop Theodore McCarrick
All Praise and All Thanksgiving:
A Pastoral Letter on the Eucharist

Word would go round the countryside that Campion had arrived, and throughout the evening Catholics of every degree, squire and labourer and deposed cleric, would stealthily assemble. He would sit up half the night receiving each in turn, hearing their confessions and resolving their difficulties. Then before dawn a room would be prepared for Mass. Watches were set in case of alarm. The congregation knelt on the rush-strewn floor. Mass was said, communion was given. Then Campion would preach.

It needs little fancy to reconstruct the scene; the audience hushed and intent, every member of whom was risking liberty and fortune, perhaps his life, by attendance. The dusk lightened and the candles paled on the improvised altar, the tree tops outside the window took fire, as Campion spoke. The thrilling tones, the profusion of imagery, the polish and precision, the balanced, pointed argument, the whole structure and rich ornament of rhetoric which had stirred the lecture halls and collegiate chapels of Oxford and Douai, Rome, Prague and Rheims, inspired now with more than human artistry, rang through the summer dawn. And when the discourse had mounted to its peroration and the fiery voice had dropped to the quiet, traditional words of the blessing, a long silence while the priest disrobed and assumed once more his secular disguise; a hurried packing away of the altar furniture, a few words of leave taking, and then the horses' hooves clattered once more in the cobbled yard; Campion was on his way, and the Catholics dispersed to their homes.

Evelyn Waugh
Edmund Campion

It was in the Blessed Eucharist above all that Sister Marie-Bernard, true to her faith, sought this living Jesus. Members of the Community bore eloquent testimony to the recollected manner in which she prepared for Holy Communion, and her complete absorption in the Divine Presence during her thanksgiving. To the question, "What do you do that you take so long over your thanksgiving?" she replied: "I think that Our Lady is giving me the Child Jesus. I welcome Him and I talk to Him, and He talks to me." Her spiritual notes give a more enlightening glimpse: "I was nothing, and of this nothing, Jesus has made something great." "It is because through Holy Communion I partake of the Godhead in some way. Jesus gives me His Heart, I am thus linked closely with Him, spouse of Jesus, friend of Jesus, that is to say, another Jesus."

Some of her companions stated that during her thanksgiving, the face of Sister Marie-Bernard would "light up—as during the apparitions at Massabielle." The parish priest, not over-imaginative, had already mentioned something similar with regard to his little parishioner. Without doubt, Holy Communion, or rather, Holy Mass, was the culminating point of Sister Marie-Bernard's spiritual life; to be deprived of it during her illnesses cost her more than all her sufferings. "If one must go from Tabor to Calvary, one returns from Calvary to Tabor with Jesus, that is our foretaste of heaven." If instead of Tabor we say the Blessed Eucharist, then this saying of Sister Marie-Bernard will best express the source of her spiritual happiness, her hope and her love.

Fr. Andre Ravier, SJ
Bernadette and Her Rosary

Meditate on the miracle of the multiplication of the loaves. Jesus Christ takes this lifeless thing, this tiny, coarse object, this bread, and by His blessing, it becomes food and life for the entire crowd.

Why should I not be, in these same divine hands, the poor instrument for another such work? Why should I not be given by God to souls to uphold and revive them? I am only feebleness, but strength will come from Him alone who uses me; I will let myself be distributed by Him to souls, and will serve them only in the measure that He wills. Sweet divine benediction, descend upon me! Multiply my prayers, sacrifices, and acts of charity! Let these fragments of Thy love in me become warmth and comfort for the spiritually starved, until the blessed time when Thou, the one Living Bread, shalt come Thyself to revive and save them.

Elizabeth Leseur
My Spirit Rejoices

June 5 (the chapel). This evening the Lord is neither standing nor sitting. We are united. It's good to pause with Him.

—Where are you, Lord?

—*In you, in Pierre. I'm at home in you.*

I wait. At the moment Pierre raises the Host, the image of Christ's face from the Holy Shroud appears on the Host.

—Lord, is what I'm seeing really true? I feel very calm but I can hardly believe what I'm seeing, nor do I dare say it.

—*Dare.*

I tell it to the others.

—Why are you giving me all this, Lord?

—*To make all of you free of care so that you care only for me.*

Nicole Gausseron
The Little Notebook

Sunday, February 20. During Mass, after the Consecration, Jesus came, so entrancingly beautiful.

"Tell Me what you have to offer Me for the souls I have confided to you. Put it all in the wound of My heart, so that your offering may acquire an infinite value."

I told Him that He could take everything, for all I do is for these souls.

"Tell it to Me in detail."

Then I began an enumeration of everything: my holy hour, my little mortifications and penances, the suffering of the Crown of Thorns, every breath I draw, my work, my fears, my weakness and nothingness, everything I do and think—"It is for love and for souls, Lord, and it is little indeed."

At nine-o'clock Mass He came back with His Heart aflame.

"Look," He said, "these souls are safe now, deep in My Heart."

Sr. Josefa Menendez
The Way of Divine Love

As though this paralysis was not a sufficient Calvary for her, Marthe [Robin] ceased eating altogether. This extraordinary phenomenon may be incredible, but it has also been known in the cases of other mystics, Christian, Hindu, and Moslem. From 1928 to 1981, the year of her death, Marthe did not consume anything except the Eucharist that was brought to her once or twice a week. The host, entering into her, instantly disappeared without any normal ingestion. Marthe could not swallow anything else. As far back as the beginning of that year, when her mother had brought her a cup of coffee, it had immediately flowed back out of her mouth. Mrs. Robin groaned, "Look at my poor little one, in what a state she is!" And Marthe's father wept, "But she has done nothing bad!" He was pitiful, a childhood friend of Marthe's told me.

Thenceforth, Marthe had no ingestive or digestive processes whatever, and, in addition, she entirely ceased to sleep; she was completely stripped. According to medical men, a total loss of sleep is even more extraordinary than not taking any food or drink.

One does not enter into such a state without agony. It appears that at this time Fr. Netton began to come to visit and console Marthe. And it was at this point that the Blessed Virgin began to increase the frequency of her apparitions. What did her heavenly mother say to her? Marthe remained quite silent on this subject, but the fact of the apparition is attested to by her sister from Saint-Sorlin, Mrs. Serve.

Fr. Raymond Peyret
The Cross and the Joy

From the Eucharistic Prayer on which we have been medi-
tating throughout this book, it is clear that the radical
source, center and summit of the whole life of a Eucharist-hearted people is the mystery of Christ's presence, which is
most fully manifest in his "gift of self" in the Eucharistic sacrifice. At the Last Supper, Jesus did not merely say: "Love one
another"; he added those significant and vital words: "as I have
loved you." Thus, the task in bringing about the "wholeness"
of this new culture of life does not consist merely in our human striving to do away with poverty and disease or to overcome divisions and class distinctions, but rather, in realizing
our unity in woundedness—a unity with Christ the Savior who
heals our deepest wound of self-centered pride by becoming
one with us in his own "gift of self."

Evangelization, which is intrinsic to the reality of our life
together in Christ as brothers and sisters, therefore, takes on a
profound "Eucharist-hearted" significance in this environment
of the grace of Christ's presence to humanity in the Eucharistic
sacrifice: it becomes a matter of "one beggar telling another
beggar where to get bread."

Michael L. Gaudoin-Parker
Heart in Pilgrimage

"Look at Jesus as He loves, works, prays, suffers and immolates Himself, from his descent into my virginal womb to his ascent upon the Cross, in this his unceasing priestly action, so that you may understand how I am above all Mother of Jesus, the Priest.

I am therefore also true Mother of the Most Blessed Eucharist. Not because I beget Him again to the mysterious reality upon the altar. *That task is reserved only to you, my beloved sons!* Nevertheless it is a task which assimilates you very closely to my maternal function because you also, during holy Mass and by means of the words of Consecration, truly beget my Son. For me, the cold manger of a poor and bare cave received Him; for you, it is now the cold stone of an altar which welcomes Him. But you also, as I, give birth to my Son. This is why you cannot but be sons of a special, indeed a most special, predilection on the part of her who is Mother, true Mother of her Son Jesus.

But I am also true Mother of the Eucharist, because Jesus becomes truly present, at the moment of the Consecration, through your priestly action. By your human *yes* to the powerful action of the Spirit, which transforms the matter of the bread and the wine into the Body and the Blood of Christ, you make possible for Him this new and Real Presence of His among you." (Words of Our Lady, August 8, 1986)

Fr. Stefano Gobbi
To the Priests: Our Lady's Beloved Sons

I had four abortions before I was married; had a nervous breakdown at eighteen; and became addicted to drugs and alcohol in my twenties. I attempted suicide seven times, unable to understand why I had to live a life without meaning. My husband, chosen by my parents, was an atheist.

Once a Catholic priest taught me two lines of prayer that turned my life around: "Jesus, may all that is You, flow into me. May Your Body and Blood be my food and drink."

Meanwhile, I was diagnosed with leukemia. This was in addition to diabetes that I had for twenty years. I knew the key to my healing was finding a place where I could receive the real Body and Blood of Jesus. Something inside kept telling me that if I could receive the Body and Blood of Jesus I would be healed.

I found it in a Catholic church during my first healing Mass, which I attended with a friend. At the Consecration I saw a vision of a lamb slain on the altar. It was the Lamb of God. I knew then that this was where I would find the Body and Blood of Jesus, and that it would bring me healing. I was received into the Catholic Church in May 1985.

When I met Father DeGrandis in 1985 he told me I needed to forgive my father for some ways he hurt me as a child. I began a regular program of saying the "Forgiveness Prayer." On his retreat I was healed of diabetes and the leukemia went into remission.

I thank God for my second chance. I especially thank the Lord for allowing me to receive Him in the Eucharist. "Take this," He said. "This is My Body" (Mk 14:22). (Ella's story)

Fr. Robert De Grandis, SJJ
Healing through the Mass

Gabriel Gargam was a postal worker assigned to the Bordeaux-Paris express trains. In a railway wreck on December 18, 1899, he was thrown about sixty feet from the tracks by the force of the collision. Upon being brought to the hospital, it was found that he had broken his clavicle, his legs, and that he also had received some head injuries. The shock had created serious internal troubles, and he was paralyzed from his hips down. He could not eat and his weight had gone down from 160 to 72 pounds. At the medical examination conducted by the doctors of the railroad, it was learned that he was a total disability case. All his organs were afflicted, and only his mind was left intact.

In 1901, although his condition was hopeless, his mother took him to Lourdes. He was immersed in the water, apparently without result. His nurse quipped that there was no reason for him to be blessed by the Sacrament during the procession because by that time he would be dead. At this moment the man declared dead rose, and in his bare feet, clad only in his long shirt, he walked behind the baldachin placed over the Eucharist. Immediately, sixty-three doctors examined this "human ghost," as they called him, and checked the official diagnosis, which stated that his entire organism was destroyed. His heart, liver, kidneys had malfunctioned, yet without convalescence he had been totally and entirely cured. And he died in 1953 at the rather ripe old age of eighty. After his miraculous cure he became one of the *brancardiers* in Lourdes, performing the heaviest and most difficult work.

Zsolt Aradi
The Book of Miracles

The *Spiritual Diary* attests that Ignatius' trinitarian and christocentric mysticism developed almost exclusively in the atmosphere of the Mass. This is also true of his mysticism of loving reverence, of discernment, of election, of confirmation, and of extraordinary mystical experiences. Ignatius focused his entire day on the Mass. The multifarious daily mystical graces occurred while thinking about which Mass to say, while preparing for Mass both interiorly and exteriorly, while saying Mass, and during his thanksgiving after Mass. In fact, many of the mystical favors he received throughout the day extended or complemented his Eucharistic graces. The *Spiritual Diary* notes and associates almost every mystical grace he received with the Mass said that day.

It must be emphasized that for Ignatius the Mass was the milieu in which he decided important matters for himself and for the Society. One commentator hits the mark when he writes that "the infused favors showered upon Ignatius were graces centered about Christ's sacrifice of the Mass, and dominated by the Most Holy Trinity to whom this sacrifice gives us access."

Fr. Harvey D. Egan, SJ
Ignatius Loyola the Mystic

"If you would know what grace and what gifts you receive, you would prepare yourselves for it each day for an hour at least," Our Blessed Mother told the seers at Medjugorje. "Let the Holy Mass be your life. I wish that the Holy Mass be for you the gift of the day. Attend it, wish for it to begin. Jesus gives Himself to you during Mass. Thus, look forward to that moment when you are cleansed. The Mass is the most important and the most holy moment in your lives. Mass is the greatest prayer of God. You will never be able to understand its greatness."

Michael H. Brown
Secrets of the Eucharist

Over the past five years, Christina [Gallagher] has repeatedly received messages from Our Lord and Our Lady encouraging frequent use of the sacraments. On February 28, 1988, Our Lady instructed, "My child, tell all my children to *come back to me and my Son*. We are waiting and we love all our children. Repent, go to Confession. Unburden yourselves of all sin and receive my Son's Body and Blood worthily. Pray and make sacrifice. In return, I will give you peace in your hearts."

Ever available, peace through the Sacraments is rejected by many, and this brings pain and sorrow to the Blessed Mother. From a message on July 1, 1988, the Blessed Mother informed Christina even some consecrated souls did not believe that "Jesus' Body and Blood are present in the Consecration of the Mass. They do not believe that the bread and wine are changed into His Body and Blood. . . . We must love Jesus in the Mass and Holy Communion."

Just two weeks later on July 14, 1988, Our Lady admonished her children: "Do not go to Holy Mass out of habit. Love my Son when you are at Holy Mass." Our Holy Mother wanted to make sure we didn't misunderstand her. On August 11, 1988, she implored Christina to understand that, more than anything else, Our Lord wishes to meet us at His table: "My children, go to Holy Mass. Offer it to the Father, console the Heart of my Son Jesus."

Thomas W. Petrisko
The Sorrow, The Sacrifice and The Triumph:
Prophecies of Christina Gallagher

The danger and the difficulty of saying Mass became a reality for us in the lumber camps of the Urals. We began then to do what we probably should have done before: we began to prepare ourselves to say the Mass by heart. We were afraid we would lose our Mass kit, the chalice or the missal; but we were determined that as long as we had bread and wine we would try to say Mass somehow. Over and over again in the evenings, when others were chatting or reading or playing cards, we would repeat to each other the prayers of the Mass until we had learned them by heart. How often, in the years that followed, I thanked God for this interlude in the lumber camps of the Urals and the time of training and of grace that was given to me to prepare for the years ahead.

After a few months, when Father Victor and I had adjusted somewhat to barracks existence as a way of life, we were able to find more and more occasions to say Mass. We would walk out together, for example, into the forest and there offer Mass on a stump of a tree. I could not help thinking how the forests sometimes resembled a cathedral—the tall rows of towering trees arching over us, the hushed silence, the natural beauty around us, the silent whiteness of the snow in winter. Even time seemed to stand still as we offered the eternal sacrifice of Calvary for the many intentions that filled our thoughts and our hearts, not the least of which was the thought of the deprived thousands of the Church of silence here in this once Christian land for whom we had come to work as priests in secret. I shall never forget, as long as I am a priest, those Masses in the forests in the Urals.

Fr. Walter J. Ciszek, sj, with Fr. Daniel Flaherty, sj
He Leadeth Me

"My children, do I ignore you? No, then stop ignoring Me! During the Mass I lay up here on the altar in the broken body of My Son and I am ignored. How can you ignore the broken body of your Savior who is lying on the altar in front of you?

Reflect today on the Real Presence of Christ in the Host, and remember where the Son is so is the Father. Think about His blood and how it was shed on Calvary. It is not enough just to receive. You must receive and believe, to live. If you don't believe, you put up a barrier to My life, supernatural life.

My children you are body and soul and you have a duty to feed both. The best food for the soul is the Body and Blood of your Savior and Lord Jesus Christ, but you must accept it worthily and knowledgeably. To accept it worthily you must be in the state of grace. To accept it knowledgeably you must understand, and acknowledge, and believe, that My son Jesus Christ's Body, Blood, soul and divinity are present in that Host.

It is only by recognizing what really takes place in Mass that you can obtain the full benefits, My children. If you don't understand the importance of the Eucharist, read, there are good books. Ignorance must be overcome My children, you are chosen to bring the world back to My love: and the way is by the Eucharist.

Make the Eucharist the center of your lives and all will be well." (Words of God the Father, June 14, 1993)

Matthew Kelly
Words from God

Monday morning found Matt at Mass again. Because work at the brickyard began at 6 AM, Matt attended the 5 AM Mass. He thought of how he had spent his first sober Sunday. He had stayed for all the Masses, had gone home for dinner and had returned to church. Matt felt secure there. A church was the only place in all of Dublin where Matt felt safe enough from himself. He decided that he would fight his sobriety struggle in the presence of the Eucharist. As the penitent continued his lonely vigil with the Lord, he reflected on the nights he had squandered at the pub. He had gone home routinely in the early morning, arriving at work on time the next day at 6 AM. If he could deprive his body of sleep for alcohol, why couldn't he do it so that the Lord might grant him the gift of sobriety until death? From the time of his conversion, Matt permitted himself only four hours of sleep nightly.

Matt rose early to pray and read. And when he could not bring himself to do those things, he sat quietly, his big eyes looking sadly at nothing in particular. He wanted to leave the craving for alcohol far behind, but it was there waiting for him in the morning, lurking in his shadow during each day, taunting him when he went to bed at night. "It's just no use," Matt said to his mother. "I can't stay sober for three months. I can't win this fight. There aren't enough churches in Dublin to hide me from myself."

Elizabeth Talbot encouraged her son. She understood and sympathized. She prayed for him. She believed that he could win with God's help.

Susan Helen Wallace, FSP
Matt Talbot: His Struggle and His Victory Over Alcoholism

After twelve years of Catholic education all I could remember was that God was the Father Almighty which meant to me that He could do anything, and Jesus Christ is present in the Blessed Sacrament. I had little trust in doctors and believed that only God could help me. One day I decided to go to church and make a visit. As I sat there in front of the tabernacle, I recalled all the things I had done in life to be happy. My thoughts lead me back to when I was seventeen. At that time I was very happy and began wondering why. So I asked myself what was missing that I had then that I don't have now. The answer immediately flashed in my heart: God! Soon after my visit I went to confession, but because I was ashamed I neglected to tell all. I stepped out of the confessional and sat there in the church saying, "Jesus I love you," repeating the words the priest had told me to say for my penance.

Then as I sat in church looking at the tabernacle I felt a gentle call to return and confess what I neglected. So I went back into the confessional and confessed that I was a drug dealer and abused myself with drugs. I'll never forget the excitement and happiness in the priest's voice as he said, "That's OK. I'm glad you came back. You don't have to say any extra prayers, but consider coming to confession more often. Now I'll absolve you." As the priest raised his hand to make the sign of the cross a wonderful sensation came over me, my whole body became so light. My legs felt like rubber and I could hardly stand up.

Thomas R. Hyatt
*Come to Me: Forgiveness, Inner Healing
and Deliverance through Confession*

When I visit the Blessed Sacrament it is I who go to the Savior, in order to rest with Him awhile. How good it feels! How beneficial for the weary mind to go aside a little from the society of men. . . . O how empty and superficial so many of those associations are! Oh this tiresome levity of countless souls, who become bored as soon as one speaks a word about God, who show active interest only in the vanities of the world and the pleasures of sense. Then that wild chase after earthly goods!. . . and then to see how sinners are often pursued by good fortune, whereas virtue has only oppression and humiliation for its share. And then there is that icy coldness of so many hearts, who are dulled to all Christian charity! My soul would finally lose courage altogether and become sick, would be submerged in a sea of doubts, could I not daily visit my Savior and Comforter in the Blessed Sacrament. There I live in quite another atmosphere; there, thanks be to God, I find quite other interests.

It does me so much good—this visit! When with Jesus I feel that I am in the right place. Virtue, sanctity, a spirit of sacrifice there shine forth before me in all their charming beauty. I again find myself reconciled with life.

Oh, if all Christian souls but knew what it means daily to visit our dearest Savior in the Blessed Sacrament.

Msgr. William Reyna
Eucharistic Reflections

On Palm Sunday, after Communion, my [St. Teresa of Avila's] faculties were completely suspended, so that I was not able even to swallow the Sacred Form and, finding It in my mouth, when I had come round a little, I really thought that my mouth was full of blood. I also thought my face and my whole body were covered with it, as though the Lord had just shed it. It seemed warm to me and made me feel excessively tender. And the Lord said to me: "Daughter, it is My will that My blood shall profit thee; be not afraid that My mercy will fail thee. To shed this Blood cost Me great pain and, as thou seest, thou hast the fruition of it with great joy: I am rewarding thee well for the welcome thou hast given Me this day."

This He said because for more than thirty years I had communicated on that day, if I had been able, and had striven to prepare my soul to act as host to the Lord. For I thought the Jews had acted very cruelly to Him in letting Him go so far for His food after giving Him so great a reception, and I used to think of Him as staying with me—in a poor enough inn, as I now see. So I used to make these silly meditations—and yet the Lord must have accepted them, because this is one of the visions the genuineness of which I regard as most certain and, when I have been making my Communion, it has been of great help to me.

Msgr. William J. Doheny, CSC
Selected Writings of St. Teresa of Avila

Feast of St. Peter Damian
1000-1072

Peter Damian lost both father and mother shortly after his birth. One of his brothers adopted him, but treated him with unnatural harshness, forcing him to work hard and giving him poor food and scanty clothing.

One day, Peter found a silver piece that represented to him a small fortune. A friend told him that he could conscientiously use it for himself as the owner could not be found. The only difficulty Peter had was to choose what it was he most needed, for he was in sore need of many things.

While turning the matter over in his young mind, it struck him that he could do a still better thing, viz., have a Mass said for the Holy Souls in Purgatory, especially for the souls of his dear parents. At the cost of a great sacrifice, he put this thought into effect and had the Mass offered.

A complete change at once became noticeable in his fortunes. His eldest brother called at the house where he lived and, horrified at the brutal hardships the little fellow was subjected to, arranged that he be handed over to his own care. He clad him and fed him as his own child, educated and cared for him most affectionately. Blessing followed on blessing. Peter's wonderful talents became known, and he was rapidly promoted to the priesthood; some time after, he was raised to the episcopacy and finally created a Cardinal. Miracles attested his great sanctity so that after death he was canonized and declared a Doctor of the Church. These wonderful graces flowed, as from a fount, from that one Mass.

Fr. Paul O'Sullivan, OP
The Wonders of the Mass

Feast of the Chair of St. Peter

The church is hushed as the words fall silently from the sacramental lips of the priest. In answer to these words Jesus Christ opens the gates of heaven and descends upon the altar with a mighty retinue of angels and saints. On the altar, He is as truly present as when upon the Cross, where He appeared for us; as truly present as He is in heaven, where He continues to appear for us before the Eternal Father. In the priest's elevated hands we see Christ, our Redeemer. There is no moment on earth more holy than this! Let us look at the Host and at the Chalice, saying with the faith of St. Thomas: "My Lord and my God."

He is veiled by the appearance of bread and wine, but we know that He is there to show His love for us, and to win our love in return. Remember that He called the first Apostles while they were about to fish. He did not judge them by their catch. So will He reward our good intentions. "And Jesus, walking by the Sea of Galilee, saw two brothers, Simon, who is called Peter, and Andrew his brother, casting a net into the sea, for they were fishers. And He said to them, 'Come after Me, and I will make you fishers of men'" (Mt 4:18-19).

This is the time to promise Him loyalty and obedience. In the days of chivalry, the young candidate for knighthood spent the night before the Blessed Sacrament. After that, he placed his hands between the hands of his lord, and swore loyalty, saying: "I am your man." This was called "doing homage." Let us be equally generous as we gaze upon the Sacred Host.

Fr. John T. McMahon
Live the Mass

Eight to nine thousand Masses are going on right now! Right now I can unite myself with the Lord Jesus as the Holy Eucharist is being offered to the Father. In addition, I can unite myself with Jesus present in the thousands of tabernacles around the world. The prophetic word given through Malachi is really being fulfilled: "For from the rising of the sun, even to its setting, My name is great among the nations; and everywhere they bring sacrifice to My name, a pure offering: for great is My name among all the nations says the Lord of hosts" (Malachi 2:11).

The third Eucharistic Prayer addresses the Father, paraphrasing this prophecy: "From age to age You gather a people to Yourself, so that from east to west, a perfect offering may be made to the glory of Your name." This means at each moment and in every circumstance I can offer the Eucharist. I can offer the Immaculate Victim and in union with Him I can offer myself. As a royal priest I can offer my whole being—body, soul, and spirit. I can offer "always and everywhere" even the least of my sufferings, or rather *especially* my little sufferings, because those are often the only ones I have. In union with the Immaculate Victim, the Eucharistically offered Victim, the eternal Priest and Victim, Jesus Christ, Who offered Himself on Calvary for the salvation of us all—in union with Him my smallest offerings become His and so of the greatest worth and power.

Nothing is too small to offer, nothing insignificant when offered Eucharistically, when offered in union with Jesus for the salvation of souls to the glory of the Father. It is called intercession. We are all called to it.

Fr. George W. Kosicki, CSB
Intercession

We have seen that the vital point of his day was the Mass; all the rest started from that and moved under that initial impulse. He said it not too fast—out of reverence—not too slowly—from fear of attracting notice; besides, as the Abbe Monnin tells us, "he consulted the general convenience rather than his own desire and his own piety." A pilgrim who several times served his Mass noticed that the only point at which he took longer than the ordinary priest was before the Communion. The liturgical prayers being ended, there was a secret colloquy between Our Lord and His servant. M. Vianney gazed lovingly upon the sacred Host. His mouth shaped words; he stopped, listened, seemed to speak again, and with a visible effort—as of a friend parting from a friend—after an instant's hesitation, he consumed the sacred species.

"He remained as though in an ecstasy for as much as five minutes," related another—and he shed tears. He was seen to look at the Host, "sometimes in tears, sometimes with a smile."

One day, even, as he naively confesses, he dared to say to Our Lord: "My God, if I knew that I must have the misfortune not to see You for all eternity, I should never let You out of my hands."

He remained "lost in God" till the end of his thanksgiving. "When one has received Communion," he cried in one of his catechisms, "the soul buries itself in the sweetness of love like a bee in flowers."

Henri Gheon
The Secret of the Cure D'Ars

Conchita asked the Lord: "If the Redemption satisfied Your justice to efface sin, if by it the distance between man and the divinity was overcome, why did You perpetuate this same sacrifice of the Cross on the altars?"

The Lord answered her: "Solely out of love, solely out of charity, I remain on the altars because burning thirst consumes the Word made flesh who rejoices in His immolation for the sake of man.

"I have stayed on the altars to perfect in their souls by My life as a victim what is wanting of sacrifice in them. I have stayed thereon to continue expiation for man's ingratitude through a perpetual sacrifice. I have stayed thereon since I am the only pure victim.

"Without Me every immolation would be futile, by My perpetuating My sacrifices, forgiveness is likewise perpetuated, giving their value to the sacrifices of men when they are offered in union with Mine.

"I have stayed thereon to bring souls, through My example, to become lovers of pain under all its forms. I have stayed thereon due to the pleasure the Incarnate Word feels from the proximity of His creature."

"In the Mass is perpetuated the same immolation of the same Victim, Me, on Calvary. It is not a prolongation or a repetition of My sacrifice, but the same sacrifice though unbloody, the same living crucifixion with the same and only loving will of the Father to give His own Son, His only Son, for the salvation of the world."

M. M. Philipon, OP
Conchita: A Mother's Spiritual Diary

An article in *USA Today* reported that meditation reduces stress, lowers blood pressure, improves work performance, slows aging, cultivates sanity, and brings well-being to our lives. These therapeutic values have generated interest among discussion groups, hospitals, business leaders, and even the Pentagon.

Pope John Paul II takes us beyond the ideals of this newspaper article. He focuses on the most therapeutic of all forms of prayers: meditation and adoration before the Blessed Sacrament, and he does so in the context of "the task of the new evangelization." Calling that task the "greatest challenge facing the Church today," he tells us that it can be most effectively accomplished by "evangelizing for the Eucharist, in the Eucharist, and from the Eucharist."

In, for, and from the Eucharist is exactly how Jesus evangelized the two disciples He met on the road to Emmaus: "While He was with them at table, He took bread, and said the blessing, broke it, and gave it to them. With that their eyes were opened, and they recognized Him . . . He was made known to them in the breaking of the bread" (Lk 24:30-35). In anticipation of the Great Jubilee Year 2000, John Paul wants to see us evangelizing in exactly that same way: "In order to highlight the living and saving presence [of Christ] in the Church and the world, an International Eucharistic Congress will take place in Rome on the occasion of the Great Jubilee. The year 2000 will be intensely Eucharistic. In the Sacrament of the Eucharist, the Savior, who took flesh in Mary's womb twenty centuries ago, continues to offer Himself to humanity as the source of divine life."

Fr. Tom Forrest, CSSR
The Vine, March 1996

Thus St. Gertrude, in all the joys of her contemplation, knows the fundamental truth of the mystic life, that the giving up of our own will, however pious its aspirations, is the one great condition of union with God. When she asks Our Lord why He so often deprives souls of spiritual consolation on feast days or at the moment of Holy Communion, He replies that He prefers good intentions and humility to sensible devotion, and she is reminded that "sufferings of body and mind are proofs of the spiritual espousals of God and the soul." Despite all the extraordinary graces showered on her, she is often overwhelmed with sadness, and never ceases to bewail the enormity of her faults.

H. C. Graef
The Way of the Mystics

Feast of Bl. Angela of Foligno
1248-1309

Blessed Angela of Foligno was favored with seven visions of the Eucharist. She was privileged to contemplate the Lord under the Sacramental Species, sometimes in the form of a child of marvelous beauty and again bleeding, crucified and dying, and other times surrounded with ineffable glory. She found the joys of Christmas, the sorrows of Calvary, the glories of Tabor, all the mysteries, united in the Eucharist. One day when she longed to communicate and could not get a priest to bring her Holy Communion, angels brought the Sacred Host to her. She received Holy Communion every day, and for twelve years, in fact, it was her only food.

"It is the Sacrament of Love," she says, "that excites the soul to ardent prayer. It stirs up the virtue of impetration and, as it were, forces God to grant our petition. It deepens the abyss of humility, above all it enkindles the flame of love in the heart; hence the Sacrament is the Gift of Gifts, and the Grace of Graces. When the almighty and eternal God comes to us with all the perfection of His thrice holy humanity and His divinity, He surely does not come empty-handed. Provided that you have proved yourself as the apostle enjoins, He remits your temporal punishment, strengthens you against temptation, weakens the powers of your enemies and increases your merits. Therefore I recommend you in the reception of the Holy Sacrament of the Altar both frequency and reverence."

Fr. Hugh F. Blunt, LLD
Witnesses to the Eucharist

How great it is! In appearance, indeed, it is smaller even than the palm of my hand; but ah! Its influence extends over the whole earth; from it there issues the very life, the very soul, of Christendom.

Without the Sacred Host our beautiful churches and magnificent cathedrals would cease to be what they are, they would become spacious halls of emptiness, cold, cheerless; Christian art would sink down and die; virtue would faint and fade away; there would be a priesthood without a sacrifice and without an altar; and souls would wander aimlessly in loveless darkness, only to lose themselves on the broad path that leads to perdition.

The sun never sets upon the kingdom of the Sacred Host. Its throne is the only one that has never tottered, that never will totter. It may be that there are monarchs without subjects. But one thing shall never be: the Sacred Host shall never want adorers!

And I am here in its presence. How poor and little I feel before greatness such as this! O Jesus, so great! How can You find Your joy in me? How can You invite me, nay, command me, to stay very near to You? O little Host . . . And yet so great! . . . Imagination fails me . . . I humble myself . . . I adore.

Msgr. William Reyna
Eucharistic Reflections

Only His glorious presence in the Messianic banquet will be greater than this actual presence of His in a piece of bread, which I shut up in my traveller's pack as I walk the roads of the kingdom.

You can carry It with you. Oh, how I hope that the time will soon come when after Mass every Christian will carry the Eucharist home with him! When every Christian will construct a tiny oratory to honor the presence of God in the intimacy of his home, so he can gain from this mystery the strength to love and the joy to live.

In the mystery of the Eucharist, in the sacrament of the Bread of Life, God truly becomes everything to everybody. Everyone can see Him, touch Him, take Him, eat Him, contemplate Him, locate Him, and finally, if he wishes, spend as much time with Him as love urges him to. All this without agitation, without false fears, without the dangerous pressures of our senses, without the sloppiness caused by sentimentality.

If He were before us in another way—more striking, more pleasurable, more triumphal—we should be oppressed by it, or at least afraid. So, under the sign of bread He leaves us completely free; He acts only on our faith, of which it is the great mystery; He stimulates our hope, of which He is the "memorial"; He revives our charity, of which He is the nourishment and the model.

Carlo Carretto
The God Who Comes

D id you ever wonder why we call the Eucharist the *Most Blessed Sacrament*? They are all blessed, of course, because they all render Jesus present in a certain sense. But the *Most Blessed Sacrament* of the altar, the Holy Eucharist, makes Jesus himself really, truly and substantially present to us.

Is this a miracle? No it's not, because we can't see it. Is it a mystery? You bet. How does He do this? We don't know, but He says in Scripture that He would do this, and so we believe He has.

In the Most Blessed Sacrament of the Eucharist, the Body and Blood together with the Soul and Divinity of our Lord, Jesus Christ, is really, truly and substantially contained. The Council of Trent confirmed that in 1551. We say it's the *Real Presence* not because we mean the other ways He is present to us are not real. We call it *a Real Presence* because it is presence in the fullest sense.

Let me draw a loose analogy. You and I are present to each other when we talk to each other on the phone, when we think about each other, when we write letters to each other. Those are all ways in which one person can be present to another. But when I say you are really present, I mean you are here, all of you, physically with me. That's the substantial presence which Christ in the Eucharist, as God and man, makes Himself wholly and entirely present.

Bishop Thomas G. Doran
The Observer, October 4, 1996

Father Damien volunteered to go to the island of Molokai, where lepers were ostracized from both family and friends because the disease was so contagious and, at that time, incurable. After Father Damien was there for a period of time a friend wrote him a letter and asked how Father Damien was able to stay so long among the lepers. Father Damien's reply was: "Without my daily holy hour in the presence of the Blessed Sacrament, I would not be able to have stayed here a single day."

When Father Damien arrived the lepers did not notice. They were in a drunken stupor and had a sexual orgy each night to help them forget the rotting flesh of leprosy, dooming them to a life of oblivion and a death without consolation.

The first thing Father Damien did was build a chapel where he took each leper and the gospel scene was repeated over and over again: "A leper came to Him [and kneeling down] begged Him and said, "If you wish, you can make me clean." Moved with pity, He stretched out His hand, touched him, and said to him, "I do will it. Be made clean." The leprosy left him immediately and he was made clean" (Mk 1:40).

Jesus stretched out His hand and touched each one, making each one whole in His love, making each one innocent in His Blood. And innocence recaptured is more precious in the eyes of God than innocence never lost.

Oh, they kept their rotten flesh, but it didn't matter anymore. Their souls were made clean with the innocence of His Blood. They didn't need drink, because they became intoxicated with His love. Sex was no longer a need, because they had the intimacy of His Heart.

Msgr. Josefino S. Ramirez
Letters to a Brother Priest

E ileen and Jesus were together at the Communion. They sat beside a brook, which reflected their countenances. Jesus threw a pebble into the brook. Because of the ripples their faces were distorted.

Jesus said: "This is what Capi (*Capitano*, the little captain, Lucifer) is doing in the Church. He is distorting the image of the Son and His Father by the ideas which liberal theologians are introducing."

The Father told Eileen that He was giving her a new mission, to make Him known to His people. He explained that this was their last chance. He had sent His Son and He had been rejected; His Word (Scripture) was distorted so that the Father and the Son could not be clearly seen in it. His Son's Eucharist had been despised and ridiculed. He had sent His Son's Mother and she had been rejected. He had sent His Spirit (the Charismatic movement) with the same result.

Now He had no one else to send. He would come Himself through her. She would make Him known to His people. If they rejected Him, then the river of hope separating the two contending forces would dry up and Armageddon would take place. He showed her the two forces: those in black, ugly, under their leader, Lucifer, and at the head of the forces of God, Michael. Michael would do battle with his sword and the defeated army would go into eternal loss.

Eileen George
Conversations in Heaven

"Soaking" in Scripture and in the presence of Jesus in the Blessed Sacrament are the only ways to keep the next generation of Catholics from being swept away from the Faith, according to the keynote speaker at Sunday's Diocesan Eucharistic Congress.

Scott Hahn, an assistant professor of theology and Scripture at the Franciscan University of Steubenville, Ohio, spoke for almost an hour on the meaning of the Eucharist and its role in family life. Hahn, a former Presbyterian minister who joined the Catholic Church six years ago, said he was still amazed to be speaking to a Catholic gathering because "for years and years I was a committed anti-Catholic." At that time, he considered Catholic teaching about the Eucharist to be just one of its many "errors." "There was no (other) denomination on earth that worshiped a wafer and said that it was God," he said.

Through years of studying the Scriptures, however, Hahn discovered the roots of Catholic doctrine about the Eucharist. He pointed out that the New Testament compares the sacrificial death of Jesus with the sacrifice of a lamb for the Jewish Passover feast. "Jesus Christ wasn't done giving of himself when he died on the cross," he said. "If he is sacrificed as a Passover lamb, then we, too, must eat the lamb.". . .

Hahn drew his biggest round of applause when he challenged the audience with the question, "Do you really believe that Jesus Christ is present in the Holy Eucharist? Do you really believe that?"

Elaine Krewer
The Catholic Post, June 28, 1992

Feast of St. Colette
1381-1447

During her long life, Colette was to raise from the dead no less than four people. This gift of the highest form of miracle . . . placed beyond any doubt, by the fact that these four resurrections were cited during the process of her beatification.

The second person whom she raised from the dead also belonged to Besancon. He was named Jehan Boisot, and was fifteen years old. At the time that Perrine was writing her biography he was still alive. His heartbroken parents could not resign themselves to lose their boy, and the powers attributed to Colette seemed to offer a last chance of holding him from death. At all events, they decided to make the attempt. They carried the bier to the convent chapel, and the father and mother implored Colette to give them back their son. It was early in the morning. Colette made no reply and went to hear Mass. And then, as if she had made use of the Holy Sacrifice on behalf of this child, she commanded him to arise, and he lifted himself off the bier and walked.

Madame Ste. Marie Perrin
St. Colette and Her Reform

One summer's day, I was celebrating Mass in a convent. The gospel passage was Matthew 12, I shall never forget the impression these words of Jesus made on me: "Behold, something greater than Jonah is here . . . Something greater than Solomon is here." Surely I was hearing them for the first time! I understood that the word "here" really meant here, in this precise place, at this precise moment, and not only when Jesus was on earth many centuries ago. A shudder ran through me and I was shaken out of my torpor: right there in front of me was something greater than Jonah, something greater than Solomon, than Abraham, than Moses: there was the Son of the living God! I understood the meaning of the words: "Lo, I am with you always . . ." (Mt 28:20).

Ever since that summer's day, these words have become dear and familiar to me in a new way. Very often during Mass, when I genuflect after the Consecration I say to myself: "Behold, something greater than Jonah is here! Something greater than Solomon is here!"

Raniero Cantalamessa
The Eucharist: Our Sanctification

With a time and a place set aside for prayer, Frances [of Rome 1384-1440] began to grow more deeply drawn to the Spirit. She and Vannuzza increased their visits to the various churches in Rome. The two were familiar figures to the people as they walked to and from Mass in the early morning at the church in the Forum. They attended the festivals at the local chapels to celebrate the patron saints' feasts.

Between her obligations to her husband and the Ponziano family business, Frances made certain that she had plenty of time to devote to God. Much to her surprise, she began to have visions during the different Masses she attended. The visions often related to the feast day.

The visions increased Frances' desire to reach out to others. Soon, she and Vannuzza were a daily sight carrying food to the hungry in the city and helping the many pilgrims who had become stranded in Rome.

Her life became centered in the liturgy of the day. The liturgical cycle became quite important to both women and to their spiritual lives. They continued to faithfully celebrate the Mass daily and to participate in the Olivetan prayers at the monastery.

Daniel F. Stramara, OSB OLIV.
Driven by the Spirit

Feast of Dominic Savio
1842-1857

I n regard to his actual reception of Holy Communion, he used to say a special prayer of preparation the night before. In the morning he prepared with the other boys during Mass, and with his own particular devotion; but his thanksgiving cannot be said to have ever terminated. It was quite an ordinary occurrence that, if not specially called or aroused, he would not remember breakfast-time or even school-time, remaining in prayer, or rather in a sort of contemplation and adoration of the goodness of Our Divine Lord, who communicates with souls in His own ineffable manner.

If he could spend an hour during the day in the presence of the Blessed Sacrament, it was his utmost delight; but he always found time for a visit every day, and got someone to go with him if possible. His favorite prayers were a series of acts in reparation to the Sacred Heart of Jesus . . . in order that his Communions might be more fruitful and meritorious, and that there might be a motive of renewed fervor every day, he always had a definite intention in view. His intentions were thus distributed over the week: *Sunday*—In honor of the Blessed Trinity. *Monday*—For the welfare of spiritual and temporal benefactors. *Tuesday*—In honor of my Patron Saint, Saint Dominic, and of my Guardian Angel. *Wednesday*—In honor of Our Lady's Seven Dolours, for the conversion of sinners. *Thursday*—For the Souls in Purgatory. *Friday*—In honor of the Sacred Passion of Christ. *Saturday*—In honor of Our Lady, to obtain her protection in life and death.

(St.) **John Bosco**
The Life Of Dominic Savio

On November 7, 1995, Our Lord once again called Michael to come before Him, where He is truly present in the tabernacle. Michael states, "I was overwhelmingly drawn to Him; to love Him; to adore Him." A short time into being before the tabernacle, Our Lord spoke to Michael, asking him, "Will you stay with Me and ease the pains of My heart caused by the ingratitude of so many?"

Michael said that at these words he was overcome with love for our Lord. Love consumed him in those moments and for a time after. Michael wished to share this experience because he says that we are *all* called by Our Lord to come to Him and spend time with Him before His Real Presence in the Holy Eucharist. Jesus wishes for all of us to come to Him so that we may love Him and He may love us in return.

On November 14, 1995, while Michael was in prayer contemplating the Holy Eucharist, Michael said, "Our Lord spoke to me with great seriousness and power, engraving His words upon my heart." Our Lord said: "I am here . . . for all." Our Lord was referring to His *true* presence in the Most Blessed Sacrament when He said, "I am there," and then "for all," meaning for all people.

May we love and adore Jesus, Our Lord and Savior, in the Most Blessed Sacrament of the Altar. Let us thank Him everyday for this most wonderful gift.

Michael McColgan
Open Your Hearts:
Messages from Our Lord Jesus and His Blessed Mother

What should be the subject of our meditation during the adoration hour? Yes, routine creeps even into our love of God, and we grow weary of repeating the same prayer. But Father Eymard's wisdom has given us a remedy against this new danger: "Do you wish to learn the secret of true Eucharistic prayer?—Consider, then, all the mysteries in the light of the Blessed Sacrament. It is a divine prism through which they can all be studied. The Holy Eucharist is, indeed, 'Jesus Christ, yesterday, and today, and the same forever'" (Heb 13:8). In this Sacrament He glorifies all the mysteries of His life and prolongs, as it were, the exercise of all His virtues. The Eucharist is, in a word, the great Mystery of our faith to which all Catholic truths lead. . . . "

Developing his thought at greater length, the Servant of God continued: "What is easier than to establish the connection between the birth of Jesus in Bethlehem, and His sacramental birth on our altars and in our hearts? Who does not understand that the hidden life of Jesus in the tabernacle is a continuation of His hidden and retired life at Nazareth? Who does not believe that the Holy Sacrifice of the Mass offered at every moment of the day is the renewal of Christ's death on Calvary? Is not our Lord as meek and humble in the Blessed Sacrament as He was during His life on earth? Is He not always the Good Shepherd, the Divine Consoler, the Changeless Friend? Happy the soul that knows how to find Jesus in the Holy Eucharist, and in the Eucharist all things!"

Fr. Albert Tesniere, SSS
Blessed Peter Julian Eymard: The Priest of the Eucharist

Merton first came to learn something about this in the books he read. He worked hard at internalizing what he read. He spent time regularly in meditation. He used the traditional forms of the Rosary and the Stations of the Cross. He guided himself through the *Exercises* of St. Ignatius. He came to know the power of the Mass above all by participation. During the summer of 1939 at Olean, New York, living in what he later described as an early hippie commune, intent upon producing a novel, he contented himself with Sunday Mass. In the following summer he withdrew to some extent from the general activities of the commune—for a couple of weeks he even went to live in a dorm with young Franciscan novices at Saint Bonaventure's College—and got to bed early so that he could be up and off to Mass in town or at the college each morning.

Entering more and more deeply into the meaning of the Mass, Tom began to conceive a desire to be a priest. Yet there were other considerations: his past and his present. Would a past such as his be a lifetime impediment to such a ministry of holiness? And wasn't he still too much of a man of the world, drawn to the things of the world and in need of them? Could he give them up? And if he gave them up, could he live in the world and stay away from them? Many questions, plus the fear to answer them.

M. Basil Pennington, OCSO
Thomas Merton, Brother Monk

S r. Briege McKenna, OSC, at the priests' retreat at International Falls, Minnesota, on April 26, 1990, spoke this word she heard coming from the Lord.

"Come to Me in My Eucharistic presence. There is a time coming in which there will be a great denial of My presence, denial that I am truly present among My people. But I invite you to spend time with Me. I invite you to lead your people to come to Me. There will flow life-giving waters. I will refresh you and free you. I will pray that angels protect you. I will give you My angels to go with you and before you. No one will rob you of what I have given you if you stay close to Me. Come and taste the Bread of Life. Invite your people to come and in this way you will prepare for the darkness that will come upon the Church. For evil forces will try to destroy my people. I invite you to come to Me often. Come and let Me cleanse you of your sinfulness. Do not accept the darkness in your own life. Do not allow yourself to be deceived. New life means that I love you, that I long to make you spotless. Come to Me often. Confess to one another and allow Me to minister through each other and I will give you the wisdom that you need to confront the enemy."

Fr. Robert De Grandis, SSJ
Healing through the Mass

When celebrating Mass in this healing way, people are healed not only interiorly but also physically (1 Cor 11:17-34). The Eucharistic prayers expect healing of the whole person. Before Communion the priest prays, "Let this not serve unto condemnation but unto health of mind and body." This prayer for healing is followed by the centurion's, "Lord, I am not worthy to receive you, but only say the word and I shall be healed." Even St. Augustine, who believed that the physical healing occurred only in earlier times, had to retract his views because he saw the Eucharist, as well as other means, bring physical healing. As a chaplain bringing the Eucharist, I too have witnessed physical healings even recorded on heart monitors.

Whether speaking about healing that can be recorded on heart monitors or healing that involves a change of heart toward a pastor, Eucharistic healing occurs when we give Christ our hardened, unforgiving hearts and receive his heart of flesh opened on Calvary. There He released to us His forgiving Spirit as promised: "A new heart I will give you and a new Spirit I will put within you; and I will take out of your flesh the heart of stone and give you a heart of flesh" (Ez 36:26). Memories are healed when hearts are exchanged on Calvary.

The Eucharist has a built-in pattern for exchanging hearts on Calvary.

Matthew Linn, sj, and Dennis Linn
Healing Life's Hurts:
Healing Memories through the Five Stages of Forgiveness

March 15

Feast of St. Clement Maria Hofbauer
1751-1820

The apostolate of our saint has been called a Eucharistic Apostolate, and not without reason. The Real Presence of the God-man Jesus Christ in the Blessed Sacrament is the center of all Catholic faith and devotion. The Blessed Eucharist will, therefore, occupy an important place in the life of every one of God's saints. Aside from this, if the devotion to the Blessed Sacrament occupied in the life and labors of Hofbauer a place unusually prominent even for a saint, we must seek the reason for this in the condition of the times.

The "Illuminati" and the protagonists of Jansenism had removed this beautiful Mystery of Faith and Love to an almost unapproachable distance from the eyes and the hearts of the faithful. At Warsaw, the saint deliberately attacked . . . the Jansenistic school, which had won over to its ranks the officials of the city. The Countess Choloniewska writes: "He regarded it as his greatest happiness to be able to assist in spreading devotion to the Blessed Sacrament over the whole world, and to awaken in the hearts of the faithful an ardent desire to receive their Eucharistic Lord frequently in Holy Communion. Filled with the longing to see the Blessed Sacrament surrounded all over the world with all the pomp and grandeur that love could inspire, he introduced the solemn adoration of the Blessed Sacrament in Warsaw, where he had found . . . the most woeful lack of all true devotion. The daily adoration of Our Savior hidden in the Sacrament of the Altar soon produced among the people in that city the richest fruits of piety."

Fr. John Hofer, CSSR
St. Clement Maria Hofbauer: A Biography

I n the ancient days of Christianity before churches were as immense as they are now and before Christians were numbered in the thousands, the faithful assisting at Mass expressed this act of offering themselves with Christ, not merely in words, but even in actions. In our Masses today there is only one procession of the faithful to the altar to take part in the Mass—and too many do not take part even in that—at the Communion. Then the faithful come to the altar to receive, to partake of the fruits of the Sacrifice of the Mass. In the olden days there were two processions, one, to the altar to give, the other, to receive at Communion time.

The faithful of those days understood well that they partook both in the offering and in the receiving of the Eucharist. They approached the altar each one in person and presented their part in the sacrifice; some gave bread and wine, flour or fruits. Others offered gold or other precious gifts according to their means. But their gift even then was a sign of the inner spiritual gift of themselves which each one made to God. By it they showed their readiness to sacrifice whatever God asked of them in their lives. Some of these gifts were used for the Consecration—the bread and the wine. Others were kept for the adornment of the church, the altar, the sacred vessels, and what remained was set aside for the poor.

John N. McCormick, CSSR
John A. Treinan, CSSR
What Is the Mass?

From midnight of November 7, until 8 AM, I prayed with all my heart. I recited fifteen decades of the Rosary, up to the moment when I was to make a contract with obligations. I was still unsure about many things. At about 6 AM, Pancho and I received Communion at the Church of St. John of God. Right after, both of us returned home to get everything ready. I prayed to Jesus to help me be a good wife and make happy the man He was giving me as a companion. I put on my white wedding dress embroidered with orange blossoms. Later I offered up part of my dress to the Immaculate Virgin and the rest I used to decorate the *prie-Dieu* of my future children on their First Communion and to fashion pillows for the poor on Christmas Eve. They placed a veil and a crown on me. Thus garbed, I knelt down to ask for my parents' blessing. They gave it to me whole heartedly but in tears.

I remember that at the wedding banquet, when toasts were being made, I got the idea to ask him, who was now my husband, to promise he would do two things for me: allow me to receive Communion every day and never to be jealous. Poor soul! He was so good that many a year later, he stayed home with the children waiting for me to come back from church. During his last illness, he asked me whether I had gone to receive Our Lord. God must have rewarded him for this favor which made up my whole life.

M.M. Philipon, OP
Conchita: A Mother's Spiritual Diary

We will . . . rest content with recalling the testimony offered by St. Cyril of Jerusalem, who wrote the following memorable words for the neophytes whom he was instructing: "After the spiritual sacrifice, the unbloody act of worship, has been completed, we bend over this propitiatory offering and beg God to grant peace to all the churches, to give harmony to the whole world, to bless our rulers, our soldiers and our companions, to aid the sick and afflicted . . . we all pray for all these intentions and we offer this victim for them . . . and last of all for our deceased holy forefathers and bishops and for all those who have lived among us. For we have a deep conviction that great help will be afforded those souls for whom prayers are offered while this holy and awesome victim is present."

In support of this, this holy Doctor offers the example of a crown made for an emperor in order to win a pardon for some exiles, and he concludes his talk with these words: "In the same fashion, when we offer our prayers to God for the dead, even those who are sinners, we are not just making a crown but instead are offering Christ who was slaughtered for our sins, and thus begging the merciful God to take pity both on them and on ourselves." St. Augustine attests that this custom of offering the "sacrifice which ransomed us" also for the dead was observed in the Church at Rome, and he mentions at the same time that the universal Church observed this custom as something handed down from the Fathers.

Pope Paul VI
Mysterium Fidei

Feast of St. Joseph

For the Feast of Saint Joseph, I [Mother Cabrini] had a very high temperature, and I felt as though I were about to die; but, on the eve of the feast, Saint Joseph consoled me in a very extraordinary manner. I seemed to see him on a beautiful white altar around which we all knelt. We wished to celebrate that day in a very special manner in his honor. So, since I had chosen him as the spiritual director of the sisters, I told him it would be better that he should address the sisters. It was not necessary to ask him a second time, for he started immediately to give an exhortation on all the virtues to be acquired without which we cannot be saints. While he spoke, sparks of fire darted from his mouth and flew upon those nuns who were the best disposed to hear him. Sometimes the saint appeared to take the form of Our Lady, and from this, as though in a dream, I drew the conclusion that his momentary apparition meant to convey that he possessed many virtues like those of the Blessed Mother.

During this dream I asked Saint Joseph to relieve me of the high temperature so that I might go down to receive Holy Communion, as I was longing so much to do. What would you expect? I awoke without the temperature I had had for seven consecutive days, and I was thus able to go down to receive Holy Communion. After a few hours, the temperature returned; but it was not so high, and at the end of the month I was able to resume my work and go on my travels again.

Mother Saverio DeMaria, MSC
Mother Frances Xavier Cabrini

My experience as spiritual director of Christina [Gallagher] has been one of an infinite deepening of devotion and an awareness of the wonder of the Mass. I look back with sadness on that part of my life when I just said the Mass. Of course, I always loved and believed in the Mass, but I did not profit from so much grace that God would have wanted to give me. I lost out on so much grace flowing from the sacrifice of Jesus in the Mass.

The one message that I have that has been burned very deeply into my own soul through all of this is that the Mass really is the sacrifice of Jesus, the sacrifice which is timeless and everlasting. I feel very sad that today so many priests concentrate on the Mass as somehow a kind of get-together or some kind of celebration, without emphasizing its sacrificial nature. The Mass is only a sacred banquet because it is first a sacrifice. We wouldn't have the Body and Blood of Jesus to share if He first did not surrender His life in an act of infinite love and in a passion of indescribable pain and suffering in order to provide this gift for us. I am saddened by so much casualness about the Mass and so much positive disrespect toward the Real Presence.

People are not to be blamed because people take their cue from the priest. *The faith of the priest will influence the faith of the people and strengthen it. Priests have a lot to answer to God for; we priests are largely responsible for the condition of the faith of our people.*

Fr. Gerard McGinnity
Signs of the Times, April/May/June 1994

I f only we Christians would realize that we eat our Lord's Body and drink his Blood, not only so that He can communicate His divine life to us, but also so that in us and through us He can continue His self-giving to the world and for the world. When we eat our Lord's Body and drink His Blood, He forms His own sacrificial love in us. Our mission of Christian love is a continuation of His own self-giving on the cross.

Thus when He says, "Take and eat, take and drink," He is saying, "Become one with Me in My self-giving, merge your sacrificial giving of yourself into My sacrificial giving of Myself. Become one body with Me, one with Me in My self-giving, one sacrificial offering with Me. By your self-giving love for My people, continue My self-giving love for them.

"Thus continue My supreme act of evangelization, My perfect proclamation of God's love for the world. Just as I revealed God's love to the world in My self-giving, so manifest that love to the world in your self-giving in union with Me. Thus by loving one another as I have loved you, you will be, along with me, the revelation of God's love for the world. You will proclaim His love for the world by loving the world with His love, with My love. Thus your love for one another as I have loved you is your fundamental and your supreme act of evangelization."

Fr. Paul Hinnebusch, OP
Homiletic and Pastoral Review, January 1995

Under Father Maximilian's spiritual leadership, the friars of Niepokalanow and *Mugenzai no Sono* had incredible success in their press apostolate. Their secret for success was a community life of prayer centered on the Eucharist.

In the mid-1930s, when the friars of Niepokalanow were about to inaugurate their first newspaper, the *Maly Dziennik* (*Little Journal*), they had formidable opponents in the secular press of Poland. For nine days before the appearance of this first issue, the friars prayed day and night before the Blessed Sacrament. The newspaper venture met with a tremendous success.

Years later, Father Maximilian initiated a program of perpetual adoration (i.e., during the day but not at night) of the Eucharist at Niepokalanow. This began on December 8, 1939, the day on which Father Maximilian and the friars were released from a three-month imprisonment by their Nazi captors. When they returned to Niepokalanow, which had been ransacked and plundered by the Nazis, Father Maximilian had no illusions. He did not wish to lose one minute of the precious time that was left for him. He immediately introduced perpetual adoration of the Eucharist in order to increase his "active forces of prayer." Every half hour, day after day, a fresh group of four friars took its place before our Lord in the tabernacle. This became the friars' primary apostolate, inasmuch as the Nazis only permitted one more issue of the *Knight of the Immaculata* to appear during the war.

Fr. James McCurry, OFM CONV.
Kolbe Novena in Honor of the Immaculate Conception

"My dear ones, I am here with you again this night as your Lord and Savior to plead with you. Listen to what I have asked, to what My mother continues to ask. Rededicate yourself, each of you, to prayer. You have become, My dear ones, so scattered. Come again before Me in My Most Blessed Sacrament. Come to Me in that precious gift of Mine and My Father's, and Our Spirit's to you. I see within your hearts and there is such a lack of forgiveness. My dear ones, look upon the crucifix. Remember what I have done for you. Imprint that picture within your mind. Press it to your heart and then see how terrible it is when you refuse to forgive yourself. I have died for you. Isn't that proof that you are forgiven?

Come to Me through the sacrament of reconciliation and receive again My healing and My forgiveness. My dear ones, your lack of forgiveness of yourself blocks the mercy, and the joy, and the peace that I wish to give to you. Come to Me. Present yourself again to Me in My Most Blessed Sacrament. I want with all of My heart to heal you, to strengthen you. With My strength you will forgive yourself, and so this night I bless you with the strength that you need, with the courage of My Holy Spirit. You again, this night, as you come to Me, can be a new creation. Be at peace now. Fear is useless." (Words of Our Lord to Fr. Jack Spaulding, June 16, 1994)

Queenship Publishing
I Am Your Jesus of Mercy, Vol. V

As we have seen, many people who knew Padre Pio insist that the most impressive feature of his ministry was his Mass, which, according to one Italian journal, made worshipers feel as if they were at the foot of the cross. A Salesian priest observed that when Padre Pio celebrated, "the most intimate fibers of my being vibrated with feelings of emotion and sweetness which I had never before experienced." Another witness said that it seemed as if Padre Pio, in saying Mass, "came from another humanity superior to ours, speaking . . . through an atmosphere beyond this life." Padre Gerardo Di Flumeri described Padre Pio's Mass as "a supernatural Mass."

What made the Mass supernatural? Padre Pio, who defined the Mass as "a sacred fix with the Passion of Jesus," in which "all Calvary" was presented again, extended into the present, admitted to an intense mystical involvement with the unseen world. Apart from any merit or worthiness on his part, he was allowed to relive Jesus' Passion in a direct way. "All that Jesus has suffered in His Passion, inadequately I also suffer, as far as is possible for a human being. And all this against my unworthiness, and thanks only to His goodness."

C. Bernard Ruffin
Padre Pio: The True Story

March 25

Feast of the Annunciation

On the morning of March 25 of the year 1679, patches of field were still white with untrodden snow and islands of breaking ice floated heavily on the St. Lawrence; but the stir of spring was in the air and in the thawing earth. The new bell from France had arrived in exchange for the long collected beaver furs, and all four bells were ringing together for Our Lady's Annunciation. The chapel was crowded for the eight o'clock Mass and a slender figure wrapped in a long blue shawl was kneeling motionless, not far from the communion rail. As always when at prayer, Kateri was oblivious of everything around her; but today a new light burned in her eyes, and her whole face glowed in its radiance. This was the day dedicated to her vow of virginity, the culmination of years of inner growing toward an ideal that was supernatural.

A few moments after she received Holy Communion on this the very day commemorating Mary's tremendous words of surrender, this daughter of the Mohawks, renouncing forever the human happiness of marriage, chose Christ alone for her Spouse, making to God the same complete dedication that Christ's Mother had made, also against the traditions of her race. It was to honor Mary that Kateri united with her vow a double consecration, offering herself first of all to Christ, then to His Blessed Mother. With this act the greatest desire of her life was fulfilled. She no longer belonged to herself nor did she seem any longer to belong to this world.

Marie Cecilia Buehrle
Kateri of the Mohawks

Ignatius had great respect for the efficacy of the Mass. He often said Mass for discernment, special graces, benefactors, and the like. For example, he requested of his brother Jesuits that 3,000 Masses be said with the intention that the *Constitutions* be approved by the Holy See.

The *Spiritual Diary* reveals that Ignatius received numerous explicitly Eucharistic and priestly graces, although less in number than trinitarian and Christ-centered mystical experiences. For example, during the Consecration, Ignatius saw how Mary's "flesh was in that of her Son." A mystically given "thought" or "judgement" illuminated him that he "ought to live or be like an angel for the privilege of saying Mass."

Another mystical thought came to him about pronouncing the name of God during Mass with profound respect, surrender, and loving reverence. Furthermore, Ignatius realized that if he made good use of the experience of loving reverence "throughout the day without distraction," he would experience it even more deeply during Mass. His mysticism of loving reverence, therefore, is related intrinsically to his Eucharistic and priestly mysticism.

Harvey D. Egan, SJ
Ignatius Loyola the Mystic

The holy Gospels tell us again and again that while the Savior was visibly with us on earth He healed the sick by His mere passing by; and with an only word He raised the dead to life. If such was His active goodness then— and who would venture even to think of doubting it?—what works of charity must He do now, in His Eucharistic life! Oh, He does not merely pass before me now, He does not only speak to me—nay, He actually enters under my roof and transforms me into Himself.

It is not enough for Jesus to increase in me the life of grace in Holy Communion. No; He gives me even His own life. And so it happens that it is no longer that I live, but Jesus that lives within me. And therefore it is that in the eyes of God every action of mine appears clothed in all the beauty and adorned with all the worth of the actions of Jesus.

Hence, if my Communion is truly holy and worthy, if Jesus does not find in me the obstacle of sin, He, in a certain sense, deifies me and all my works . . . then everything—even things that would otherwise have no value whatsoever—becomes of infinite and supernatural value within me, thanks to Holy Communion. So, for instance, my recreations, my work, become the recreations and the work of Jesus; the breath I take at rest and in toil becomes the breath of Jesus. When I come and go, Jesus comes and goes; when I sit at table, Jesus sits at table. In short, no matter what I do, it is Jesus Who does it.

Msgr. William Reyna
Eucharistic Reflections

I urge priests, religious and lay people to continue and redouble their efforts to teach the younger generations the meaning and value of Eucharistic adoration and devotion. How will young people be able to know the Lord if they are not introduced to the mystery of His presence? Like the young Samuel, by learning the words of the prayer of the heart, they will be closer to the Lord, who will accompany them in the spiritual and human growth, and in the missionary witness that they must give throughout their life. The Eucharistic mystery is in fact the "summit of evangelization" (*Lumen Gentium*, no. 28), for it is the most eminent testimony to Christ's Resurrection.

All interior life needs silence and intimacy with Christ in order to develop. This gradual familiarity with the Lord will enable certain young people to be involved in serving as acolytes and to taking a more active part in Mass; for young boys, to be near the altar is also a privileged opportunity to hear Christ's call to follow him more radically in the priestly ministry.

Pope John Paul II
Letter to Bishop Albert Houssiau, Bishop of Liege,
Belgium, 750th Anniversary of the Feast of Corpus Christi

September 25 (the chapel). —Gather me into yourself, Lord, because I'm not managing to place myself in your presence.

—*I will gather you in.*

I feel hopelessly scattered. My mind doesn't obey me and goes wandering off in all directions. This evening's dinner, Laurette's homework, tomorrow's shopping. If I keep on this way, he won't come. So I try as hard as I can to quiet down. Ouf! At the Consecration I'm finally more ready to receive him.

—It would be stupid to miss a meeting with you, Lord.

He doesn't reply. After the Consecration, I finally have some peace and quiet.

—Thank you.

—*Keep your eyes wide open to the world, to the events and people that I place in your life. But keep your eyes closed when you're on the way. I will lead you on the way. Don't worry. Be like a child and let yourself be led.*

I need to look inward, to listen to his word and follow his road.

Nicole Gausseron
The Little Notebook

Not too long ago three of us got together and decided to pray together in front of the Blessed Sacrament. This was about three months ago. Well our numbers have grown and now we are as many as sixteen people.

Our spiritual life has grown as well for each of us. I know mine has. I'm attending Mass, not only on Sunday, but on every Saturday and as often as I can get to Mass during the week. My prayer time at home has doubled. My personal life has changed. I've devoted more of my time to bringing people to the Blessed Sacrament and to the task of opening more churches for perpetual adoration.

I was very, very active socially. I belonged to yacht clubs, went skiing, did a lot of entertaining at my house, enjoyed life, loved life, had many friends, did a lot of wonderful, exciting things. Yet, I don't feel the excitement for these same things any longer. I now realize that many of these material things did not fulfil me, did not touch my soul. It's as if the more I had, the more I wanted. I felt like a person in a little boat that has drifted away from land where all the people were standing. Sometimes I've felt alone in the boat except for my God who is with me. It is said, "our treasure is where our heart is." We spend our time where our heart is and my heart is with God.

Claudia Blache
Perpetual Eucharistic Adoration newsletter, March 1995

Gertrude's own preparation for Holy Communion included special watchfulness against sins committed by the tongue. "A person who receives Communion after sins of speech is like one who invites a guest and then heaps up a great pile of stones at the door."

The saint's desire for the Blessed Sacrament was so strong that she would have forced her way to it through drawn swords. While she watched the other nuns receiving Communion, it seemed to her that it was not the priest but Christ who was giving himself, the priest merely making the sign of the cross over each Host.

One of the most striking expressions of Christ's indwelling occurred when at the time of Communion He said to Gertrude: "I will clothe myself with you that I may be able to extend my hand to sinners. . . . And I will also clothe you with Myself in order that all those for whom you pray and those who by nature are like you may be made worthy to receive My innumerable benefits."

Sr. Mary Jeremy, OP
Scholars and Mystics

The wonderful gift we are given, the real meaning of what Jesus is saying in Scripture, is that the Eucharist is real. It is Christ. It is not a memorial or just a re-membrance of something that happened. It is a wonderful gift we are given. When we enter the doors for Mass, time stands still, and we enter the timelessness of God. As far as God, Our Father, is concerned, there is no time. God is only in the present. That is why Mass is said in the present tense. The priest says, "This *is* My body. This *is* the cup of My blood." Right before our eyes Christ comes to us. The words pale as they try to cap-ture how amazing it is to think that, not only did God become one of us through Mary, not only did He become such a part of us that He wanted also to die for us; He also becomes our food. Who would have thought of it? No wonder the Jewish people had such a hard time taking the words of Jesus to heart. How can this be, that He would give His own Flesh and Blood for us? I cannot explain it, but I would die for it.

Oftentimes when I distribute the Holy Eucharist I am brought to tears because, for whatever reason, at that particular time, the Lord lets me understand what He is allowing me to do. He is allowing me to feed His people with Himself. Some-times when I receive the Eucharist I am also reduced to tears. To think that the Son of God, my Savior, would want to come to me as my food.

Fr. Jack Spaulding
Hope for the Journey

With God's help and by the gift of myself, I have been seemingly worldly and outwardly gay; I have renounced much for some time and especially during these last days. And while I talk and smile and force myself to be gracious, in the depths of my soul there is an unspeakable longing for solitude and recollectedness, and I cry from within to the kind Master, "Thou seest how I thirst for prayer and calm, and how ardently I desire to live only for Thee and for a few persons who are dear to me. Thou knowest how heavily the world weighs upon me, how I hold the spirit of it in horror; but since it is Thy Will that I should live not for the world but in the world, since the duties of my state and my ardent desire for the apostolate keep me there in spite of all my longing to be free, then permit these many sacrifices. It is for this that I offer Thee so much conversation without interest, so many activities devoid of consolation for me, so much costly amiability. Accept it all, take it all, use it all for souls and for those I love."

Then at the first opportunity I retire quickly into my inner "cell," and there I pray and adore and lie at the feet of my Savior. My three Communions each week and the few minutes of meditation each morning prepare me for my daily activity; and every day when I offer Him in advance all the activity and suffering that makes up my days, everything that later happens is gathered up by our good God, and nothing is lost; no, nothing, not even this great boredom with worldly occupations hidden beneath the veil of charity.

Elizabeth Leseur
My Spirit Rejoices

Francis was ordained priest by the Bishop of Calahorra on Saturday in Whitsun week, 1551. He did not, however, say his first Mass until the 1st of the following August, the feast of St. Peter's Chains. It was celebrated in the chapel of the Castle of Loyola, the splendid vestment he wore on the occasion being the work of his sister, Dona Louisa Borgia, Countess of Ribargorca. This vestment was preserved in the Jesuit house at Vergara, and many striking miracles have been accomplished through its application to sick persons, whose maladies have been by this means instantly and completely cured. Don John Borgia was present at the Mass, and partook of Holy Communion. "Thus," as Father Ribadeneira remarks, "did the son receive from his father's hand the most precious gift that heaven or earth can bestow." Pope Julius III, granted a Plenary Indulgence on the usual conditions to all those who should assist at Francis' first public Mass.

A. M. Clark
The Life of St. Francis Borgia of the Society of Jesus

Years ago I used to receive letters from an Indian convert. He had become a Catholic when, as a young man, he had served as a secretary to a Catholic priest.

The young man read the reviews and papers this priest received. Reading them, he became convinced of the truth of the Catholic faith and asked for baptism. At a time when missionaries work to "nativize" local liturgies, and emphasize Catholicism's similarity to existing religious belief, *it is interesting to note that my Indian convert friend was brought to the Church by its most unique reality: the Presence of Christ in the Blessed Sacrament.*

The Church still has much work to accomplish in India. But my friend believes the faith could be easily upheld in India and the world through promotion of greater devotion towards the Most Blessed Sacrament. His plea is simple but profound: There should be much more public adoration of the Blessed Sacrament; Holy Mass should be offered with very great veneration; the faithful should assist in the same spirit; processions should be held; and Christ should be adored more fervently in the tabernacle.

Besides this, priests should preach more often about the Blessed Sacrament, always explaining it in accordance with the doctrine of the Church.

John P. M. van der Ploeg, OP
Signs of the Times, April/May/June 1994

Feast of St. Juliana of Mount Cornillon
1192-1258

I n 1246, Robert of Thourotte, your distant predecessor in the see of Liege, instituted in his Diocese the Eucharistic feast now known as *Corpus Christi*, at the request of Juliana of Cornillon, who had already composed an office for *Corpus Christi*, Eve of St. Martin and other women of Liege. A few years later in 1264, Pope Urban IV made this feast of the *Body of Christ* a holy day of obligation for the universal church, thereby expressing the importance of venerating the Eucharistic Body of our Savior. On the occasion of the 750th anniversary of the institution of this feast, as I join all the pilgrims who will be participating in the jubilee ceremonies and the faithful all over the world who ceaselessly pray before the Blessed Sacrament, I raise a fervent prayer of thanksgiving to the Lord.

Pope John Paul II
Letter to Bishop Albert Houssiau, Bishop of Liege,
Belgium, 750th Anniversary of the Feast of Corpus Christi

When I went forward to receive Jesus in the Eucharist, the Lord gave me a greater love for Charlie. I knew that this love could help create an opening for God to begin working in Charlie's life, too. I returned to my seat and began to cry. Jesus had worked a great healing in me and I wanted to tell someone. How I wished I could go home and tell Charlie!

As soon as we got home I phoned Charlie at his motel. When he answered I said: "Honey, I want you to know that I love you just the way you are and that it doesn't matter to me where you go or how long you stay or who you go with. I'll be waiting for you." Then I hung up.

Charlie says that he just stood there in the motel room not knowing what to do. When he had heard my voice on the phone, he had expected me to tell him that he was a sorry excuse for a man and that three lawyers would be waiting for him when he returned. He would have known how to handle that. But he didn't know how to handle love or how to respond to it.

That was November 14, 1976. The following February 8, Charlie Osburn, the "wild man of Warrington," the man who could never change, the man that I "had to teach a lesson to," went down on his knees with Father Jim Smith, surrendered his life to the Lord Jesus, and asked for the infilling of God's Holy Spirit. (Jeanne Osburn)

Charlie Osburn, with Fred Lily
The Charlie Osburn Story

Jesus Christ is at the center of our worship. In the Holy Eucharist, His redemptive act of love is remembered and made present. It is through the words of the ordained priest that His sacrifice, His death and resurrection, and thus His love are made sacramentally but truly present to us.

The result of sincere worship at the Holy Eucharist and the reception of Holy Communion brings about a special grace, a unique result, for all who are assembled—those who share in the priesthood of Christ through Baptism, which is all of us, the priest included; and those of us who share in the priesthood of Christ through Holy Orders. We ourselves become offered. All of us should leave the Eucharist confirmed in our self-giving to God and to our brothers and sisters. How can we assemble at the Eucharist where we are drawn deeply into His self-giving without giving ourselves to others. This is the purpose of the Holy Eucharist. It is not to "tell our story." It is not to "contemplate one another." It is not to "enter into the choreography." It is not to divide us or eliminate an essential role. It is so that we all may be offered to God, to carrying out His will, to His service, and to be reminded of our final goal. When we all understand this, our unity will be strengthened.

Bishop John M. D'Arcy
The Eucharist: A Response

" I long for My people to participate in the Mass and to receive Me worthily! Think of it! I, Who am your God, long to come to you each day! In the Eucharist I come to you in My Body, Blood, Soul, and Divinity. Present within you, I long to take you close to My Sacred Heart—this Heart which is truly within you. The more you allow Me to do so, the more closely I press you to this Heart. I shower you with its riches. I abundantly give you great graces which increasingly form you in My likeness.

"I am Lord and Master! Please listen to My words. Pray, pray for a deeper understanding of the Mass. In union with Mary, approach Me daily in the Eucharist. I, your God, long to come to you. How much do you long to receive Me?" (Words of Our Lord)

Fr. Edward Carter, SJ
Tell My People

A little boy was brought to this outdoor Mass who was suffering from very severe burns and sores on his body. I remember thinking, "My goodness, there's really nothing that can be done. It's so bad. We have no doctors or medicine here."

I admired the priest. We prayed with the little boy, then the priest said to the old woman who had carried him to the Mass, "Just leave him under the table here and let's continue with the celebration of the Eucharist."

As we approached the Consecration, I had my eyes closed. When I opened them, I discovered that people were prostrate on the ground. They lifted up their eyes to adore the Lord. The look on their faces made me think, "They really believe that this is Jesus." Then when I looked at the sacred Host, in my own imagination, I got the most beautiful image of Jesus with his two hands out. He was smiling with great love and compassion. He was embracing these poor people and saying, "Come to me, all who are weary, and I will give you life and faith." After the Mass, I went around to see how the little boy was. I looked at the child and he was fine. There wasn't a thing wrong with his little body.

During this Mass as in all Masses, the priest had put his hands over the bread and wine, and he called upon the action of the Spirit to make this action holy "that it may become the Body and Blood" of Jesus. When the priest said this prayer, the Holy Spirit came, but He of course was not limited to do only what the priest asked. The Spirit also put His power over the little boy and the boy was changed. He was healed and made whole.

Sr. Briege McKenna, OSC
Miracles Do Happen

" **M**y son, I tell you once again that it is in a living prayer that you will find peace and victory. In no way should you abandon fellowship with God because of the external world. You should begin each new day in communion with God. Let the things of the world yield first before the demands of your life in Christ; and when you pray, do not omit anything of what is your duty. This is what the Lord is expecting of you. Do not omit your morning prayers, no matter what should stand in your path.

All through the entire day, look for occasions to be united with God. In this fashion, you shall protect yourself from sin and conclude the day with giving thanks to the Lord. In every prayerful occasion, ask the Lord for forgiveness of everything that you have done before God. Confess your sins and disobedience to God always. You will be given forgiveness and cleansing in the Precious Blood of Jesus during the Eucharist. Remember this: that the prayer of faith was given by the Lord Himself in order to protect the communion of Christians with God, in order to help reveal the will of God to those who believe, and in order to bring the victory of Christ to the ones who endure all things. Amen." (Words of Our Lady)

Josyp Terelya
In the Kingdom of the Spirit

April 11

We read in the lives of different saints that, as sometimes they were unable to go to the Church for Holy Communion, God made use of an angel who, to satisfy their hunger for the Blessed Eucharist, acted instead of the priest and took the consecrated species to them. It appears that Our Savior Himself willed to take this great gift to Gemma; and that happened quite three times. Here is how it is told us by one who was an eyewitness.

"On the morning of the Friday on which dear Gemma for the first time underwent the cruel punishment of the scourging, on seeing her horribly lacerated all over, I forbade her to get up. The poor child obeyed, and collecting her thoughts she set to prepare herself for a spiritual Communion, for which she used to make her preparation in the same way as for her sacramental Communion in the Church. She went into ecstasy and, at a given moment, I saw her join her hands and return to herself, while her eyes sparkled and her face suddenly lit up as usually happened when she had some extraordinary vision. At the same moment she put out her tongue and soon withdrew it, returning into ecstasy to make her usual thanksgiving. The same thing happened at other times as well, but I was not then a witness. I learned from Gemma herself, who quite candidly told me of it, that it was Jesus and not an angel Who came to communicate her."

Father Germanus, CP
The Life of Gemma Galgani

I am sure that the main reason why I felt at home becoming a Jewish Catholic was a personal experience. Once during the time that I was reading the Gospels I took a short nap. I had a powerful dream. I entered a large room with a long banquet table in it. I was down at one end, but I could see at the head of it the figures of Jesus and Mary. They beckoned to me and asked in Hebrew if I would sit down between them. I awoke with a euphoric sense of belonging.

I longed to be a Catholic, but I did not think I had enough faith to take the step. I had been praying that I might have the grace to believe in such a way that I could fully commit myself to Christ. I was told that I must leap into the arms of Christ and that this would require a moment of courage. Then it seemed that Christ Himself took my hand and led me across the gulf between doubt and total faith. After a session with a priest for formal instructions in the Catholic faith, I was walking down the street and suddenly I believed totally and simply and happily.

Then, I lived in anticipation of Baptism, which took place on January 4, 1959. My godparents were Professor Schwarz and his wife Leni, whose love and kindness and patience with me then and still today are indescribable. After the ceremony I burst into a flood of tears in gratitude for my salvation.

I have now been a Catholic for twenty-five years. I love the sacraments. Daily liturgy and Communion is the mainstay and joy of my life. I teach Catholic philosophy, write books about spirituality and ethics, give lectures, retreats and try to bring Jesus into the family. (Ronda Chervin)

Robert Baram, Ed.
Spiritual Journeys

When you are in our Lord's presence, would you be noble, disinterested in your love of Him? Speak to Him, then, of Himself, of His heavenly Father, of all that He has done for His Father's glory. You will thus gladden His Heart. Speak to Him, moreover, of His love for man, and you will touch Him to the quick; speak to Him of His Mother, and you will exalt His filial affection; speak to Him of all the saints, and you will thus magnify His divine grace that has made them such.

And after speaking to our Lord of Himself and of the things which concern Him, pay an attentive ear, He will speak to you of yourself, of your own interests. Under the influence of this colloquy your heart will expand with peace and joy, like the flower that bathed and refreshed by the dews of night opens its corolla to the morning sun. In silence and repose you will listen to the sweet voice of Jesus penetrating into your soul. There is more. Your very silence and repose will be changed into the eminent activity of love: *You will become one with Him.*

Fr. Albert Tesniere, sss
Blessed Peter Julian Eymard

I make a Holy Hour each day in the presence of Jesus in the Blessed Sacrament. All my sisters of the Missionaries of Charity make a daily Holy Hour, as well, because we find that through our daily Holy Hour our love for Jesus becomes more intimate, our love for each other more understanding, and our love for the poor more compassionate. Our adoration has doubled the number of our vocations. In 1963 we were making a weekly holy hour together, but it was not until 1973, when we began our daily Holy Hour, that our community started to grow and blossom.

Nowhere on earth are you more welcomed, nowhere on earth are you more loved, than by Jesus, living and truly present in the most Blessed Sacrament. The time you spend with Jesus in the Blessed Sacrament is the best time that you will spend on earth. Each moment that you spend with Jesus will deepen your union with Him and make your soul everlastingly more glorious and beautiful in heaven, and will help bring about an everlasting peace on earth.

When you look at the crucifix you understand how much Jesus loved you. When you look at the Sacred Host you understand how much Jesus loves you NOW. This is why you should ask your parish priest to have perpetual adoration in your parish. Even if he cannot begin perpetual adoration immediately, start at least, with a holy hour once a week. I beg the Blessed Mother to touch the hearts of all parish priests that they may have perpetual Eucharistic Adoration in their parishes, and that it may spread throughout the entire world.

Mother Teresa
Immaculata magazine
Special Eucharistic Adoration Issue

There were other struggles as well, inner struggles. During the first three months of Matt's conversion, the fear of not persevering in sobriety was constantly with him. One Sunday morning he was in the front pew, and as time for the reception of Holy Communion drew near, a feeling of evil crawled through Matt. It was a mysterious sensation that overwhelmed him. His forehead was bathed in perspiration as he stood up. He felt pushed and pulled at the same time and found himself at the entrance of the church, then out on the street. He paced up and down outside, struggling with his own unworthiness. He reminded himself that he had gone to confession, that he was continuing to receive the sacrament of reconciliation every Saturday evening. He told himself that the Lord welcomed him to receive Holy Communion. Still he could not direct his steps toward the church.

Matt stood in front of the large building and looked up at the cross. He felt the rosary in his pocket and clutched it in the palm of his hand. "Holy Mother," he prayed, "help me to receive your Son." Talbot ascended the church steps and slipped inside. Another Mass was just beginning. He participated in the responses and prepared to receive his Lord. This time he approached the altar and the Eucharist was placed on his tongue. Peace flooded his soul as he returned to his pew.

Susan Helen Wallace, FSP
Matt Talbot: His Struggle and His Victory Over Alcoholism

Feast of St. Bernadette Soubirous
1844-1879

"The Holy Eucharist was the breath of her soul." How beautiful and eloquent is this testimony from Sister Dalias! She drew from it "the strength to endure in peace of soul her indescribable sufferings," as Mother Cassagnes said. She saw in it the fount of all purification and of every virtue. Sister Robert confessed to her one day; "How hard it is to correct one's faults!" Sister Marie-Bernard, opening her eyes wide, replied spiritedly: "How can one receive the Bread of the Strong and not be more courageous?" Canon Perreau, who often gave Bernadette Holy Communion, was able to judge how deep was her faith and her love. Her eyes as she gazed on the Sacred Host "profoundly moved" the priest, especially when he saw her approaching "with heaving breast." He had often to wait "until the emotion had subsided a little."

She looked upon "this moment of Holy Communion as a most precious time; she always found it too short." Sister Vincent Garros asked her: "How do you manage to remain so long at your thanksgiving?" She answered: "I think to myself that the Blessed Virgin is giving me the Infant Jesus, I welcome Him, I speak to Him and He speaks to me." To encourage her young compatriot to greater recollection, for she was subject to sudden distractions and uneasy at not feeling any sense of God's presence in her thanksgiving, Sister Marie-Bernard said nicely: "You must give God a good reception. We have every interest in welcoming Him for then He has to pay us for His lodging."

Francis Trochu
Saint Bernadette Soubirous

On the evening of the last day of the novena, after the singing of the litany, one of the priests exposed the Most Blessed Sacrament in the monstrance. When he placed It on the altar, I immediately saw the Infant Jesus stretching out His little arms, first of all toward (a picture of) His Mother who, at that time, had taken on a living appearance. When the Mother of God was speaking to me, Jesus stretched out His tiny hands toward the congregation. The Blessed Mother was telling me to accept all that God asked of me like a little child, without questioning; otherwise it would not be pleasing to God.

Then the Infant Jesus vanished, and the Mother of God was again as if lifeless, and Her picture was the same as it had been before. But my soul was filled with great joy and gladness and I said to the Lord, "Do with me as You please; I am ready for everything, but You, O Lord, must not abandon me even for a moment."

Bl. M. Faustina Kowalska
Perpetual Eucharistic Adoration newsletter, October 1992

O n that April 11, a twenty-month-old baby, Julius Stephi, was literally pulling his hair out in the agony of meningitis. The child also had pneumonia. Both were complications from a severe attack of measles. Three physicians had fought for the child's life—and lost. The little one was in prolonged death throes when his grandmother, Mary Magdalena Vogel, came into Pittsburgh and stopped by on her way to Mass at St. Augustine's Church. . . .

During the Mass, the pain-racked little body in the crib was continuously before her eyes. Just as the priest reached the solemn moment of the Mass when the bread and wine offered are changed into the Body and Blood of Christ, Mrs. Vogel suddenly saw another face in her mind: Father Seelos, who had been her confessor years earlier. Redemptorist John Vaughn relates: "In this particular church they would ring the bell in the church tower at the moment of the Consecration during the Sunday High Mass. As the bell rang she said: 'Father Seelos, while you were on earth you had the power to change bread and wine into the Body and Blood of Christ. Now that you are in heaven, you are not less powerful. Please ask God to heal my grandchild.' Then she promised to make a novena in honor of Father Seelos and have a Mass said if the child would either end his agony by a quick death or recover."

Mass ended and Mrs. Vogel rushed back to her grandson. Her daughter met her at the door. Just after the Consecration bell rang in the tower of St. Augustine's, little Julius stopped writhing. An hour later the toddler, who had refused all food for two days, woke up ravenous—and well.

Patricia Treece
Nothing Short of a Miracle

When she came to Mass, very weak and longing for spiritual communion, it happened that the priest who had taken the Body of Christ to a sick person was returning from the village. At the sound of the bell, she was filled with desire and said to the Lord: "Oh, how gladly would I receive you now, life of my soul, at least spiritually, had I but a little time in which to prepare myself!" He replied: "The eyes of My divine love will prepare you most fittingly. Upon which she saw the Lord looking at her, directing rays as of sunlight into her soul and saying, "I will fix My eyes upon thee" (Ps 31:8). By these words she understood that three things were effected in the soul by the divine gaze, which was like the sun, and that there were three ways in which the soul should prepare to receive them.

First, the look of divine love, like the sun, takes away all stains from the soul, purifying it and making it whiter than snow (cf. Ps 50:9). And this effect can be gained by the humble recognition of one's own defects. Second, the look of divine love melts the soul and fits it to receive spiritual gifts, just as wax is melted by the sun's heat and made ready to take the imprint of a seal. And this effect the soul obtains by devout intentions. Third, the look of divine love makes the soul fruitful, so as to bring forth flowers of virtue, just as the sun gives fecundity to the earth so as to bring forth and multiply its various fruits. And this effect is obtained by faithful trust; for if a person abandons himself wholly to God, faithfully trusting in God's boundless love, everything, whether in adversity or in prosperity, will work together unto good (cf. Rom 8:28).

Margaret Winkworth, Trans. and Ed.
Gertrude of Helfta: The Herald of Divine Love

If Marthe's [Robin] last years were blessed by numerous apparitions of the Blessed Virgin, it cannot be doubted that she had particular need of this consoling presence, because Satan increased his attacks, striking her savagely and trying to make her believe that her sufferings were in vain, and worse, that she was obstructing the growth of God's kingdom.

On Monday, February 2, 1981, the feast of the Blessed Virgin, Marthe said to Fr. Finet: "The demon tells me that he will stay with me to the very end."

On the evening of Wednesday, February 4, Marthe prepared, as she did each week, to receive Communion. The many people who gathered around her on that evening recited the prayers she loved: the Litany of the Blessed Virgin, the Consecration of Saint Louis-Marie Grignion de Montfort, a Prayer to Saint Joseph, invocations, the Rosary, the Prayer of Pius XII, the prayer of the angel at Fatima, and several more invocations. Then Marthe received the Body of Christ and entered into an ecstasy, as she did every Wednesday.

Fr. Raymond Peyret
The Cross and the Joy

Francis' devotion to Christ was, as we know, the very center of his life. He had set out to follow Christ and to obey each one of His commands, however costly this might be. In many ways he felt as close to his Master as the first disciples had felt. Everything that Jesus had said and done was familiar to him, made so by his constant meditation on the Gospels. He felt particularly close to Christ in everything that was connected with His sufferings, and he prayed that he might share in them (so far as such a thing was humanly possible) and was rewarded by the long agony of the stigmata.

Francis's passion to be with Christ in all that he did, and in the life which he had chosen to live, gave him a special devotion to the Eucharist, which he saw as a unique meeting-place with Christ where he came as near as it was possible to see and to touch Him. Jesus had told His disciples that the bread and wine of the Eucharist were, in fact, His Body and His Blood, His physical being; and Francis had taken this literally. That was why he was so insistent that people should show respect for the priests, and especially to their hands, since it was they who made possible this physical contact with the Risen Christ.

John R. H. Moorman
The Spirituality Of St. Francis Of Assisi:
Richest of Poor Men

While he was thus thinking, a change came over the worship. A priest, or at least an assistant, had mounted for a moment above the altar, and removed a chalice or vessel that stood there; he could not see distinctly. A cloud of incense was rising on high; the people suddenly all bowed low; what could it mean? The truth flashed on him, fearfully yet sweetly; it was the Blessed Sacrament—it was the Lord Incarnate who was on the altar, who had come to visit and to bless His people. It was the Great Presence, which makes a Catholic Church different from every other place in the world; which makes it, as no other place can be—holy.

It was Sunday morning about seven o'clock, and Charles had been admitted into the communion of the Catholic Church about an hour since. He was still kneeling in the church of the Passionists before the tabernacle, in the possession of a deep peace and serenity of mind, which he had not thought possible on earth. It was more like the stillness that almost sensibly affects the ears when a bell that has long been tolling stops, or when a vessel, after much tossing at sea, finds itself in harbour. It was such as to throw him back in memory on his earliest years, as if he were really beginning life again. But there was more than the happiness of childhood in his heart; he seemed to feel a rock under his feet; it was the soliditas *Cathedrae Petri*. He went on kneeling, as if he were already in heaven, with the throne of God before him, and angels around, and as if to move were to lose his privilege.

John Henry Cardinal Newman
Loss and Gain: The Story of a Convert

When they finally got to the letter "W" and read my name, I responded by saying: "I am a priest and I am staying. While one hostage remains, I, too, remain."

There was a rather long silence, and then the head of the [Peruvian] terrorist group, Comandante Cerpa, responded: "If you want to stay, stay." The other hostages applauded, and this response confirmed me in my decision.

I was not sure what the repercussion of my decision would be outside the residence. I feared that my family would suffer from my decision, and wondered if my brother Jesuits would really understand the reasons for my decision. Soon after, I heard from my family, from my Jesuit brothers, and from many friends, all of whom strongly supported my decision.

I believe I stayed, then, to share this unjust situation with my fellow hostages, to be with them as a priest. I knew that if I left they would not be able to receive the sacraments, especially the Eucharist, and so for me it was both an act of human solidarity and also a service of the Church, that, with the help of God, I could offer.

There was something very divine that entered into my decision; I wanted to accompany Jesus Christ who was present in my fellow prisoners. I recalled the words from the Eucharist, "Do this in memory of Me," and realized that God was asking me to do this in memory of His Son. Looking back, I don't believe that I every prayed so intensely or so truthfully. (Words of Fr. Juan Julio Wicht, SJ, from an interview)

Fr. James O'Leary, SJ
Company

I n the presence of Jesus in the Blessed Sacrament I invariably find something that the world always hides from me, namely knowledge of self. In the light of the Holy Eucharist all my faults and failings and all my sins, past and present, become clear to me; and then from the very depths of my heart there wells up a cleansing, purifying fount of sorrow. Oh, how poor and miserable I appear to myself when in the presence of Jesus! And yet how sweet and salutary are the tears that I shed at the sight of transgressions!

If I cannot find it here, then where in the world can I find it—a little patch of earth, I mean, one to be watered by my tears so that thereon the tender blossoms of hope may grow? Who, if not Jesus, can say to me, "Go in peace, thy sins are forgiven thee"?

In vain do the fallen look for comfort and consolation from the proud ones of this world; they receive naught but the humiliation of contempt. Jesus alone knows how to extend to the fallen who are trying to arise again the helping hand divine. Jesus alone gives unto them the kiss of renewed friendship.

The tabernacles of sinners are no longer for me. To find peace, I must share my dwelling with Jesus.

Msgr. William Reyna
Eucharistic Reflections

It was hard to attend my son's First Communion because of our painful family circumstances. I was divorced and my ex-husband sat with his girlfriend in the family section. I stayed towards the back, fighting tears and wishing I could leave. As I turned to greet the people in my vicinity during the sign of peace, a gray-haired woman took my hand in hers and said gently, "Oh my dear, keep up your courage. You are doing just fine." They were the most perfect words anyone could have said. This gentle stranger, who apparently knew about my circumstances, gave me fresh courage and hope. Jesus knew all about my pain and probably prompted her to sit behind me and pray for me during my son's First Communion. Jesus reached out to heal me that day, through that woman. (A mother's story)

Fr. Robert DeGrandis, SSJ
Healing through the Mass

Alphonse, accompanied by Father de Villefort and Baron de Bussierre, was conducted to the principal entrance to the church, wearing a long robe of white damask. He held a Rosary tightly clasped in his hands, his eyes frequently bent on the medal attached to it. (For the information of non-Catholic readers, it may be explained that on the medal rays of light stream from Our Lady's hands.) First came the Exorcisms, and never had this mysterious liturgy seemed more truly divine than in the scene of imposing solemnity.

"What do you ask of the Church of God?"

"Faith!"

A sigh of unspeakable bliss, a smile of heavenly joy, and Marie Alphonse Ratisbonne raised his head still wet with the waters of Baptism. He had crossed the abyss, he was a Christian!

The Sacrament of Confirmation immediately followed to set the seal on this outpouring of graces. Then the Abbe Dupanloup proceeded to congratulate the newly made Christian in the name of the great Catholic family which welcomed him into her bosom. The Holy Sacrifice of the Mass then began.

Marie Alphonse followed the service deeply absorbed in prayer. When the solemn moment was reached and the Cardinal, his hand trembling with emotion, laid the sacred Host on the tongue of the neophyte, Ratisbonne, hitherto so calm and self-controlled in all his fervour, burst into sobs. At last the Te Deum rang out in a torrent of sound from the hearts of all present; it was no mere solemn rhythmic chant, but the loud acclamation of a multitude swept by the enthusiasm of their faith.

L. M. Leggatt, Trans.
A Nineteenth Century Miracle: The Brothers Ratisbonne

"I was never lonely," Father Martin Lucia says of his boyhood years spent at a boarding school run by nuns who encouraged him to spend time on Sundays with the Blessed Sacrament. When he was ten, his father died. Martin's mother was suddenly a single parent to Martin and two younger children. She decided it was best to enroll him a school away from home so that she could better meet her young family's needs.

That early experience of finding consolation, peace and inspiration in front of the Eucharist stayed with him. No one really taught the boy how to pray before the Blessed Sacrament or how to revere the sacred presence of Jesus who was truly there in the guise of bread. The young Lucia simply learned to pour out his heart to the listening Lord and listen, in return, to Jesus in the quiet.

Whenever he had a decision to make or a problem that needed to be dealt with, he would take it before Jesus in the Blessed Sacrament, explained Father Lucia, who was ordained in 1970. He knew, of course, that he wanted to dedicate his priesthood to the promotion of perpetual adoration of the Eucharist.

Catherine M. Odell
Columbia magazine, August 1995

Feast of St. Louis de Montfort
1673-1716

After Holy Communion, close your eyes and recollect yourself. Then usher Jesus into the heart of Mary; you are giving Him to his Mother who will receive Him with great love and give Him the place of honour, adore Him profoundly, show Him perfect love, embrace Him intimately in spirit and in truth, and perform many offices for Him of which we, in our ignorance, would know nothing.

Or, maintain a profoundly humble heart in the presence of Jesus dwelling in Mary. Or, be in attendance like a slave at the gate of the royal palace, where the King is speaking with the Queen. While they are talking to each other, with no need of you, go in spirit to heaven and to the whole world, and call upon all creatures to thank, adore and love Jesus and Mary for you. "Come, let us adore" (Ps 94:6).

Or, ask Jesus living in Mary that His kingdom may come upon earth through His holy Mother. Ask for divine wisdom, divine love, the forgiveness of your sins, or any other grace, but always through Mary and in Mary. Cast a look of reproach upon yourself and say, "Lord, do not look at my sins, let Your eyes see nothing in me but the virtues and merits of Mary."

St. Louis de Montfort
True Devotion to the Blessed Virgin

Feast of St. Catherine of Siena
1347-1380

Catherine came home from Pisa bearing the invisible stigmata and the pain and weakness that accompanied them. Getting out of bed was hard for her practically every morning now. She still did not sleep more than an hour most nights, but she did rest in the early morning hours. After her rest, her body often felt weak. Later in the day she might find more energy, but never in the morning. Only the strength of her loyal friends among the Mantellate and the prospect of receiving the Eucharist could get her out of bed most mornings.

Receiving the Eucharist was the central event in Catherine's day. For many years it was her only food. It fed her physically and spiritually, and she hungered for it in both her body and her soul. When priests refused to give her the Holy Sacrament, as they often did before Raymond came to Siena, it caused her physical and spiritual anguish.

Anne B. Baldwin
Catherine of Siena: A Biography

This beautiful home included a chapel where the Blessed Sacrament was always reserved. She loved to visit the chapel and kneel there for hours without moving! She was only eight years old when she felt led to repeat the vow over and over: "Oh my God, I dedicate to You my purity and I make to You a vow of perpetual chastity."

When her godmother died, Margaret [Mary Alacoque] returned to her own house, but shortly afterwards, her father died. The children were sent off to religious schools and Margaret went to a convent school. The sisters soon noticed that this girl who was so rowdy at games loved to pray before the Blessed Sacrament. Often she would interrupt play to run to the chapel or to hide in some small corner.

This pleasant life underwent an abrupt change when Margaret came down with rheumatic fever, leaving her bedridden for four years. During this time she made a vow that if the Blessed Virgin cured her she would one day become one of her daughters. After this promise, Margaret was healed. It seemed to her that the Blessed Virgin taught her day by day how to do God's will.

But then came fresh trials. Various relatives had taken over the Alacoque household to substitute for the deceased father and the weak-willed mother. They refused to let Margaret go to Mass during the week, assuming that such trips must be pretexts for meeting boyfriends.

To compensate, Margaret spent ten years hiding in the fields and gazing at the church where she knew her beloved Christ was to be found inside the tabernacle.

Ronda Chervin
Prayers of the Women Mystics

"May is Mary's month. The Mother of God. The most beautiful creature I ever created. In Mary you will find care and concern for even the smallest details. Mary is a mother, she knows what you need. You are her son, she loves you as she loved Jesus. When she wept for Jesus she also wept for you. She is, the 'Mother of the World' and is greatly disturbed that her household has strayed.

But in any household there is one or two that keep the faith and in time bring the rest of the family back to My love. Bring her family, the world, back to your Heavenly Father's love, little by little.

She has revealed to others the way in which this should be done: prayer; the Mass; the Rosary; and, fasting. Her love is stronger than all the love and attention you have ever been shown put together. All this love will come to you every moment of every day if you open yourself to her.

In this month of May, try especially in the area of devotion to Mary. Love, Love, Love is the answer. Mary is your mother and she loves you dearly, consecrate yourself to her each day and the graces of her love will flow through your work, prayer and relationships." (Words of God the Father, May 14, 1993)

Matthew Kelly
Words from God

We have said that Holy Communion is God's return to us for the honor, praise, gratitude, reparation and petition we have rendered to Him. Communion is God giving us not merely a grace and divine life, Himself. It is true that we can believe that our Blessed Lady had received Communion at the Last Supper with the apostles, and she continued to receive daily her own Son from the hands of His best-loved apostle, St. John. But Mary's return for her part in the sacrifice of Calvary was even more wonderful than Holy Communion. Since she redeemed mankind with her Son, since every grace that Christ merited by His Passion, she also merited by her compassion; since she with Christ paid the purchase-price of grace for our salvation, not merely by giving Christ a humanity in which to suffer, but even more so by suffering with Him, she ought to have a part in the distribution of grace. Her Communion in that first Mass, her Communion in every Mass that has followed lies in this: that Christ communicated to her the disposing, as she sees fit, of all the graces which they together have merited upon Calvary.

She is the invisible communicant at every altar in every Mass, receiving all from an affectionate divine Son for distribution to other poorer, weaker, helpless children—you and me.

John N. McCormink, CSSR
John A. Treinen, CSSR
What Is the Mass?

The sacraments and especially the Eucharist is the heart of evangelization, which is the primary mission of the Church. We learn to live fully in a human way only through and because of God's love. Learning to love—to live in love—entails more than a journey of the mind. It calls for a response of our whole selves: the surrender of our senses, imagination, emotions, intelligence, power of self determination, dynamism to value or will—as well as our endeavors to communicate daily in words and deeds. Anything less than this surrender of our whole selves would be selfishness—not love. But paradoxically in surrendering ourselves entirely to Christ we are made whole: we discover the wholesomeness or peace of being in harmony with the whole of creation in God. The love of Christ calls and empowers us to journey to the heart of reality. This is the pilgrimage of the heart, in which our inmost being becomes gradually oriented toward the depths of God.

The Spirit of truth, whom Jesus promised at the Last Supper, transforms not merely the gifts of bread and wine, but our whole lives because He creates our hearts anew to be worshippers whom the Father seeks. In the worship of the Eucharistic community especially we discover our worth in taking responsibility for one another and the whole of creation. Here we learn to receive and communicate forgiveness and the vital art of trust, without which there can be no solidarity in society. Here we are strengthened through the support of others' faith in Christ to journey beyond the barriers of our fears to risk the cost of loving and of venturing forward not merely to the horizons of the unknown, but to the mystery of God's presence.

Michael L. Gaudoin-Parker
Heart in Pilgrimage

I celebrated a healing Mass for the people of Naga in the chapel of the Carmelite Monastery on a Saturday morning. I did not know the condition of any of the people at the Mass as no one had asked me to pray for any special intention. I stressed the importance of forgiveness, led them in *The Forgiveness Prayer*, and gave everyone general absolution. During the homily I was led to tell the people to look up during the elevation of the Body and Blood of Christ. "As you are looking at the Lord Jesus . . . in faith," I said, "pray for healing. Especially if you pray for others," I added, "you will be healed."

One woman, Nena Bichara, took my words as gospel truth. She had been suffering from a goiter for three years. The doctors could do nothing about it except to recommend surgery that, of course, she did not want to undergo. During the elevation of the Body of Christ she prayed for different people. Then she added, "and also, Lord, do not forget my goiter." At once she felt a power hit her. She knew instantly that she was healed. She nudged her son next to her and said, "I am healed." He answered, "Be quiet, mommy. People will think you are crazy." After the Mass she called her doctor and insisted on an examination. He told her to come next week as it was already Saturday afternoon, but, like the persistent widow in the gospel, she got her way. The doctor could find no trace of goiter! Three months later in Manila she went to another doctor who did not know her case. She asked for a complete examination and asked the doctor to be sure to check for goiters. The doctor told her, "You do not have any sign of a goiter. You have never had one." Praise God!

Fr. Robert DeGrandis, SSJ
Healing through the Mass

On Sunday, February 2—twelve days after the incident of which we have spoken—Father Eymard, on his return to La Favorite where he was temporarily acting as novice-master, paid a short visit to the Sanctuary of Our Lady of Fourviere. It was two o'clock in the afternoon; the church was deserted. The Servant of God placed himself in the nave, a little behind the pulpit, and there he poured out his soul to his Tabernacled Lord. In all probability, his prayers centered on the thought which had been absorbing him during these twelve days.

"As I was praying," he afterwards confided to the author of this biography, "I was absorbed by so strong a thought that I became unconscious of everything else: Our Lord in the Blessed Sacrament had no religious Congregation whose sole purpose was the glorification of His Mystery of Love. There was need of such a Congregation!"

This thought amazed and ravished Father Eymard. He must have remained for a long time in this state, for, to the above words, he added in an indescribable tone: "What hours I spent there that afternoon!"—His companion then said: "Then you must have seen the Blessed Virgin to have been so enraptured?" Father Eymard did not expect such an embarrassing question. A "yes," extorted by truth and checked out of humility, was muttered in reply; but it did not escape the ears of his questioner: "His answer is still fresh in my ear, and stands out very clearly in my mind; for it was what I wished to learn when I put the question. It may have seemed indiscreet on my part; but it was of the highest importance to me."

Fr. Albert Tesniere, SSS
Blessed Peter Julian Eymard

"*I am the Mother of adoration and of reparation.* Beside every tabernacle of the earth there is always my motherly presence. It forms a new and loving tabernacle for the solitary presence of my Son Jesus; it builds a garden of love for his permanent residence among you; it forms a celestial harmony which surrounds Him with all the enchantment of paradise in the adoring choirs of angels, in the blessed prayer of the saints, in the painful aspiration of the many souls who are being purified in purgatory. In my Immaculate Heart all form a concert of perennial adoration, of unceasing prayer and of profound love for Jesus, really present in every tabernacle on earth.

Today my motherly heart is saddened and is deeply wounded because I see that, about the divine presence of Jesus in the Eucharist, there is so much emptiness, so much abandonment, so much neglect, so much silence.

O Church, pilgrim and suffering, of which I am the Mother, Church who are the family of all my children, ark of the new alliance, people of God, you must understand that the center of your life, the fount of your grace, the source of your light, the beginning of your apostolic action is found only here in the tabernacle where Jesus is truly kept. And Jesus is present to teach you how to grow, to help you to walk, to strengthen you in giving witness, to give you courage in evangelizing, to be a support for all your sufferings." (Words of Our Lady, August 21, 1987)

Fr. Stefano Gobbi
To the Priests: Our Lady's Beloved Sons

A young boy about to make his first Communion was questioned by the pastor. "What will you receive next Sunday?" he was asked. "Bread and wine." "Try again, it's not just bread and wine, is it, Johnny?"

"It is bread and wine! It looks like bread. It tastes like bread and it feels like bread. It is bread! And that wine business—it looks, tastes and smells like wine, and that's what it is. It's wine! So it is bread and wine!"

The pastor refused to let Johnny receive the sacrament, so the boy was sent to me. "What is your problem, Johnny?" I asked. "I don't have a problem. The priest has the problem. He thinks that bread and wine is Jesus," he said defiantly.

I smiled at the stubbornness of this very intelligent eight-year old. "I believe it is Jesus too, Johnny," I said. "Then you gotta problem too!" was his quick answer.

It is a problem understanding Christ's Real Presence under the appearance of bread and wine. It's a mystery! Electricity is truly present in the radio, the television, the lightbulb, and the air conditioner. The things it touches have not changed but the power is contained within these things. Yet we can see them working. At least we see the effects of the electricity's presence.

How about radiation? If I exposed bread and wine to radiation, the bread would still taste like bread, look like bread, feel like bread. The wine would still taste like wine, look like wine, smell like wine. But I had better not eat or drink them—I would become radioactive! It would be radioactive power under the appearance of bread and wine. And none of my senses could tell me that. *But you better believe it.*

Fr. Ken Roberts
You Better Believe It

I t struck me recently that the first person who had the right to say of Jesus, "This is my body. This is my blood," was Mary. Even before Jesus was to say this at the Last Supper, even before we are to say this during this Mass, Mary could say this as Jesus was hanging on the cross. Mary could look at Christ and say, "This is my Body. This is my Blood. This is my sacrifice. I am joined in Him." This is what we do in the Eucharistic sacrifice. When the priest says, "This is My Body" over a piece of bread and "This is My Blood" over a cup of wine, the same Holy Spirit comes down upon these elements that came down upon the tent in the desert, that came down upon Mary. The same Holy Spirit comes down on these elements and brings forth the same Son, now not the Word carved in stone, the Ten Commandments, but the Word actually become flesh. This is the heart of the Consecration of the Mass.

John Cardinal O'Connor
Homily in St. Patrick's Cathedral, December 22, 1996

Christ, then, had not omitted to supply this fundamental need of human nature. When He left us, He appointed representatives to answer men's questions concerning faith and morals and to carry on His sanctifying work on earth, forgiving sins, administering the cleansing waters of Baptism, and distributing the Body which He had immolated for us on the Cross. With His deep understanding of mankind, He had inaugurated visible rites and had chosen to confer invisible graces by means of them. It was thoroughly characteristic of Our Lord to require us to do small physical acts evidencing a little faith and a little humility, and then to recompense them with enormous spiritual rewards. It was part of the logic of the Incarnation that He should give Himself to us in Holy Communion, not only by spiritual indwelling in the soul, but sensibly under the appearances of the bread and wine. With ineffable joy I read that He had actually done so: that the Word had been made flesh not only for Peter and James and John, but for all posterity. One could still adore God visibly in the Eucharist. One could still be united physically to His Sacred Person—both human and divine—more closely (in a sense) than was Our Lady when she had carried the Infant Jesus in her womb.

Fr. Avery Dulles, SJ
A Testimonial to Grace

Duran Mass, at which St. Gertrude communicated, she beheld the Mother of God, gloriously adorned with every virtue. She prostrated humbly at her feet, beseeching her to dispose her to receive worthily the august Sacrament of the Body and Blood of her Divine Son. The Blessed Virgin then gave her a magnificent necklace, which had seven rays or points, to each of which a precious stone was attached and these stones indicated the signal virtues that had pleased our Lord most in His Blessed Mother. The first was her exquisite purity, the second her faithful humility, the third her ardent desires, the fourth her clear knowledge, the fifth her unquenchable love, the sixth the sovereign pleasure that she took in God, the seventh her peaceful tranquility. When St. Gertrude appeared before our Lord with this necklace, He was so won by the brilliancy of her virtues, that He inclined lovingly towards her. Drawing her to Himself and enclosing her as it were in His bosom, He honored her with His pure and holy caresses.

Msgr. William J. Doheny, CSC
The Revelations of St. Gertrude

The presence of the whole Trinity in the Eucharist, affirmed by theology, has sometimes been actively experienced by the saints. A great mystic wrote in her diary: "It seemed that in the most Holy Sacrament, as on a throne, I saw the one and triune God: the Father in His omnipotence, the Son in His wisdom, the Holy Spirit in His love. Every time we communicate, our souls and hearts become the temple of the most Holy Trinity, and when God comes to us, the whole of paradise comes. On seeing God enclosed in the Host, I was transported with joy for the whole day. If I had to give my life to confirm this truth, I would do so a thousand times" (St. Veronica Giuliani).

Therefore, we enter into a mysterious communion, real and deep, with the whole Trinity: with the Father, through Christ, in the Holy Spirit. The whole Trinity is invisibly present round the altar. This is depicted in A. Rublev's well-known icon of the Trinity in which the Father, Son and Holy Spirit, symbolized by the three angels that appeared to Abraham under the oak of Mamre, form a sort of mystic circle round the altar and they seem to say to us: "May you all be one, as we are one!"

Fr. Raniero Cantalamessa
The Eucharist: Our Sanctification

Another night, Nonette Silla was in the chapel praying from 2 AM to 3 AM, the hour before mine. Three weeks before she had lifted up to the Heart of Jesus a man she knew who was destroying the moral life of many of her girl-friends. Her prayer included this man because she knew Jesus loved him, too. Her prayer ended with an exclamation point that she wanted Jesus to bring him to the chapel so that she would know for sure that he was converted.

Three weeks later while she was in prayer at the chapel she heard someone sobbing in the back. She turned around and it was he. He explained that for three weeks his mind was con-fused. What he thought was right now looked like it was wrong. He could not sleep. That night he began to drive around the city. He lived in Makati. When he passed the church of San Miguel he saw the light on in the chapel. The light was invit-ing, welcoming. He decided to stop and come in. What he met was not condemnation for his sins. Instead, he experienced ten-der mercy from the Blessed Sacrament. That is why he wept.

When I came at 3 AM, he told me his story. I heard his con-fession, gave him absolution, and he has been a daily commu-nicant ever since.

Msgr. Josefino S. Ramirez
Letters to a Brother Priest

Feast of Our Lady of the Blessed Sacrament
Feast of Our Lady of Fatima

I cannot end a discourse on the Eucharist without linking it to the great Queen, for there is no secret how the Blessed Virgin is related to the Eucharist. It is very simple. It was she who gave Him His Body and His Blood, and she is the channel of divine grace who draws men to her Son. As Pope John Paul II says in his encyclical *Redemptoris Mater*: "Mary guides the faithful to the Eucharist." Indeed, in a decree dated September 12, 1963, his predecessor Pope Paul VI declared the Most Blessed Virgin Mary as "Our Lady of the Most Blessed Sacrament, the principal and heavenly Patron of the Congregation of the Fathers of the Blessed Sacrament." This Congregation was founded by St. Peter Julian Eymard (1811-1868).

Significantly, it was on that feast day, the feast of Our Lady of the Blessed Sacrament, that she chose to open her apparitions in Fatima. It was on May 13, 1917. The Eucharist is the Sacrament of the new and everlasting Covenant and Our Lady of the Blessed Sacrament is the Tabernacle of the Most High. She is the Ark of the Covenant.

The ancient Ark of the old Covenant, which was kept in the Holy of Holies in Solomon's Temple, contained some of the miraculous manna that fell from heaven. But the Tabernacle on the altars of Catholic churches houses the Eucharist behind small doors, frequently covered by a veil like in the days of old. This is the new Holy of Holies that contains the true Bread of Life, the Lawgiver Himself, the Mediator of the new and everlasting Covenant.

Dr. Courtenay Bartholomew
A Scientist Researches Mary: The Ark of the Covenant

At Fatima today, pilgrims from distant lands are some times surprised to see that the great golden statue in the heart of the Cova da Iria, where Our Lady appeared, is not a statue of Our Lady of Fatima, but a statue of the Sacred Heart. By contrast, the statue of Our Lady of Fatima is a much smaller, wooden statue in an almost insignificant little chapel, off to one side.

Pilgrims are sometimes even further surprised to see that the great demonstrations of faith at Fatima are centered primarily in the Blessed Sacrament.

When pilgrims come to Fatima they think at once of the spot where Our Lady appeared, and they flock to that little chapel and realize with awe that they are on sacred, visited ground. But when the ceremonies begin, the statue is taken from that little chapel and carried in procession, attracting the attention and devotion of all to Our Lady, and then it leads to the great altar in front of the Basilica, is put to one side, and the real devotion of Fatima begins, with Mass, Communion, and Benediction of the Blessed Sacrament.

John Mathias Haffert
Sign of Her Heart

I used to think that the concept of the Real Presence of Christ in the Eucharist had been invented sometime during the Dark Ages as a ploy of the priesthood to gain power. Yet this truth is such a mystery that it seems unlikely anyone would invent it. Further, the most elementary reading of primary sources from the first three centuries of Christianity will show this theory of priestly invention to be the result of ignorance of almost unbelievable proportions.

In the Early Church, everyone who wrote anything about the Eucharist believed in the Real Presence of Christ in the elements of Communion. Ignatius was the second bishop of Antioch and died a martyr at about the same time the Apostle John died. Speaking of the Docetist heretics, who denied the humanity of Jesus, he wrote, "They confess not the Eucharist to be the flesh of our Savior Jesus Christ, which suffered for our sins, and which the Father, of His goodness, raised up again" (Ignatius of Antioch, *Epistle of Ignatius to the Smyrnaeans*, 7). I thought that I had seen something new in John 6, until I noticed that Ignatius equated the flesh of the Eucharist with the flesh of the Cross, just as John had recorded Jesus as doing.

David B. Currie
Born Fundamentalist, Born Again Catholic

"It was August 26, 1861. I was praying in Holy Rosary Church in La Granja during my hour of adoration at seven o'clock in the evening. Then the Lord granted me the great grace of the sacramental species abiding in my breast. I now bear day and night within me the adorable Eucharist. I must therefore be always recollected and cultivate the interior life. Moreover, according to the Lord's command I must try to arrest by prayer and in other ways the evil rampant in Spain." A little farther below we read another entry on the same subject. "About a quarter past four on May 16, 1862 during prayer I casually thought of the notes I had made the previous day, concerning the indwelling of the Blessed Sacrament granted me August 26 of the last year. I was tempted yesterday and today to erase them. The Blessed Virgin however made me understand I was to let them remain; and afterwards during Mass Our Lord assured me that He had really granted me the grace of the sacramental indwelling in my breast."

Fr. Thomas, CMF
Saint Anthony Mary Claret: A Sketch of His Life and Works

Feast of St. Pascal Baylon
1540-1592

The sectaries addressed this question to their prisoner with scornful hate: "Papist, do you believe that God is in the Sacrament that you consecrate and call the Mass?" To affirm the Catholic doctrine on this point was to sign his death-warrant. "Yes," exclaims Paschal, "I do believe it, and I most firmly maintain that God is as really present in the consecrated Host as He is in the glory of Heaven." At this spirited reply of the Confessor of the Faith, the sectaries foam with rage. They fancied that fear would extort some weak concession from this wretched monk and that, in order to escape death, he would have recourse to equivocation or subterfuge. They had not realized what kind of a person they had to deal with.

Not wishing to acknowledge defeat, the heretics challenged Paschal to a formal disputation on the subject of the Eucharist. The man of God was not one to shirk the encounter, especially as it was a question of defending the Blessed Sacrament. With that deft manipulation, peculiar to heresy, the sectaries, hiding the hollowness of the arguments under an imposing pile of Biblical texts, endeavoured to prove that the bread after Consecration still remained bread, and that the Sacrifice of the Mass was useless, derogatory to the Passion of Christ, and the occasion of the most monstrous idolatry. Paschal listened in sadness to this long string of blasphemies. When his turn to speak came, he replied to all these fallacies in due order, refuting each one with such powerful arguments, so well grounded on the Holy Scriptures, that the Protestant thesis went utterly to pieces.

Fr. Louis-Antoine de Porrentruy
The Saint of the Eucharist: Saint Paschal Baylon

B y continuing my knotted-string calendar I counted down to what I thought was Easter and celebrated Eucharist in my closet. I suppose there was some poignancy in spending Holy Week as a hostage in chains, celebrating it a week early. Now I learned I had been mistaken in my calculations. Yet I knew there was only one thing to do about it: celebrate it again!

And so I did. Chained to a wall in the guards' presence, I had to rise very early to avoid their surveillance, celebrating Eucharist for my second Easter in pre-dawn darkness.

I always retained a piece of the Eucharistic Christ, clinging to the Lord especially in moments of violence, sadness, boredom, or fear. One day I was holding Christ's Body in a closed hand and one of the guards noticed and asked, "What do you have in your hand?" Opening my clenched fist, I showed him the small piece of bread and said, "This is Jesus." He stood in uncomprehending silence.

Lawrence Martin Jenco, OSM
Bound to Forgive

A mystic once related: "As Jesus is truly in heaven, so also is He truly present on earth in the Eucharist with His Body, His Blood, His Soul and His Divinity."

So coming into the presence of the Eucharist to intercede is to come into the presence of the Lord Himself. We enter into the radiance of His presence that penetrates us and transforms our intercession. Coming into the presence of the Lord in the Eucharist is like being irradiated with the rays of the sun. So, in a sense, our intercession before the Blessed Sacrament is above all a presence—our presence to His presence, like a plant in the sun drawing energy to grow and bear fruit.

The more we expose ourselves to His radiating presence, the more we are transformed into His image. Through us then, Jesus makes Himself present again, immolates Himself anew and gives Himself to souls. In this way we become truly intercessors before the Father. Would that we be fully transformed and radiate His presence!

Various mystics have related that a time is coming when the Church and world will be renewed and we will be a Eucharistic people. I think this means that Jesus in the Eucharist will be the focal point of our lives—that our gatherings, our worship, and intercessions will center on His Eucharistic presence among us.

Fr. George W. Kosicki, CSB
Intercession

Mostly Bernadette's thoughts were fixed beyond this earth. "During her long nights," reported Canon Perreau, "she used to say the Rosary." At other times she placed herself as it were in adoration before the Tabernacle. On her curtains had been fastened the picture of a monstrance. "I am happy in my sleepless hours," she confided to Mother Audidier, "uniting myself with our Lord. One glance at this picture gives me the longing and the strength to immolate myself, when I am feeling my loneliness and my pains." But "her great happiness," asserts Canon Perreau, "was to join in spirit in the Holy Sacrifices which, at that very moment, were being celebrated in this or that part of the world." She used to note the country where priests were going up to the altar at that moment; and for this she used another well-known pious picture: a clock-face on which could be read the hours of Mass in every part of the globe. She loved also to gaze at a simple print, likewise fastened to the bed curtains, representing the Elevation of the Host. Bowing down behind the celebrant was a darling little altar-boy, and Bernadette would sometimes call out to him: "Now then, ring the bell!"

Francis Trochu
Saint Bernadette Soubirous

S harp, intense pain, going straight to the core of my heart, is what I have had to offer to Jesus glorified, together with the struggle against myself and outside agitations. During this month devoted to Mary, which is also devoted to Jesus in the Blessed Sacrament, to the Sacred Heart, and to the Holy Spirit, I want to make a courageous effort toward holiness. To be silent, to forget myself; to think of others and devote myself to them; to care for and accomplish nothing but the divine Will; to be the apostle of the Sacred Heart, an adoring and atoning soul; my eyes and my heart fixed on the tabernacle and on Heaven, to seek there only Jesus and to lead to Him all of the souls He will place in my path.

Above all, an apostolate of prayer and suffering. Humble, discreet action; unalterable gentleness, friendliness and kindness.

Elizabeth Leseur
My Spirit Rejoices

The witnesses of the Process [of beatification] tell us that it was a wonderful thing to hear her speak on God and on His attributes, as though she had studied the most difficult points of theology, although she was able neither to read nor write. Christ Jesus had stolen the heart of Rita—He alone possessed it. He had made her heart His heart; and under the white veils of the Eucharist He was for her soul, as He is for all loving hearts, heaven upon earth. How sweet is the moment in which poor humanity, wearied and afflicted, may remain alone, with Jesus alone, in the Sacrament of Love; for there the Lord, with His flaming heart open, calls unto all, "You that are burdened and heavy laden, come unto Me and I will refresh you." Happy are those hearts that know how to satisfy the unquenchable hunger and thirst in this heavenly banquet!

And in truth our Rita had such a heart. So thoroughly was it inflamed with love for the Bread of Angels that the more she partook of that Bread the more she felt new desires to partake more often. Rather than lose one single Holy Communion she would have preferred to lose life itself; and when in her old age she was broken by sickness and could no longer by herself approach the Holy Table, she seemed transformed into an eager angel of love to those good Sisters who accompanied her and held her in their arms. Her tears and sighs, her groans, her words of affection burst forth as from the heart itself, and she longed for the moment when she should receive from the hands of the priest Christ Jesus in the Sacrament.

Fr. M. J. Corcoran, OSA
Our Own St. Rita: A Life of the Saint of the Impossible

I n the ancient Eucharistic Liturgy, I find the place where the crushing mystery of our mortal existence, with all of its bliss and its agony, touches the Eternal Mystery. There is no answer at all to the riddle of human existence, and especially of human suffering and human sin, if it is not to be found in the mystery of oblation—of sacrifice—of offering. All Christian believers find that mystery brought to a point at the Cross. Here we find the God who reveals Himself, not as the One Who will speak the formula that unlocks the riddle, but rather as the One Who takes on Himself the whole of our suffering and our sin. And—mystery of mysteries—He invites us into His own self-immolation there. "You are a royal priesthood," says St. Peter. "I am crucified with Christ," says St. Paul, and, "I fill up that which is behind of the suffering of Christ."

Surely if these words mean anything at all, they mean that we are invited into the mystery of Christ's own self-offering, to make our lives and our sufferings one with His, not merely for our own comfort, but for the life of the world. Do we add something to His merits? Certainly not. But the Church shares His priesthood; the Church is His Body, which has no purpose other than to be broken, like bread, for the life of the world. This is what the Mass is about. This is what the mystery of worship brings us to. A merely verbalist, propositionalist, disembodied religion of preaching does not go to the heart of the Gospel. (Thomas Howard)

Robert Baram, Ed.
Spiritual Journeys

Three miraculous communions are mentioned in the biographies of St. Mary Magdalen de Pazzi (d. 1607). The earliest occurred on Holy Thursday in the year 1585 when the saint was nineteen years of age and a novice in the Carmelite Order. She was then already experiencing ecstasies and participating in Our Lord's sufferings. During one of her ecstasies, while she was following the events of the Passion, she was seen to assume the position of a communicant; with great devotion she opened and closed her mouth, and then bowed her head. When she emerged from the ecstasy she confided to the sisters what had taken place, namely, that she had received Holy Communion from the hands of the Savior, Himself.

That same year, during Mass on the feast of St. Albert of the Carmelite Order (August 7), while reciting the *Domine non sum dignus* ("Lord, I am not worthy"), St. Mary Magdalen de Pazzi opened her mouth and, while in ecstasy, participated in a long discussion with Our Lord. Afterward she revealed that she had once again received Holy Communion at the hands of the Redeemer.

The third occasion occurred on Holy Thursday of the year 1592, when the saint again received Holy Communion miraculously. This occurred while she was participating in the passion of the Saviour.

Joan Carroll Cruz
Eucharistic Miracles

Feast of St. Madeleine Sophie Barat
1770-1865

Today, the feast of our blessed mother [Madeleine Sophie Barat], I went into her cell many times to whisper a little prayer to her, and once (I was in my blue working apron) I just stood for a moment and said: "O Mother, once more I ask you to make me very humble, that I may be your true daughter!" There was no one in the room and this little invocation escaped me out loud. Suddenly I became aware of the presence of an unknown nun. She took my head in her two hands, and pressed it lovingly, saying: "My child, commit all your frailties to the Heart of Jesus, love the Heart of Jesus, rest in the Heart of Jesus and be faithful to the Heart of Jesus."

I took her hand to kiss it, then with two fingers she made the sign of the Cross in blessing on my forehead, and disappeared.

This first meeting was followed by many others. Up and down the cloisters of Les Feuillants that her feet had so often trod, in her cell, in the shadow of the tabernacle where she prayed, St. Madeleine Sophie showed herself to her child, with the same vivacious and ardent expression of countenance she was known to have had on earth, but now stamped with the light of glory. Josefa spoke to her with the same confidence and simplicity with which she had recourse to her mother on earth. She listened to her counsels, confided all her difficulties to her, and under such motherly guardianship she felt her vocation safe.

Sr. Josefa Menendez
The Way of Divine Love

While celebrating his first Mass, St. Philip Neri (1515-1595) was so overwhelmed with consolation and joy that he was scarcely able to pour the wine and water into the chalice because of the excessive trembling of his hands, which continued until the end of the Holy Sacrifice. His ecstasies, especially at the elevation and Communion, were so intense that he frequently found it necessary to lean against the altar to avoid collapsing. So frequent were his raptures during Holy Mass that the Sacrifice occupied two hours or more. For this reason he was obliged to offer Mass in a private chapel.

It was St. Philip's practice from time to time after receiving the Eucharist to cover his face with a linen cloth so that he might pray and enjoy the presence of his Heavenly Guest without being distracted and without having his enraptured expression observed by his companions. During St. Philip's illnesses, it often proved beneficial for him to receive the Holy Eucharist, which served as a healing agent.

During the last five years of his life, whenever St. Philip offered Holy Mass in his private chapel, the server would leave the chapel at the *Agnus Dei* ("Lamb of God") shortly before Communion, lock the doors, and hang up a sign that read: "Silence, the Father is saying Mass." When the server returned in two or more hours, the saint would be so absorbed in God that he seemed to be at the point of death.

Joan Carroll Cruz
Eucharistic Miracles

"There stood by the Cross of Jesus, his mother" (Jn 19: 25). At Bethlehem she gave birth to Him physically, without pain. On Calvary she gave birth to His Mystical Body in sorrow and suffering. Mary's name is inseparable from the Sacrifice of Christ, Her Son.

Let us bring Mary with us to Mass. She will kneel beside us at the Consecration and we shall feel her intense devotion, admire her heroic courage, and yearn for her spirit of self-sacrifice. Mary knows that the more a soul gives itself into His hands, the more perfectly does He work for its sanctity. No one has abandoned herself to Him as Mary has.

Mary knows me far better than I know myself. She knows why I am reluctant to be subject to Him, why I hestitate to surrender myself to Him, and she will help me to beat down the resistance I put in His way. Mary understands the sacrifice of giving, for, next to Him, she gave most; more than any of the martyrs.

Let us, in imagination, assist at the Mass said by St. John in the presence of Mary, in their humble home at Ephesus, where St. John had taken her. What an acceptable offering that must have been! What better companions can we have to walk to Mass with than Mary and St. John, who walked together the bitter road to Calvary! What better guides can we have to stand beside us at the Consecration than Mary and St. John, who stood by the Cross on Calvary!

Fr. John T. McMahon
Live the Mass

The example of well-known saints, as well as that of ordinary people, has helped us see the beauty of the sacrificial love that is found most perfectly in the sacrifice of Calvary and of the Mass. The life of St. Maximilian Kolbe offers us such an example. While a prisoner at Auschwitz during World War II, this priest offered his life to save the life of a man who had a family. During the long period when Maximilian and those condemned with him were being starved to death, he ministered to them, led them in prayer and helped lift their faith and their spirits. When the soldiers decided to execute the few remaining prisoners by lethal injection and finally came to him, St. Maximilian joyfully held up his arm to receive the needle because he knew that Jesus would not leave his love unrewarded.

The account of this beautiful death helps us know the power that Christ's sacrifice can have in our lives. Because we are joined to Calvary, we can have the courage and strength to offer our own lives for others. We can take up our crosses daily to follow Him. Life's pains and struggles, as well as its smaller inconveniences, can become occasions for showing our love for God and for one another when we join them to Jesus' own self-giving.

Bishop John J. Myers
Pastoral Letter to the People of the Diocese of Peoria

In 1832, two years after the apparition of Our Lady to Catherine Laboure in Paris, Fr. Charles des Gennettes was the parish priest of Our Lady of Victories. For a century and a half, the parishioners were known for their devotion to the Blessed Virgin. However, with the anti-clerical French Revolution . . . scarcely anyone came to Mass or received the sacraments.

On Sunday, December 3, 1836, Fr. Charles began to say Mass in an almost empty church, when he was seized by the conviction that he must resign. . . . At that moment he heard a soft distinct voice say very solemnly: "Consecrate your parish to the Most Holy and Immaculate Heart of Mary." Convincing himself that it had been his imagination, he knelt to say his prayers. Again, he heard the words: "Consecrate your parish to the Most Holy and Immaculate Heart of Mary."

Taking up a pen, he composed the rules for a Confraternity of Our Lady. The Bishop approved the rules that same week. The following Sunday, Father des Gennettes told the ten people at Mass about his project. He said that there would be vespers of Our Lady that evening and that he would give them the full details of the Confraternity. When he entered the church that evening more than four hundred people were there.

People began to come to Our Lady of Victories from all parts of Paris, and then from all of France, and soon the fame of the shrine was world-wide. In 1838 Pope Gregory XVI made the Confraternity the "Archconfraternity of the Holy and Immaculate Heart of Mary for the Conversion of Sinners." Today, thousands of plaques in thanksgiving for cures line the walls of the church.

Dr. Courtenay Bartholomew
A Scientist Researches Mary: The Ark of the Covenant

A s St. Albert the Great says in his book on the Mass: "The congregation is not offering merely material gifts. He who offers something is offering himself to the priest at the same time, so that he, too, can become an offering made to God." In the sacrifice Jesus Christ Himself, present after the Consecration under the appearances of bread and wine, offers himself, innocent though He is, for our sins. The least we sinners can do is to offer ourselves with him in his sacrifice because, at least in part, we were the cause of his death on Calvary. We are not offering ourselves by shedding our blood, but we must do it by a total surrender to God, so that He can do with us whatever He pleases.

The offering of the faithful should symbolize for each one of us our complete availability, as Christians, for whatever God wants of us. We want to play whatever part He has given us in His redemptive plan. The offertory signifies our self-surrender, that of the Church as the Mystical Body united to Christ its Head, and of each of the faithful who are members of the Mystical Body. We hand over our gifts for God to use, not only bread and wine, not only alms for the poor, but the gifts God has given us to enrich our lives. We offer our sight and hearing and all our senses, our mind and will, our health, and our sickness too, because that can be a sharing in Christ's passion and so have redemptive value. We put everything at God's disposal.

Federico Suarez
The Sacrifice of the Altar

Q. What has Our Lady taught you about Our Lord's presence in the Holy Eucharist?

A. On the second apparition, when Our Blessed Mother came from a distance, there was a Light over her heart. Then, when Our Holy Mother came close up, I could see it was the Holy Eucharist and the Light was radiating from it. Our Lady was joyous and drew my attention to look down as she was looking down.

After that, I was wondering why the Holy Eucharist was over Our Blessed Mother's heart. It's only been these last couple of months that I thought about it. So I prayed and said, "Holy Mother, if you want me to know the meaning of what that was all about, then you'll reveal it." She didn't reveal it in words; it was revealed inwardly. I was aware that she held Jesus over her heart, meaning that she loved Jesus in the Holy Eucharist. Our Lady would give reverence to Him by carrying Him over her heart, meaning that we should carry Him over our hearts and in our hearts. The Light around it, for me, signified the graces we can receive by receiving the Holy Eucharist, worthily—in a proper way. Our Holy Mother said we can receive the Holy Eucharist only when we have made a proper Confession. Our Blessed Mother desires her children to unburden themselves of all sin and receive her Son's Body and Blood worthily.

When Our Blessed Mother spoke about the Holy Eucharist and the sacraments, she was talking about the Mass itself. Mass, with the celebration of the Holy Eucharist, is the reality of Jesus. It is to love Jesus in prayer and adoration.

Thomas W. Petrisko
The Sorrow, The Sacrifice and The Triumph:
Prophecies of Christina Gallagher

June 1

T
he earliest documentation of the Liturgies of the Eucharist and of the Word cojoined is found in the *First Apology*, written in 150 AD by St. Justin Martyr. In the *Apology*, Justin explains the liturgy to Greek-speaking Roman citizens, giving two accounts: one after baptism and another a Sunday morning celebration, "the day on which Jesus Christ our Savior rose from the dead." The liturgy Justin describes is so like our own as to be astonishing. It clearly includes the Offertory, Preface and Canon, Great Amen and Holy Communion.

Liturgy of the Word: "The memoirs of the apostles [the four Gospels] or the writings of the prophets are read as long as there is time." *Sermon*: "When the reader has finished, the president of the assembly verbally admonishes and invites all to imitate such examples of virtue." *Offertory*: "We all stand up together and offer up prayers; bread and wine and water are presented." *Preface and Canon*: "He who presides over the brethren . . . offers prayer . . . and he utters a lengthy thanksgiving because the Father has judged us worthy of these gifts." *Great Amen*: "And the people express their approval by saying, 'Amen.'" *Holy Communion*. "The Eucharistic elements are distributed and consumed by those present, and to those who are absent they are sent through the deacons." Notice that the second century community has a distinct Catholic understanding of the Real Presence of Christ in the consecrated elements. Says Justin, "The food over which the thanksgiving has been spoken becomes the flesh and blood of the incarnate Jesus."

Daniel Gallio

Immaculata, January/February 1996

"My beloved friend, tell My people that they are living in the Age of the Two Hearts—that of My Heart and My Mother's heart. My people live in the initial stages of this great era. I call all My people to take up their refuge in My Heart and My Mother's heart. In Our Hearts they will become more and more transformed into My likeness.

The greatest source for growth in devotion to Our Hearts is the Eucharist. I wish My people to attend Mass often, daily if possible. What a great gift I have given to My people in the Eucharist! Yet many of My people are indifferent to the treasures contained in the Mass. Think of it! My people are privileged to offer the Sacrifice of the Mass together with Me! And yet how many prefer to do other things rather than attend Mass. How this attitude offends My Sacred Heart!" (Words of Our Lord)

Fr. Edward Carter, SJ
Tell My People: Messages from Jesus and Mary

T he Mass is mine. Through the Mass, the fruits and benefits of Calvary can and do become mine. The Mass is from me to God but also for me from God.

In human societies we know that the more we contribute the more we draw out of the society. Our profits or dividends are proportionate to our investment. Likewise is this the case in the supernatural organization of prayer, the Mass. The more actively and intimately we participate in the action of the sacrifice, the more fruit we derive from it.

And the first fruits of the Mass are intended for Our Father Who is in heaven. Picture the Mass as a mighty tree lifting its head high above the clouds of the earth, rising even into heaven before the throne of God Himself. From that divine tree God plucks the infinite fruits of adoration, praise, thanksgiving and propitiation. These first fruits, though they are from us, have actually an infinite value, for the infinitely perfect God does not spoil their perfection as they issue from the infinite heart of Christ, our divine head.

Other fruits from this infinitely laden tree fall to earth upon our souls. These are the graces that we need for ourselves. These are the fruits of petition for our body and soul; the fruits of pardon for sin and its punishment; the fruits of actual graces and the increase of sanctifying grace. The pity is that though these fruits could be infinite by virtue of the infinite power of the Mass, nevertheless because of our lack of devotion or because we bring only a thimble-soul to the altar, we carry away from the tree of the Mass only a very limited supply of fruit.

John N. McCormick, CSSR
John A. Treinan, CSSR
What Is the Mass?

Heavenly Father, when Your priest holds up the host and says "the Body of Christ" let my soul bow in humble adoration before the love and humility of Jesus. Let my heart be a pure resting place for Your Son. I desire, dear Father, that the image of Jesus grow brighter in my soul after every Communion. At that tremendous moment God and I are one. My Jesus, so shine in me that together we may glorify the Father by bearing fruit in abundance. Let us go out into the world together and radiate Your love and kindness.

I am a child of God through Baptism and my resemblance to Him has grown stronger through Holy Communion. Somewhere, someplace, there is a Mass being said—a Calvary to be present at—a Communion to receive, either sacramentally or spiritually—an opportunity to be more like Jesus, the privilege of helping my neighbor, a time to say "I thank You, God," a situation to choose Jesus over myself or a chance to make a sacrifice. Truly, the Mass will go on and on until one day the Father will say, as His Son once said, "It is finished." Yes, the Lamb of God shall reign triumphantly with all those who have been washed clean in His Blood.

Mother Angelica
The Mass in My Life

Because the Eucharist or the Lord's Supper makes present the central mystery of the Christian faith—the passion, death and resurrection of the Lord Jesus—Catholics consider it the highest form of Christian prayer. (This is not to exclude the "Our Father" which is an important part of the Mass). It is not just the prayer of the individual, nor of the priest who presides over it, but it is truly the prayer of the whole church, gathered to worship Jesus, our Savior and Great High Priest (Heb 7:26, 27, 8:1).

The Second Vatican Council's *Constitution on the Sacred Liturgy* affirms this when it says that: "the liturgy (the Mass) is the summit toward which the activity of the Church is directed; at the same time it is the fountain from which all her power flows. For the goal of apostolic works is that all who are made sons of God by faith and baptism should come together to praise God in the midst of His church, to take part in her sacrifice and to eat the Lord's Supper" (no. 10).

All the power of the church flows from the death and resurrection of Jesus Christ. All the church's many activities are brought together and offered to God as a sacrifice of praise in the liturgy of the Mass. The Mass reminds Catholics that all gifts and power in the church come from God and that the purpose of our lives is to worship God, to be nourished by God, and to offer all that we do back to Him as a pleasing sacrifice by uniting it with the one truly acceptable sacrifice, the sacrifice of Jesus Christ.

Dr. Alan Schreck
Catholic and Christian

St. Norbert had a special liking for the Eucharist, hence it is that he is usually pictured as holding in his hand a monstrance—although the use of the monstrance as such belongs to later times. The monstrance is always the sign of Norbert's devotion to the Eucharist, and a reminder of his victory over the teachings of the heretic Tanchelm and the Sacramentarian heresy in Antwerp.

His biographers tell us that he never undertook any important work without saying Mass and spending hours before the tabernacle. The very first chapter of his Constitution treats of the "Tremendous Sacrament of the Altar," and tells the religious how to gain from it zeal for souls. One of his three favorite counsels to the religious was, "Cleanliness about the altar, for on the altar one proves the liveliness of his faith and the fervor of his love."

It is related in his life, that, during his stay at the new abbey, which he had established at Floreffe, when he was saying Mass he noticed upon the paten just before communion a large drop of the Precious Blood, all red and surrounded by rays of light, which came from the Sacred Heart. He turned to his deacon and said, "Brother, do you see what I see?" "I do, Father," he replied. The altar stone upon which the miracle occurred has always been kept in the Monastery at Floreffe.

Fr. Hugh F. Blunt, LLD
Witnesses to the Eucharist

It is likewise our most fervent desire that all who profess themselves Christians and are seriously engaged in the effort to establish the kingdom of Christ on earth will consider the practice of devotion to the Heart of Jesus as the source and symbol of unity, salvation and peace. Let no one think, however, that by such a practice anything is taken from the other forms of piety with which Christian people, under the guidance of the Church, have honored the Divine Redeemer. Quite the opposite. Fervent devotional practice towards the Heart of Jesus will beyond all doubt foster and advance devotion to the Holy Cross in particular, and love for the Most Holy Sacrament of the Altar. We can even assert—as the revelations made by Jesus Christ to St. Gertrude and to St. Margaret Mary clearly show—that no one really ever has a proper understanding of Christ crucified to whom the inner mysteries of His Heart have not been made known.

Nor will it be easy to understand the strength of the love which moved Christ to give Himself to us as our spiritual food save by fostering in a special way the devotion to the Eucharistic Heart of Jesus, the purpose of which is—to use the words of our predecessor of happy memory, Leo XIII—"to call to mind the act of supreme love whereby our Redeemer, pouring forth all the treasures of His Heart in order to remain with us till the end of time, instituted the adorable Sacrament of the Eucharist." For "not the least part of the revelation of that Heart is the Eucharist, which He gave to us out of the great charity of His own Heart."

Pope Pius XII
Haurietis Aquas

As a result of my ongoing relationship with the Lord through prayer and the Eucharist, and from my willingness to observe and obey His Word, Food for the Poor was born. I had already dedicated my business, Essex Exports Inc., to the Lord and had asked Jesus to be its chairman. (My staff and I gather for a prayer meeting every day before our workday begins.) I have seen my business prosper in a way that I could never have imagined.

Because I was going to daily Mass wherever I was, I always had to locate a priest and find out where he was saying Mass. My business takes me back to my native Jamaica quite often, and I began to develop a relationship with some of the missionary priests there. I went to the places where they said Mass—places I had never gone to before, orphanages and nursing homes and poor parishes.

I started to ask the priests, "What can I do to help you help these people?" It was a natural reaction because the people are so poor. Eventually I was helping about seven or eight priests in their work. (Ferdinand G. Mahfood)

Robert Baram, Ed.
Spiritual Journeys

A secular priest saying Mass in St. Ignatius' Church, sure she [Bl. Anna-Maria Taigi] was a hypocrite, had the odd idea of testing her by giving her an unconsecrated host. Anna detected the imposture, and Our Lord ordered her to inform her confessor. Father Salvatori severely reproached the priest, who confessed his fault. Another day, says Cardinal Pedicini, Annette was preparing for Holy Communion in the church of the Trinitarians. When the Irish Franciscan who was saying the Mass turned round to say the *Ecce Agnus Dei*, the Host he held in his hands left them, floated through the air, remained posed for a moment, and then came to rest on the lips of the Beata. The good Father took the matter very badly and returned to the sacristy crying out against such abuse of the Liturgy and against witchcraft. He made a note in his pocket-book of the name of the guilty party in order to denounce her to the Holy Office. Two Trinitarians who were present succeeded in pacifying him and making him see that God is Lord of the Liturgy.

Many a time at the moment of Communion she saw the Host come to life. Jesus was there, sometimes in the form of a child lying upon the petals of a white lily and saying to her: "I am the flower of the fields and the lily of the valley;" sometimes in the form of a King dressed in purple: "In this crowd of people that you see in the church," He said to her one day, "there are scarcely two souls truly sincere in their love. The others are equally ready to come to church or to go to the theatre."

Albert Bessieres, SJ
Wife, Mother and Mystic: Blessed Anna-Maria Taigi

I thought the painter of the picture of Christ knocking at the door was negligent, he didn't finish the painting, he didn't put a door knob in the picture. Jesus is outside knocking at your heart. He won't enter. The doorknob is on the inside, you have to open the door to let Him in. He won't force you to love Him in the Eucharist. It breaks my heart that we come week after week, and we don't even look towards Him in the tabernacle and say, "I love You, Lord." Oh, He's so happy, He's delighted that you're here. But did you look towards that tabernacle and pour out your love for Him? "Jesus, I want to love You. Help me." If the Holy Father was sitting there, you'd all be looking at Him. . . .

In the chapel of Anna Maria College, I was telling the sanctuary lamp, "I'm jealous of you, sanctuary lamp. You can stay by the tabernacle all day and be close to the Lord, but I have to go on my merry way. Yes, I'm jealous of you. I wish I were a sanctuary lamp." Then the Father spoke to my heart and said, "Eileen, you can be the living sanctuary lamp that walks out amongst My people, and gives new light to the world saying, 'God lives here within me.'" I think of that often. Each one of us can be the living sanctuary lamp. God lives in our hearts and dwells in us. Well if He does, be radiant in His love, be joyful in His love. You are the human torches that spread the word of Christ.

Eileen George
Beacon of God's Love: Her Teaching

I n 1861 Father Eymard was invited to preach at Saint Sulpice, in Paris, the Novena in preparation for the Feast of the Sacred Heart. Every evening, for nine days, he pointed out to a large congregation the intimate connection between the Holy Eucharist and the adorable Heart of Jesus.

It was on this occasion that he formulated this sublime definition of Jesus Christ: "Jesus Christ is God's love for man, humanized and personified in the Incarnation, and perpetuated in the Eucharist." He then showed the Heart of Jesus preparing this august Sacrament by His vehement desire, instituting it in a supreme effusion of love at the Last Supper, and forever maintaining it through love for man, in spite of his indifference and sacrilegious ingratitude. . . .

We cannot, evidently, analyze all Father Eymard's sermons. He preached unceasingly for twelve years with a zeal sustained by this ardent love, and with inestimable results. We shall, however, summarize Father Eymard's apostolic career in one word taken from his personal notes. It indicated plainly and precisely the inspiration and the purpose of his Eucharistic apostolate: "Jesus is there! Then everbody to Him!"

Fr. Albert Tesniere, sss
Blessed Peter Julian Eymard: The Priest of the Eucharist

Each time we come to the Eucharist, Jesus says to us, "Take this; this is My Body delivered up for you, this is My Blood poured out for you." And He always adds, "Do this in memory of Me." Do what? Celebrate the Eucharist, of course, but also do what the Eucharist signifies. Do for others what I have done for you. Deliver up your body, pour out your blood, in self-giving love to whomever needs you.

First of all, pour yourself out in love for those for whom I have given you a special responsibility: your spouse, your children, your parents, your siblings, your needy neighbors, your co-workers.

Love even, love especially, the unlovable! For, says Jesus, in the Eucharist I give My wounded body to you precisely in your woundedness, your helplessness, your unlovableness. So love others in their unlovableness, love them with My own redeeming love.

Only love like that can heal the wounded world. And love like that, says Jesus, can flow only from My own sacrificed body given to you in the Eucharist. Proclaim to the world the good news of My redeeming love by loving one another just as I have loved you.

Fr. Paul Hinnebusch, OP
Homiletic and Pastoral Review, January 1995

Feast of St. Anthony of Padua
1195-1231

The devotion of St. Anthony's Bread as it is practiced now came into being about 1888. At that time there lived in Toulon, France, a pious girl, Louise Bouffier. She had wished to become a Carmelite nun, but since her parents were dependent on her, she stayed at home and conducted a little shop. Her spare time was devoted to the foreign missions.

One morning she tried to enter her little shop; the lock simply would not yield. She called a locksmith, and he tried many different keys, but without avail. . . . In the meantime, Louise promised some bread to St. Anthony for the poor, and when the locksmith returned, she asked him to make just one more attempt with a key. Immediately the door swung open.

Louise told her friends about this remarkable answer to her prayer and promise; and, imitating her example, they, too, received astonishing favors through the intercession of St. Anthony. One of them bought a little statue of St. Anthony for Louise; and it was placed in the back room of her shop, where a big lamp was required to make it visible. But that dark little room was soon to become a famous shrine to St. Anthony.

The room in back of Louise Bouffier's shop was filled all day with people who came to ask St. Anthony's intercession or to thank him for favors. A box was placed at the feet of the statue, and into it all classes of men placed the alms they had promised to give to the poor. . . . In 1892 the total sum was 5,743 francs, and it supported a thousand old people and orphans.

Marion A. Habig, OFM
Everyman's Saint: Life, Cult, Virtues of St. Anthony of Padua

I n wintertime, we use a furnace to heat our homes and stay warm, and when the furnace breaks it can become rather cold if not unbearable. We are now in the winter of our lives and the world has grown so cold. During this century, we have had two world wars, Korea and Vietnam, the killing fields of Cambodia and the genocide of Auschwitz. There is abortion and euthanasia, racism and poverty. The human heart has never been so cold and human life has never been so cheap.

During this winter of our times the devotion to the Sacred Heart of Jesus has never been more important. For in the Sacred Heart of Jesus we find everything that is missing in the human heart. Draw near to the Heart of Jesus and let His heart warm our hearts. But where do we find the Heart of Jesus? The Heart of Jesus is found in the Eucharist! In the Eucharist we find the living Christ. In the Eucharist we find the love, the compassion, the gentleness and humility of His Heart. In the Eucharist, the Heart of Christ is revealed to us.

Do we really wish to have our fears, our desires, our anger and our agendas consumed in the fire of His Love? Now is the time to take a look at our hearts and what is inside of them. And then to meditate on the Sacred Heart of Jesus. Hold them up together, side by side and if you do not like what is in your own heart then pray, "Jesus, gentle and humble of heart, make my heart like Yours." Pray it everyday, with every breath until the flames of love in His Eucharistic Heart reaches out to your heart and sets it on fire with His Love!

Fr. Patrick Greenough, OFM CONV.
Homily on the Feast of the Sacred Heart, June 6, 1997

I t is this unmistakable sign of the Cross with which her [St. Margaret Mary's] life is marked that is the surest proof of the authenticity of her mysticism and of her mission. As she was constantly afraid of illusion Our Lord once told her by which signs to recognize Him. His graces, He said, would always be accompanied by some humiliation or contradiction; they would be followed by confusion and a feeling of annihilation; moreover, they would never cause her to despise others, nor would they prevent her from following her Rule. Finally, they would result in a great love of Himself, in a perfect imitation of His example, in the desire to suffer for His sake, but to suffer unobserved, and in an unquenchable thirst for Holy Communion and for being near the Blessed Sacrament. Margaret Mary spent almost every free moment before the Tabernacle. For devotion to the Sacred Heart seems to be inseparably linked to an ardent love for the Blessed Sacrament.

All the practices in honor of the Sacred Heart, the First Friday Communion, the Holy Hour, the Feast itself, after the Octave of Corpus Christi, they are all at the same time devotions to the Blessed Sacrament. St. Margaret Mary's mysticism is in a very real sense, a sacramental mysticism, centered in the hidden life of Jesus in the Host. And as the Blessed Sacrament is pre-eminently the Sacrament of Love, so the Sacred Heart is the visible sign of this Love, the Heart of flesh, which is the seat of life and whose beating registers the emotions of the soul.

H. C. Greef
The Way of the Mystics

Some years ago, on my annual retreat, I found myself under terrible temptations and discouragement. Every temptation you can think of, I had that night. On my way to Mass the next morning, I felt very battered and discouraged because of the attacks and temptations of the preceding night.

As I walked up to Communion, I made an act of faith. I said, "Jesus, I know I am receiving You, but I feel so discouraged, so downhearted, and so unworthy to receive You."

This was the way I felt as I received Communion. As I received the Sacred Host and turned to go back to my place, I received a clear image of a tent. I remember looking at the tent and thinking, "Well, that poor tent is really battered." I remember examining it and saying, "It must have gone through a terrible storm."

As I got to my pew and knelt down, I saw a man coming to go into the tent. I saw myself in the image and I was telling the man, "Oh, you can't go in there, it's a mess. It's all battered. There are big holes in it."

The man looked at me and smiled and said, "What do you mean? I live in here."

At that moment, I realized that I was the battered tent, that I had been battered with the temptations to sin and discouragement and all those things that had harassed me during the night. Now, Jesus was showing me that, battered and all, He still made His home in me—and that He had just come to me again under the appearance of the sacred Host.

Sr. Breige McKenna, OSC
Miracles Do Happen

June 15. There are three of us at Mass today. During the day we had already spoken to each other.

—*There are some rough spots along the way. Don't pay any attention to them.*

—That's not easy, Lord.

—*There's nothing to worry about.*

And this evening the Lord once again wraps us in His mantle.

—This mantle?

—*To protect all of you. You are bruised and bleeding this evening. You need My tenderness. Let My presence come into you. Taste it right now, at this very moment.*

—Why are you showing me this?

—*So that you may let yourselves be overcome by My love.*

—Lord, my Lord.

I'm just babbling, but I have the impression of melting before Him.

—I know why you're telling us this tonight. Deep down what I wanted was for You to come and calm and console and heal all the anguish I sensed in the others, in my brothers. But You tell us that we've got it all wrong, that first we must accept You, must let You come into our hearts, and not worry about doing anything on our own. And then You'll come and act in us.

—*My ways are not your ways.*

Nicole Gausseron
The Little Notebook

At Communion time I simply rested in Jesus and thanked Him for His healing love for me and for the pastor. As Jesus took on my life, I gave Him my feelings and asked to take on His mind and heart until I could live out His reactions. Slowly I began to thank Jesus for creating my new hunger to say Mass reverently and with real love for the people, for forgiving my own impersonal treatment of an impersonal and wounded pastor whom I could now love, and for revealing my own need to love myself enough to let others love and help me. I then silently adored Jesus and let Him love me. I often do this at Communion because when I look at Jesus lovingly, my prayer often goes a new direction with new dimensions of healing. Sometimes Christ may bring to mind a past hurt I need to forgive with Him while other times we just silently adore the Father. Healing happens to the degree I use the love of Jesus within me to love not only the Father but myself and whoever irritates me.

Matthew Linn, sj, and Dennis Linn
Healing Life's Hurts:
Healing Memories through the Five Stages of Forgiveness

Feast of St. Juliana Falconieri
1270-1341

I t was an era of revival of devotion to the Blessed Sacrament. St. Julianna of Mount Cornillon, who had done so much for the establishment of the Feast of Corpus Christi, was dead only a few years when Juliana Falconieri was born.

It would seem that God had raised up this second Juliana to keep the flame alive. To her it was a memorial of Christ's Passion and death, and she would spend hours before the tabernacle in the spirit of reparation. So eager was her devotion, that many a time she was seen raised from the ground in ecstacy. She would shed tears for the neglect of men towards the great Sacrament of Love. For that reason, Juliana may be regarded as one of the the founders of Reparatory Adoration, which did not become general till several centuries after her death. She received Holy Communion several times a week, and so great was her reverence that on the days she received she refused to take any other food.

From the Blessed Sacrament she got all her strength and her unbounded charity. For Juliana was an angel of mercy. The Florence of those days was a hot-bed of dissension. Strife followed on strife, and Juliana was always on hand to reconcile enemies and restore peace. She visited the sick and prepared them for the sacraments, she laid out the dead for burial, she dressed the wounds and sores of those in the hospitals; in a word, there was nothing outside the sphere of her charity.

Fr. Hugh F. Blunt, LLD
Witnesses to the Eucharist

A few weeks later, on May 27, the day after the Ascension, the Beatus was saying Mass in the same church for the intentions of the Colle family, which was at the Holy Sacrifice, when, at the moment of the Consecration, his eyes once more pierced through the veil into the beyond and saw the youth shining with glory and gladness. After Mass, he found him kneeling by his side during the final prayers; and, in the sacristy, he again stood before him with the same look; but this time he was surrounded by a band of youths who had died in that house in the odor of sanctity.

On July 3 of the same year Don Bosco wrote thus to Madame Colle: "On June 21 last, the feast of St. Aloysius Gonzaga, at Mass, after the Consecration, I saw your son as I had known him on earth, but his rosy face was shining with a radiance as dazzling as the sun's." On August 30 he wrote again to the lad's mother: "On the 25th of this month, the feast of St. Louis, King of France, at the Consecration I had the joy of seeing your son even more radiant than usual. He was in a garden with other young companions, and they were all singing with a tone and a harmony that no man can tell." And on very many other occasions, at the altar, at table, in his room and elsewhere, his unforgettable young friend appeared to him: the vision was like a flash of lightning, said the Beatus, and he added: "It could not have lasted any longer, for I should have fallen down fainting, as I could not have endured the splendor any more."

A. Auffray, SC
Blessed John Bosco

Feast of St. Aloysius Gonzaga
1568-1591

Aloysius had four special devotions. The first of these was the devotion to the Blessed Sacrament. In his father's house and in the midst of his life in the world, it had been a joy to him to serve Mass; and now in the novitiate he could do this to his heart's content. Often during the day he visited the Blessed Sacrament in the church, or in an adjoining chapel. In order to prepare well for Holy Communion, he divided the week into two parts, the first of which he devoted to thanksgiving for his last Communion, and the second to preparation for the next. On the eve of his Communion-day he would speak with piety of the happiness in store for him next morning. Many of his companions, and even those who were already priests, who wished to prepare well for Holy Mass, sought to be with him on such days, in order to be moved to greater fervor by his piety and the ardent love that his words displayed.

On the morning of the day itself, his first thought was of the Savior he was about to receive, and he passed the whole hour appointed for meditation in pious reflections upon the Blessed Sacrament. He sought out a quiet corner of the church to make his preparation and thanksgiving, and his heart overflowed with sweetest consolation. Many other worshippers who saw him, but did not know him, concluded merely from the sight of his fervor that he must have a special devotion to the Blessed Sacrament, and even that he must be a saint. He spent the whole morning after his Communion in silence and recollection, praying and reading passages from St. Augustine or St. Bernard.

Maurice Meschler, SJ
Life of St. Aloysius Gonzaga

Feast of St. Thomas More
1478-1535

Constantine the Great used to attend Mass every morning, and when he went into battle he brought with him a portable altar that the Sacrifice might be offered each day amid the tumult of war and the clash of arms. Living in this manner, he gained numerous victories.

The Emperor Lothaire satisfied his piety by attending not one but three Masses, in times of peace and war alike. The pious King of England, Henry III, who did likewise, was rewarded by God with a reign of fifty-six years. St. Louis IX, King of France, was accustomed to assist at several Masses each day. St. Wenceslaus, King of Bohemia also used to hear several Masses every day, and he would often serve them himself to the great edification of all. His veneration for the Holy Sacrifice was so great that he, himself, sowed the grain and pressed the grapes that were used to provide the bread and wine for Mass. To this end he had set aside a special field and vineyard that he cultivated with great humility and diligence.

The great St. Thomas More who was High Chancellor of the Kingdom of England, and so charged with great affairs, still found time to attend Mass daily. One day, during the Mass, a message from the King arrived, requesting his presence. With humble respect and Christian courage he sent back word asking that the King be pleased to wait until Mass would be over.

Fr. L. Chiavarino
The Greatest Treasure

Another person who received a similar shock treatment was a young man who had been dating a girl from San Giovanni Rotondo. As a condition for their marriage, she demanded that he visit Padre Pio.

One morning the young man attended Padre Pio's Mass and stood in the back of the church. For several days following, he returned to the church to attend Mass. After a week he broke down and cried. Padre Pio saw him and said: "Thank God for what you have seen, and don't tell anyone. God's secrets should be kept hidden in your heart." "Yes," the young man agreed, realizing that Padre Pio knew what he had seen. "I have seen you on the altar, crowned with thorns, first with a triple crown of thorns, and then with something like a bonnet of thorns."

Padre Pio repeated, "Go home, thank God, and tell no one." But the young man told his fiancee. He told her that each morning at Mass he had seen Padre Pio, his head crowned with thorns, his face covered with blood, but with a serene, beautiful expression on his face. The young lady could not resist telling her friends in San Giovanni Rotondo what she had heard. Miss Morcaldi, a daily visitor to the church, asked Padre Pio if the story was true. "Do you have any doubt?" Padre Pio scolded: "You are like St. Thomas."

For many years the memory of this incident disturbed Miss Morcaldi. Finally she questioned Padre Pio again. "Padre," she asked, "that crown of thorns. . . . Do you wear it throughout the Mass?" He replied: "You certainly want to know too much. Yes, before and after Mass, the crown that God has put on me is never taken off."

John A. Schug, CAP.
Padre Pio

The climax of the Cure's ardent love for the Eucharist came on Corpus Christi. On that feast, he was all smiles. He had already encouraged as many homes as possible to build altars of repose so that the parish would be blessed by a multiplicity of Benedictions. There were altar boys, flower girls, and a huge procession of all the people, for he would tolerate no spectators. Never did he weary of carrying the heavy monstrance. "Why should I be tired?" he questioned a sympathizer. "He whom I carried likewise carried me." The only joy that could approach that of Corpus Christi was the joy of Holy Thursday, when he used to remain all night on his knees in silent adoration.

Fr. Bartholomew J. O'Brien
The Cure of Ars: Patron Saint of Parish Priests

"My dear little one, I your Lord love you and give to you My Most Sacred Heart in which to rest. I betroth to you My Mother who is the Mediatrix of all graces and good cheer. My little one, I wish for My people to know that I am in their midst at all times, but in a very real way in My Most Blessed Sacrament. I invite all My people to raise their hearts to God the Father through My Blessed Sacrament. When you come before Me, be at peace. Rest in My love. Put aside all distractions, fear, worry and concern. Realize you are before Me and contemplate My love and goodness. If you will absorb My love and rest in My love, your heart, mind, and soul will be rejuvenated and will rise to an ecstasy of joy. When you rest in My Heart, a peace overcomes you, almost a state of sleep; but you are resting truly in My Most Sacred Heart where I am carrying you and sifting through all your needs and organizing all your spiritual and temporal needs for the glory of God the Father." (Words of Our Lord to Gianna Talone-Sullivan)

Queenship Publishing
I Am Your Jesus of Mercy, Vol. 5

T hat is why I say, "I believe in what Jesus said; I believe that this Bread of Life is Christ near me, Christ become bread for me, and Christ become presence in me."

I know that this act of faith is dark as the night, but nothing is clearer than this night. I have gazed for days and days at this Bread, I have lived for weeks in caves in the desert with this Presence alone, and always, always, He has said to me in faith, "It is I, do not be afraid. It is I, and I love you."

"Do not be afraid of the darkness, be a child before my words. I wanted to become bread to be eaten by men, because by eating Me, they are feeding upon eternal life. Why do you find it strange that I should have wanted to become bread through love? Have you had no experience of love?

"When you have loved, really loved, have you not wanted to become bread for your beloved? Oh, to be able to enter the body of the person you love! Would not a mother do this for her child? Does not the bridegroom do this for the bride?"

You can argue about the Eucharist as much as you like but on the day love really takes hold of you, perhaps you will understand that Jesus is not a fool or a madman.

Carlo Carretto
The God Who Comes

"Today My Mother, who is the Mother of Heaven and your Mother, and through this My little and inadequate soul (Julia) is now revealing and showing My Heart to a bishop, who seeks to follow Me and My Mother as a child, so that he can make ever more known that I am really present in the Eucharist, the sublime mystery of faith and love.

If My priests who celebrate Mass daily, would truly believe in and seek to experience this Presence with their whole heart and would live the sublime and marvelous Divine Reality such as it is, innumerable souls would be purified and would live in My merciful heart with a grace that is beyond all expectations.

Make haste to make My Real Presence known. Apostasy and infidelity are bringing this world to the brink of ruin; too many of My representatives continue to sleep. In truth, My representatives even allow themselves to be seduced by false prophets. . . .

O souls whom I have called! You will experience incomprehension and persecutions within My Church that has been wounded and divided; but I shall always abide in you to encourage and to help you. I shall always remain at your side. You need not fear; but only trust in Me and proclaim Me who live in the Eucharist." (Words of Jesus spoken to Julia Kim while in ecstacy during Communion in Naju, Korea, September 22, 1995)

Julia Yun
Heart of the Harvest

Feast of St. Irenaeus of Lyons
125-203

I renaeus was a disciple of Polycarp who remembered Polycarp's firsthand stories about the Apostle John. He used the Real Presence of Christ in the Eucharist to prove the resurrection of the Christian dead: "The Eucharist becomes the body of Christ" (Irenaeus, *Against Heresies*). "How can they say that the flesh which is nourished with the body of the Lord and with His blood passes into corruption and partakes not of life?" These texts, and many more like them, can be found in a Protestant translation, *The Ante-Nicene Fathers*, published by Eerdmans.

I had always been taught that there was a "golden thread," or remnant of true Christians, who had always believed just as modern Evangelicals do now. Yet, as I searched for anyone in the first three hundred years of the Church whose beliefs were even remotely related to Evangelical notions of the Lord's Supper, I came up empty. Christians were being persecuted and martyred during this period. Yet there exists a fair amount of literature from this time. Modern Evangelical theology, however, was nowhere to be found in it. The only way to accept the remnant theory is to accept it a priori, in spite of the facts.

For a full millennium of Christianity, there were no exceptions to this belief of the Early Church in the Real Presence. It was the universal teaching of the entire Church. Not until Rationalism (and its firstborn child, scepticism) had started to transform the thinking of Europe would any movement call into question the Real Presence of Christ in the Eucharist.

David B. Currie
Born Fundamentalist, Born Again Catholic

At Mass, as she returned thanks for the special privileges bestowed on St. Peter, and particularly his having heard these words from our Lord Himself, "Whatsoever thou shalt bind upon earth, it shall be bound also in heaven; and whatsoever thou shalt loose on earth, it shall be loosed also in heaven," the saint appeared to her, vested as a Pope and extending his hands, he gave her his benediction, that it might work in her the same effects as it had worked in others, through the power that God had given him. As she approached the holy altar and trembled for her unworthiness, St. Peter and St. Paul appeared to her, one on her right hand and the other on her left, as if to conduct her thither with great pomp. When she had reached it, the Son of God received her Himself, saying to her: "I have brought you thither with the same arms with which I embrace you. I have done this through the ministry of My Apostles, that your devotion might be fully satisfied."

Msgr. William J. Doheny, CSC
The Revelations of St. Gertrude

Feast of the First Roman Martyrs

This dreadful conflagration continued nine days; when Nero, finding that his conduct was greatly blamed, and a severe odium cast upon him, determined to lay the whole upon the Christians, at once to excuse himself and have an opportunity of glutting his sight with new cruelties. This was the occasion of the first persecution; and the barbarities exercised upon the Christians were such as even excited the commiseration of the Romans themselves. Nero even refined upon cruelty, and contrived all manner of punishments for them that the most infernal imagination could design. In particular, he had some sowed up in the skins of wild beasts, and then worried by dogs till they expired; and others dressed in shirts made stiff with wax, fixed to axle-trees, and set on fire in his gardens in order to illuminate them. This persecution was general throughout the whole Roman empire; but it rather increased than diminished the spirit of Christianity.

A. Wright
A History of the Principal and Most Distinguished Martyrs

Fifty-one years ago today it was my awesome privilege to offer the Holy Sacrifice of the Mass for the first time. During these fifty-one years, so much that I had hoped and dreamed to do, so much that I had pledged to do I have not done. During these fifty-one years, there have been many failures, many people hurt, many missed opportunities to act as Christ, many failures in preaching the Word as Christ would preach the Word, many failures in being the priest that I hoped to be. But that is not what I will reflect upon today. All of the things that I have done that I should have done, all of the things that I failed to do that I should have done—in this Mass, as in every Mass, it all starts all over again. In this Mass we experience what is of such unspeakable power: Christ spiritually and mystically dies for you and for me. His Body is broken. His Blood is poured out. He obliterates all of the past, all of my failures as a priest. All of them were anticipated by the crucifixion and death of Christ so mysteriously renewed in this Mass. This is why on this anniversary of fifty years as a priest I feel such joy!

John Cardinal O'Connor
Homily in St. Patrick's Cathedral, December 15, 1996

The greatest contemplative prayer is the Sacrifice of the Mass. The action is Jesus'. My part is contemplative: awareness, receptivity. I need to be alive to what is going on, my eyes on Jesus. All the power of God is here in the Mass. . . . As the Mass continues, we move into the power of the cross and Blood of Jesus. Jesus offers Himself to His Father, in the Holy Spirit, their mutual love and their love that embraces us. As Jesus is lifted up in the Consecration, His promise becomes effective: "When I am lifted up from the earth, I shall draw all men to Myself" (Jn 12: 32). The rebellious Israelites were bitten by serpents in the desert. God instructed Moses to make a bronze serpent and lift it up on a pole. When the sick and sinful Israelites came out of their tents and looked up at the bronze figure, power went out from it and touched them for healing and forgiveness (Nm 21: 9). Jesus said, "The Son of Man must be lifted up as Moses lifted up the serpent in the desert, so that everyone who believes may have eternal life in Him" (Jn 3: 13-15). The Consecration is this moment in faith for us. As we "look on the one whom we have pierced" (see Jn 19: 37), power goes out from Him.

At the foot of the cross we can pray, "May His blood be upon us and upon our children" (see Mt 27: 26)—not now for condemnation, but the Blood of the New Covenant, which, offered in the Mass and received in Holy Communion, ransoms, forgives, purifies, frees, and preserves me for everlasting life.

Robert Faricy, SJ, and Lucy Rooney, SND
The Contemplative Way of Prayer

Sometimes, after Holy Communion, having Our Lord within me, I [Columba Marmion] follow in spirit His life, His successive states; I adore Him in the Father's bosom, in the pure bosom of the Virgin that He chose as His abode; I go to Bethlehem, to Nazareth, to the desert, to Calvary. I unite myself in this way to Jesus in each of His states, and in this contact with Him I receive the grace of all His mysteries.

Holy Communion makes us abide in Christ and He in us. You know the story of Saint Teresa of Avila and of the Infant Jesus. Well, after Communion I say to Our Lord: "I am Columba of Jesus!" and He could say to me: "I am Jesus of Columba!"

Dom Raymund Thibaut
Abbot Columba Marmion: A Master of the Spiritual Life

On many occasions the Father spoke to me, encouraging me to engage in a gentle mental conversation with Christ. "Go today and sit in front of the tabernacle and speak to My Son Jesus. Tell Him about all your worries and fears, and He will remove all your anxieties. Tell Him about your plans for the day and the joys and the problems you expect to encounter. Too many of you only tell Him of problems. Many beautiful things are happening; share them with Him in prayer. Speak to Him about everything that is happening in your life. As your friend, He wants to know."

Too often we see Jesus as just the candy man. We rush into church, we kneel in the very last pew, and we say, "Listen up, God, your servant is speaking. I want this . . . and I want this . . . and I asked for this . . . last week and you haven't given it to me yet. And by the way, could you help Aunt Susan find her cat?" Then we rush straight back out of the church. This is not prayer. If you had a friend and you only saw that friend when he came to ask you for money, would you consider that person much of a friend?

The Father is calling us to a relationship with Jesus—Jesus, who is the Way, the Truth, and the Life; Jesus who is true God, true man, and true friend.

In one of the messages God the Father said, "All the answers are in the tabernacle."

Matthew Kelly
A Call to Joy

For nine days the crowds flocked unceasingly to the church to venerate the relics, the ninth day being marked by notable miracles.

A poor widow besought the saint [Philomena] during Mass to cure her crippled boy who was unable to stand. At the elevation of the Sacred Host, the boy jumped up from where he was and ran to the urn of the saint's relics to thank her for his cure. At the conclusion of the Holy Sacrifice, the child walked about the town, to the delight of the admiring throngs, who rang bells and beat drums and finally, seizing the boy, bore him in procession through the streets.

Fr. Paul O'Sullivan, OP
Saint Philomena the Wonder-Worker

My Dear Brother,

"God has permitted my whole life to be a series of anti-Christian acts, up to the very hour of my conversion. He has also permitted the circumstances of my life to be such, that my sudden conversion can only be explained by a miracle of Divine goodness."

Father Theodore's feelings as he read this letter cannot be described.

"Next day," he says, "I was due to preach, as it was the Feast of the Purification, but in spite of all my efforts to keep calm I broke down completely and my tears flowed upon the altar. . . . I realized that the congregation was disturbed and to reassure them I explained the reason of my emotion, and told them the story of the miraculous conversion of my brother. The account seemed to rouse their sympathies, but when the name I was trying not to reveal came from my heart in spite of myself, a mighty thrill passed over the whole assembly and with one voice all the orphan girls began to chant the *Magnificat*. I nearly fainted several times before I could finish my Mass."

That evening the church was crowded to the doors.

"When," says the Abbe Desgenettes, "Father Ratisbonne, after describing the circumstances of this astounding conversion, said 'This convert is my brother,' those present could not contain their surprise, and a loud exclamation came from the huge congregation, as if an electric shock had passed through them all. Many tears of joy were shed. For a year past they had all been praying fervently for the Ratisbonne family. . . ."

L. M. Leggatt, Trans.
The Brothers Ratisbonne: A Nineteenth Century Miracle

"After Communion, Father Rookey came down among the congregation with the monstrance containing the Host, to bless the people and to pray for our healing.

"I was at the edge of a seat, quite near the front, and he stopped right in front of me, holding the Host up above me. I remember looking at the Host and begging for healing, and suddenly I began to cry. I just sat there and I cried and cried. Then, just three rows in front of me, a young girl with cerebral palsy suddenly got out of her seat, handed her crutches to her mother and walked across the church and up onto the altar. I have never seen anything like it in my life.

"I knew I had been touched in some way, if only that my faith had been restored to me. Once I managed to stop crying I felt utterly peaceful and relaxed, a feeling that stayed with me for days. A week later I visited my doctor, as routine, and after examining me he said in great surprise that the power had come back into my leg. I said I knew this, and told him that besides this I had no pain either. He was completely taken aback."

A few weeks later she visited her specialist, one of Ireland's leading neurologists, to receive the results of the lumbar puncture.

"The specialist looked at us and eventually said that the fluid test was completely clear. He just couldn't understand it. All the symptoms, all the indications following the MRI had proven to their satisfaction that their original diagnosis was correct. Yet now, the fluid just didn't confirm this. All he could say, he finally told us, was that I did not have MS." (Susan's story)

Heather Parsons
Father Peter Rookey: Man of Miracles

"But before the tabernacle, yours should be not only a presence of prayer, but also of a *communion of life with Jesus.* Jesus is really present in the Eucharist because He wants to enter into a continual communion of life with you. When you go before Him, He sees you; when you speak to Him, He hears you; when you confide something to Him, He welcomes into his Heart your every word; when you ask something of Him, He always hears your prayer.

Go before the tabernacle to establish with Jesus a simple and daily rapport of life. With the same naturalness with which you seek out a friend, or entrust yourself to persons who are dear to you, or feel the need of friends who assist you, in that same way go before the tabernacle to seek out Jesus. Make of Jesus your dearest friend, the most trusted person, the most desired and the most loved.

Tell your love to Jesus; repeat it often because this is the one thing that makes Him immensely happy, that consoles Him for all the ingratitude, that compensates Him for all the betrayals: 'Jesus, You are our love; Jesus, You alone are our great friend; Jesus, we love You; Jesus, we are in love with You.'

Indeed the presence of Christ in the Eucharist has above all the function of making you grow in an experience of true communion of love with Him such that you never again feel yourself alone, because He has remained here below to be always with you." (Words of Our Lady, August 21, 1987)

Fr. Stefano Gobbi
To the Priests: Our Lady's Beloved Sons

B
esides the more solemn celebration of Holy Mass and the general Communion of the faithful, what is, in final analysis, a Eucharistic Congress if not a prolonged and fervent visit to the Blessed Sacrament? You have observed as we have that many in our day are neglecting this touching practice of Christian life, so dear to devout souls, which consists in recollecting oneself before the tabernacle to fill one's soul with the gifts of God. Worse still, it seems that, under the influence of ideas foreign to traditional piety, some deliberately hold this practice in disfavor.

We would wish all the Congressists of Lyons to return to their homes persuaded of the excellence of this practice and eager to have it appreciated and loved by all those around them. You have only to think of the long hours spent by St. John Vianney, at the beginning of his pastoral ministry, alone in his church before the Blessed Sacrament; of the outpouring of faith and love of this great soul at the feet of his Master, of the marvelous fruits of holiness he reaped for himself and for so many others from these fervent Eucharistic prayers. There is no doubt that a flood of grace would stream down upon your families and your country if, enlightened and sustained by the example of their priests, an ever greater number of souls were to learn a lesson on this point from the saintly Curé of Ars.

It is in adoration of the Blessed Sacrament that are enkindled and fostered the dynamics of the apostolate.

Pope John XXIII
Address to the 18th National Eucharistic Congress
of France, 1959

The spirit of the Eucharist implies willingness to offer ourselves to others. It means to oppose completely the spirit of pride and selfishness that accomplishes not peace but war, destruction, violence and killing. Christ desires that we become mutual offerings and that we offer others everything we possess or can give. Everything we give through Eucharistic love is transformed into something beautiful and new and creates a new relationship. Everything we give increases and develops Eucharistic love. The giver and the receiver create a better world that can be born only from this love.

Giving and offering oneself can set off a fatal spiral for selfishness, pride and, especially, the absence of God. Those who take possession of something or behave like owners, in the context of their own lives or in the lives of others or with regard to their possessions, can become transformed into idols, like Adam who attempted to be god and master.

Instead, when an individual's life and everything he possesses become new bread offered with love, then the time of the Messiah will come. Be careful, the time of the Messiah cannot come before the transformation of the individual. After the individual's transformation, the Messiah's time of peace and justice will come.

The basis of all renewal is perfect love accomplished in Christ's becoming bread and wine. This same love changes us and our possessions into new bread, the bread of communal life, for communal life.

Fr. Slavko Barbaric, OFM
Celebrate Mass with Your Heart

At Catholic houses they found themselves guests of the highest honor, and there they sometimes prolonged their stay for a few days, until the inevitable warning of the pursuivants' approach drove them once more on to the road. In recent years most of the houses had been furnished with secret cupboards where were stored the Mass vestments, altar stones, sacred vessels and books; these "priest-holes" were usually large enough to provide a hiding-place for the missionaries in case of a sudden raid; in some cases there were complete chapels with confessionals and priest's room. Many houses sheltered one of the old Marian priests who had left his cure at Elizabeth's succession, and now lived in nominal employment as secretary and butler.

Campion found his Catholic hosts impoverished to the verge of ruin by the recusancy fines; often the household were in mourning for one or more of their number who had been removed to prison. "No other talk but of death, flight, prison, or spoil of friends," yet everywhere he was amazed at the constancy and devotion that he found. The listless, yawning days were over, the half-hour's duty perfunctorily accorded on days of obligation. Catholics no longer chose their chaplain for his speed in saying Mass, or kept Boccaccio bound in the covers of their missals. Driven back to the life of the catacombs, the Church was recovering their temper. No one now complained of the length of the services; if a Mass did not last nearly an hour they were discontented, and if, as occasionally happened, several priests were together, the congregation would assist at five or six Masses in one morning.

Evelyn Waugh
Edmund Campion

A child goes to the candy store as often as she can to satisfy her sweet tooth. She loves candy. She craves and desires its sweetness. And she is filled.

Jesus is the sweetness of all sweetnesses. We must have the same craving for the Eucharist as the child has for the candy. In all childlike trust we must go to the Eucharist and see how sweet He is, how He fills our very being. And how can we not give off the sweetness of the Lord?

Everyone loves a birthday party. No matter how old we are, we want the sweetness of the birthday cake, of the goodies and the secret gift. Well, be as a child and run to the party of all parties, where Jesus is the host, and you are indulging, not in a beautiful cake, but in all the graces that He has to give you.

The candles of faith will be the light, and you will be filled with the Holy Spirit. Your soul will spiritually clap its hands, and its eyes will beam and be radiant. For you will be celebrating the greatest of all parties, the party of Jesus Christ coming to your hearts, your very soul.

Every morning He comes, and taps on the door of your heart, inviting you to come to the Eucharist, and to let Him enkindle in your soul the candles of the Holy Spirit.

Eileen George
Beacon of God's Love: Her Teaching

We commonly and correctly speak of Eucharistic adoration. We should, because in the Eucharist is present the whole Christ, the incarnate Son of God. During his visible stay on earth, he received the adoration of those who believed in him. What did they believe? They believed that one who looked like a man, spoke and acted like a man, was really the living God. We believe it is the same Jesus Christ now present in the Holy Eucharist. What do we see? Only what looks like bread and tastes like wine. What do we believe? We believe that this is no longer bread and wine, but Jesus Christ, the man who received his humanity from his mother Mary, but who is the Second Person of the Trinity who existed from all eternity.

Adoration, therefore, is the primary response of our faith to the Real Presence. But that is only the foundation. On this worship of adoration we should build the whole edifice of the spiritual life.

Fr. John A. Hardon, SJ
Retreat With The Lord: A Popular Guide to the Spiritual Exercises of Ignatius of Loyola

On the Monday of Holy Week Father Cholenec saw that all hope of recovery was gone. All the life left in her seemed to be in her smile.

"It is Holy Week," she whispered to the priest. "May I not perform some act of penance in honor of our Lord's Passion? Perhaps going without food for just a day?" Father Cholenec shook his head. "God will accept your good intention, my child. You must think of other things now. You have not long to live."

"Tomorrow," said Father Cholenec, making an effort to keep his voice steady, "we shall bring our Lord to you." At this added news she found no further words; but the look of ecstasy lay like a quiet light upon her face.

At the mission it was unprecedented to bring the Blessed Sacrament to a cabin. The sick were usually carried to the church on a plank or some sort of litter; but Kateri was too weak to be moved. Early on Tuesday morning Marie Therese came to her. Kateri was radiant with expectancy. She was summoning all her remaining strength to meet our Lord in Holy Communion and to do it as best she could. . . .

They could hear the little silver bell tinkling its way through the narrow streets. Father Chauchetiere accompanied Father Cholenec as he carried the Blessed Sacrament on this extraordinary journey, and all those left in the village followed in procession. After having received Holy Viaticum, Kateri offered herself in final oblation to God and gave voice to profound gratitude for the graces that had been given to her. . . .

Marie Cecilia Buehrle
Kateri of the Mohawks

July 15

A story in the Book of Exodus opens another level of recognition. The people of Israel, freshly escaped from Pharaoh, are now without food in the desert. They are not happy about it. "Then the Lord said to Moses, 'I will now rain down bread from heaven for you'" (Ex 16:4). Bread is the gift of God, tangible evidence that He cares for His people.

And then something very ordinary and yet incredibly astonishing: "The Lord Jesus, on the night He was handed over, took bread, and, after He had given thanks, broke it and said, 'This is My body that is for you. Do this in remembrance of Me'" (1 Cor 11:23-24).

We gather, often quite forgetful, at the table of the Lord's Supper. We gather as Christ's body, the presence of Christ within our own bodies. We gather as God's people, family, together with Mary, the apostles and martyrs and all the saints. The earth itself is gathered too, in the bread that is the fruit of the earth and work of human hands. Here in the sacrament all levels of meaning are compressed and then explode outward and upward, resonating from the earthy inner working of our bodies all the way to the astonishing oneness of ourselves with Christ and of Christ with God.

Leonard J. Bowman
A Retreat with St. Bonaventure

He went to Mass every morning thereafter for the rest of his life. Talbot walked into church early and knelt staring at the tabernacle. He was sober and miserable. He felt tremors run through his body and he thought he would never be able to steady himself. Perspiration bathed his face and body. He braced himself in his kneeling position by holding on tightly to the bench. He was there to worship God. He had been to confession the night before. He did not doubt his sincerity. He doubted his capacity to remain away from alcohol. Tears bathed his cheeks and still he stayed, waiting for the Lord to heal him. Matt groped for words to initiate his conversation with the Lord. He had no words. All the jolly barroom conversations danced in his mind. Ridiculous conversations. Now he had the opportunity to commune with Jesus himself and he remained arid and without emotion. How long could he hold out? He could make it through this one day. That was the Lord's message to him: take care of today, live today, face today. Just one day, that was all; that was reasonable.

After Mass, Matt lingered in the pew and thought out a simple sobriety strategy. What did he have to avoid, he asked himself. He had to keep away from the pub and from his old drinking friends. This would mean walking a different route home from the brickyard at night. He could not let himself pass in front of the tavern. That would lead him right back down the road from which he had come.

Susan Helen Wallace, FSP
Matt Talbot: His Struggle and His Victory over Alcoholism

Christ as a fish was employed in a special sense for Christ as *food*, and thus for the Eucharist. The classical proof for this is the inscription of Abercius. A large fragment of the stone bearing this inscription, which probably comes from the latter part of the second century and which is certainly to be dated before 216, was found in Asia Minor in 1883 by the English scholar William Ramsay. In 1892 it was given by the Sultan to Pope Leo XIII. It now adorns the Lateran museum.

In this inscription, which is written in Greek hexameters, Abercius states that he was "a pupil of a chaste Shepherd . . . whose great eyes see in all directions." This Shepherd had taught him "the faithful Scriptures" and had sent him to Rome. Here he saw a people "having a resplendent seal." Of his journey he remarks: "Everywhere I found companions. Faith was my guide wherever I went and everywhere furnished me with food, a very large and pure Fish from a spring, which a chaste Virgin had caught, and this she (probably, the Church) gave constantly to her friends to eat, having excellent wine mixed with water that she gave with bread."

The description of the Eucharist can be recognized at a glance: the faithful ever and again receive wine mixed with water and bread as food, but faith tells them that it is the great, pure Fish, that is, Christ born of the Virgin.

Ludwig Hertling, SJ, and Englebert Kirschbaun, SJ
The Roman Catacombs and their Martyrs

October 15, 1993. It was midnight—the beginning of the 15th of October—when I felt a very strong calling to go and pray before Our Lord. (There is a chapel nearby which has a seven-day-a-week, twenty-four-hour Exposition of the Blessed Sacrament.) I went to the chapel and knelt before Our Lord for about forty-five minutes. It was during this time that I was filled with such a great joy. I almost could not get up—my soul desired to continue to kneel before Him. The joy continued to grow in my heart to the point of overflowing. (This is the best way that I can describe it.) It was then Our Lord spoke. Each word was powerfully felt within me, as if time began to move slower.

He said, "It is here that I wish for you to come and rest. It is here that I will refresh you. Tell Me that you love Me to make up for the ingratitude of so many of My children in the world."

At this point I began to say over and over again very slowly. "I love you, Jesus, I love you, Jesus. . . ." I have never felt such a joy before. I wanted to be with Him for hours in that moment. I continued to kneel for a while more, telling Jesus that I loved Him and asking Him to have mercy on me and on all the world.

Michael McColgan
Open Your Hearts:
Messages from Our Lord Jesus and His Blessed Mother

Another thing, my Jesus, in the future I am going to receive You often in Holy Communion, and gladly. And once You are in my heart You may appropriate to Yourself all the sentiments of affection that I cherish towards my loved ones, towards my relatives, towards all who do good to me or wish me well, towards all who may be well disposed to me. They are all Yours. Accept all my feelings of attachment and love, my Savior, and offer them to God, together with the love of Your own Sacred Heart. Beg of Him to enkindle in my heart a fire that will quickly seize upon and burn to ashes every love that is unworthy of You.

And I am going to assist at Holy Mass whenever I can, every day even. For is not that the hour made all holy by the Precious Blood and by love divine? How glad I ought to be in Holy Mass to offer You all my sufferings and all my tears! Be mindful, O Jesus, that if my life has been barren of good works, it has been all the more fruitful in crosses of every description. With this adorable Sacrifice unite, I beg of You, all that I have suffered in the past, all that I suffer now, all that I am destined to suffer in the future. Use all my sufferings in offering a glorious holocaust to the Eternal Father; and beg of Him, as it arises to His throne of glory, to remember not my sins in His boundless mercy, but graciously to shower upon me that grace and forgiveness that He so lavishly showered upon the whole earth when You breathed forth Your spirit upon the infamous gibbet of the cross.

Msgr. William Reyna
Eucharistic Reflections

The Lord calls us and speaks to us and guides us in our spiritual and secular lives and sometimes He uses ordinary people for extraordinary things. I have never felt loved so greatly. I thought I had always believed in the Presence of Jesus in the Blessed Sacrament but, I think it was more intellectual than feeling the Real Presence as I do today. The more I visited Him the more I got to know Him and the more intimate the conversations. Sometimes I come bursting in with happiness, bouncing in the church door, anxious to tell Him (as if He didn't know) about something wonderful happening in my life. Or, I come in and just can't wait to thank Him for something beautiful, wonderful, lovely, that has happened. Other times I come in crying, and sobbing with my hurts and disappointments in life. Sometimes I hear an inner voice of consolation and wisdom. Other times I just need to know my God is there, that He just sits with me as I sit with Him.

Claudia Blache
Perpetual Eucharistic Adoration newsletter, March 1995

I n the Gospel we read of the woman, who, suffering from a hemorrhage for twelve years, wanted to obtain health simply by touching the hem of Our Lord's garment. By touching things used or blessed by Lawrence, many persons were cured through his intercession.

While saying Mass, Lawrence often lost himself in contemplation. . . . Tears rolled down his cheeks and saturated several handkerchiefs. In 1614, Lawrence conducted visitation of the friary at Voltaggio. D. Gio. Stephen of Ferrari, Canon of the main church of Voltaggio, secured some of these handkerchiefs, by means of which many cures took place.

The first to benefit was the Canon himself. For many years he had suffered from severe headaches. After touching the handkerchiefs he never again experienced headaches. . . . A young cleric, Julius Scorza, sustained a fractured skull in a fall. Doctors gave him up for dead, but, at the application of one of the handkerchiefs, the fracture healed and Julius lived.

The power of these handkerchiefs was best observed in Naples. A swelling started to grow in the throat of Angela Sciammarro so that on the fifteenth day she could not even swallow saliva. She was on the verge of death when one of the handkerchiefs, applied to her throat, caused the swelling to disappear. Young Adriana Rospolo, lame since birth, could only drag herself on her knees from one room to the other. With deep faith, her mother applied one of the handkerchiefs to the legs of her daughter. The girl immediately stood up and walked without any support whatever.

The Round Table of Franciscan Research

The duties and cares of the day ahead crowd about us when we awake in the morning (if they have not already dispelled our night's rest). Now arises the uneasy question: How can all this be accommodated in one day? When will I do this, when that? How shall I start on this and that? Thus agitated, we would like to run around and rush forth. We must then take the reins in hand and say, "Take it easy! Not any of this may touch me now. My first morning's hour belongs to the Lord. I will tackle the day's work with which He charges me, and He will give me the power to accomplish it."

So I will go to the altar of God. Here it is a question not of my minute, petty affairs but of the great offering of reconciliation. I may participate in that, purify myself and be made happy, and lay myself with all my doings and troubles along with the sacrifice on the altar. And when the Lord comes to me then in Holy Communion, then I may ask Him, "Lord, what do you want of me?" (St. Teresa). And after quiet dialogue, I will go to that which I see as my next duty. (Bl. Edith Stein)

Sr. Concetta Belleggia, FSP
Real Women

Then, after Karin and Birger, came all the other members of the family. She appointed all of them to be present the next morning at Mass. One of them was missing—Alphonsus. But he was acting as Bridget's messenger to Pope Gregory in Avignon.

Then came the last morning. Bridget's bed was made on the table in the middle of the room, at which she had so often sat writing. They were now all gathered round this hard bed. At the altar at the foot of the bed stood Prior Petrus saying Mass. It was the feast of Saint Apollinaris, July 23. The Gospel for the day said: "At that time Jesus said to His disciples: You are they who have continued with me in my temptations. And I dispose to you as my Father hath disposed to me, a kingdom: that you may eat and drink at my table in my kingdom and may sit upon thrones, judging the twelve tribes of Israel" (Lk 22:28-30). Did Bridget hear the words? She too, had persevered through all temptations; she too, had been a judge in Israel.

But when Prior Petrus lifted up the Sacred Host, the invitation to the heavenly banquet came to Bridget: "You shall come to your convent, that is: you shall enter into the joy of your Lord. And your body shall be laid to rest in Vadstena."

Then Bridget looked up as if to give thanks to her Creator, and saying: "Lord, into Thy hands I commend my spirit," she fell asleep. It was in the year of the Lord one thousand three hundred and seventy-three, on the twenty-third day of July as day was breaking.

Johanna Jorgensen
Saint Bridget of Sweden

The apparitions of the Lady of All Nations to Ida Peerdeman have not been denounced by the Church, and so, on Friday, July 17, 1992, when I was in Amsterdam for a meeting of the Scientific Committee of the World AIDS Foundation, I visited the home and private chapel of Ida, then in her late eighties. As I entered the hallway she told me that the day of my visit was the anniversary of her "Eucharistic experience," which occurred in 1958 when, before the celebration of the Mass began, she suddenly saw a huge and almost blindingly white Host in front of the altar: "It was white fire—magnificent." The vision slowly faded away and the altar was then bathed in a beautiful light. It all lasted for a moment.

I spent an hour in front of the oil painting of the Lady of All Nations beside the altar in Ida's private chapel. The painting was a reproduction of a vision which she saw when Mary appeared to her standing in front of the Cross of the Redeemer. It was obviously the appropriate place for the Coredemptrix. The Virgin stood on a globe around which were hundreds of sheep, both black and white, representing the peoples of the world.

She stood in front of the Cross, dressed in white and her long black hair fell loosely on her shoulders. To me, it was as though she had "let her hair down," as she said what she had to say with great authority in Amsterdam. "So be it!" she exclaimed many times. "Is that clearly understood, theologians?" she also said decisively.

Dr. Courtenay Bartholomew
A Scientist Researches Mary: The Ark of the Covenant

Then, as she desired to obtain the remission of her sins through the merits of this Apostle and as she could not undertake the pilgrimage, she approached Holy Communion. As soon as she had accomplished her design, she beheld herself seated at a table with our Divine Lord, which was laden with various delicious viands. As she offered our Lord His Precious Body, which she had received, for the increase of the beatitude and glory of this Apostle, St. James presented himself before God as a prince, to thank Him for the favors that he had received through this Adorable Sacrament. He then asked that God would work in the soul of Gertrude all the good that He had ever deigned to work in any soul through his merits, because she had offered this adorable Sacrament in his honor.

Msgr. William J. Doheny, CSC
The Revelations of St. Gertrude

May 19. The little gray and red sisters are all smiles as they welcome us. From the very beginning of Mass a sort of communion is established among us. The Lord comes to take a seat near the altar. He's dressed in white and He smiles happily.

—Lord, are you taking your place up front today?

—*Yes.*

—But why is that?

No answer. I realize that he's there just the same—seated, still, peaceful. I don't understand until after the reading of St. John, chapter 17.

—Is it to show us your Father, to send us to him?

—*Yes.*

—Lord, here I am crying again. Do you know why?

—*Yes.*

—You speak to me in the same way you and the Father speak to each other. I'm overwhelmed.

—*Yes.*

—You use the same language. It's powerful even though it's wordless.

I don't ask Him anything else. I try to be as prayerful as possible. At the moment of the Consecration, Lord, you stood up and you became one with Pierre, who was celebrating. You were two and one at the same time.

—May your will be done, Lord. Where you will, as you will.

Nicole Gausseron
The Little Notebook

Today, my preparation for the coming of Jesus is brief, but imprinted deeply with vehement love. The presence of God penetrates me and sets aflame my love for Him. There are no words; there is only interior understanding. I drown completely in God, through love. The Lord approaches the dwelling of my heart. After receiving Communion, I have just enough presence of mind to return to my kneeler. At the same time, my soul is completely lost in God, and I no longer know what is going on about me. God gives me an interior knowledge of His Divine Being. These moments are short, but penetrating. The soul leaves the chapel in profound recollection, and it is not easy to distract it. At such times, I touch the ground with only one foot, as it were. No sacrifice throughout such a day is either difficult or burdensome. Every situation evokes a new act of love. (No. 1807)

Bl. M. Faustina Kowalska
Divine Mercy in My Soul

I have often been asked how to prepare sermons, and I can only speak of my own experiences after a long life of preaching.

All my sermons are prepared in the presence of the Blessed Sacrament. As recreation is most pleasant and profitable in the sun, so homiletic creativity is best nourished before the Eucharist. The most brilliant ideas come from meeting God face to face. The Holy Spirit that presided at the Incarnation is the best atmosphere for illumination. Pope John Paul II keeps a small desk or writing pad near him whenever he is in the presence of the Blessed Sacrament; and I have done this all my life—I am sure for the same reason he does, because a lover always works better when the beloved is with him.

When the general plan of the sermon has been formulated, I will then talk my thoughts to Our Lord, or at least meditate on it, almost whispering the ideas. It is amazing how quickly one discovers the value of the proposed sermon. That is why the French speak of *l'esprit de l'escalier*—"the spirit of the stairway," or the recollection of what one *should* have said in the conversation that evening. Generally there are three different formats to any lecture or sermon: what is written; what is delivered; and what you wished you had said. That is why "giving the sermon before Our Blessed Lord" is the best way for me to discover not only its weaknesses, but also its possibilities.

Archbishop Fulton J. Sheen
Treasure in Clay

The only time that I met Marthe Robin was during the course of a retreat, in August 1970. I was then at a difficult point in my life. I expected a great deal from the visit, as I had heard astonishing things about this Drome peasant woman. Bearing the stigmata that bled every Friday, the day of Christ's Passion, she had, it appeared, sacrificed her vision at the beginning of the Second World War. She had not eaten or drunk anything since 1930, except for the Eucharistic bread. Her mystical gifts gave her prophetic precognition.

Imagine my surprise upon entering her room alone, where she was eternally bedridden in semi-darkness, to encounter a thoroughly straightforward woman. I expected to have great enlightenment shed upon my life, and instead she talked to me about rain and about good weather, suddenly relating them to the problems over which I was agonizing!

From that moment on, I understood that Marthe was an authentic mystic—even a great mystic. My certainty was soon confirmed by a very special grace I received on the last day of this week-long retreat, a grace that corresponded exactly with the problem that preoccupied me.

Is it necessary for me to add that this was for me the beginning of a profound conversion that completely changed my life, the results of which I still experience today eleven years later? This is due to the power of prayer of this ordinary-appearing woman. Because she undertook to surrender herself completely to the Lord, God brought great things about through her, as he did through Mary, to whom she was so close. (Anonymous testimony)

Fr. Raymond Peyret
The Cross and the Joy

B ut there is one means that every parish priest has at his disposal—a church, and in that church the Real Presence. He is its guardian and servant. "Let the Eucharist then," concluded Father Eymard, "become to all priests the center of their thoughts and the end of their labors. In the Blessed Sacrament they have at their disposal the most efficacious means of working conversions and of sanctifying the flock entrusted to their care." There, too, they have a friend to cheer their solitude and an invincible ally to help them in their struggles. Priestly virtues, moreover, drawing their strength from this never-failing fountain of grace, will have more telling effects because our Lord Himself will act and work through them. Their influence over souls will be doubly efficacious, and the world will look to the priest for the help that it needs during its present crisis. Hence Father Eymard used to say: "To bring about the sanctification of one priest is to effect that of thousands of faithful, for the priest is a multiplier."

In the intimacy of a private talk, he thus expressed himself: "I should like to found an association that would unite parish priests by means of prayer, certain rules, and periodic conferences, and sanctify them through the Eucharist." "Do you not see," he remarked on another occasion, "that the sanctification of priests includes everything and everybody? Win over the priests to the Eucharist, and you have the entire parish; win over the parishes and you have the whole country!"

Fr. Albert Tesniere, sss
Blessed Peter Julian Eymard

Feast of St. Ignatius of Loyola
1491-1556

At Montserrat, Ignatius put aside his worldly clothing for the "livery of Christ." He also customarily read the Passion narratives during Mass, confessed frequently, and received the Eucharist every Sunday. This latter pious practice was not customary in his day. Eventually the inquisitors questioned him about his Eucharistic theology.

When scruples about his past sins drove Ignatius to the brink of suicide, his prayer to Christ, "Lord, I will do nothing that will offend you," eventually freed him. As mentioned above, he was consumed by a tremendous desire to labor in the Holy Land for the good of souls. This desire "for the Holy Land was a longing for Jesus, the concrete Jesus and no abstract idea" (Karl Rahner, SJ).

At Manresa, on the ship to Jerusalem, in the Holy Land, in Venice and Vicenza, on the road to Padua, and especially at the end of his life, Ignatius received many visions and representations of Christ. He saw him, with mystical sight, as a white, undifferentiated body, or with white rays coming from above. He likewise saw how Christ was present in the Eucharist and he received special visions about Christ's humanity. These visions consoled Ignatius, pointed out a specific way of serving Christ, and confirmed him in this service.

Harvey D. Egan, SJ
Ignatius Loyola the Mystic

Feast of St. Alphonsus Ligouri
1696-1787

"Each day I will make at least one hour of mental prayer, and visit the Blessed Sacrament, especially in the churches where it is exposed. I will wear the cassock and tonsure and behave circumspectly, yet without affectation, singularity, or pride. I will confess at least once a week, and receive Holy Communion still more frequently," [promised St. Alphonsus.] His demeanor was marked by simplicity, and if for some time he allowed himself to be attended by a lackey, it was in deference to his father's wishes. Don Giuseppe could not resign himself at all; he carefully avoided meeting his son and, even after a year had passed, coming across him accidentally, he turned his back on him. We can imagine how much Alphonsus must have suffered from this hostility.

Baron J. Angot des Rotours
Saint Alphonsus Liguori

Now we have seen what it means to say Amen and to whom we say *Amen* at the moment of Communion. The priest proclaims: "The Body of Christ!" and we answer: *Amen!* We say Amen to the most Sacred Body of Jesus born of the Virgin Mary and Who died and rose again for us. But we also say *Amen* to His mystical body, the Church, and precisely to those close to us in life or at the Eucharistic table. We cannot separate the two bodies and accept one without the other.

To many of our brothers and sisters, perhaps to most of them, it will be no effort on our part to say *Amen*, yes, I welcome you! But there will always be among them someone that causes us suffering, whoever is to blame; someone who opposes us or criticizes or speaks badly of us. In this case it is more difficult to say *Amen*, but it hides a special grace. There is, actually, a sort of secret in this little act. When we want a more intimate communion with Jesus or we need forgiveness or a special grace from Him, this is the way to obtain it: to welcome Jesus in Communion together with that particular brother or sister. We can say, clearly, to Jesus: "Jesus, I receive You today together with . . . (better if we here name the person); I'll keep him or her in my heart with You; I shall be happy if You bring him or her with You." This little act is very pleasing to Jesus because He knows that it causes us to die a little.

Fr. Raniero Cantalamessa
The Eucharist: Our Sanctification

Feast of St. Peter Julian Eymard
1811-1868

Afew months later, he [St. Peter Julian] wrote in the same vein: "It is necessary to set about this work quickly to save souls by the divine Eucharist, and to awaken France and Europe, stupefied in their sleep of indifference because they know not the gift of God, Jesus the Eucharistic Emmanuel. We must apply the torch of love to the lukewarm souls that think themselves devout but are not so, because they have not fixed their center of life in Jesus in the tabernacle. Devotion that has not a tent on Calvary and one near the tabernacle, will not result in solid piety and will never accomplish anything great. I find that we do not bring the Eucharist close enough to the faithful, that we do not preach enough on this Mystery of Love par excellence. As a result, souls suffer, become sensual and material in their piety, and are inordinately attached to creatures because they fail to find their consolation and strength in Our Lord."

Fr. Martin Dempsey
Champion of the Blessed Sacrament:
Saint Peter Julian Eymard

Feast of St. John Vianney
1786-1859

The zeal for prayer of St. Jean Marie Vianney, who can almost be said to have spent the last thirty years of his life in church, where he was kept by the tremendous number of penitents, was distinguished by a special quality, in that it was directed particularly toward the Eucharist. His ardent piety toward Christ the Lord, hidden behind the Eucharistic veils, almost surpasses belief.

"There," he said, "is the One who loves us so much. Why should we not love Him in return?" He really had a burning charity toward the adorable Sacrament of the Altar. His soul was drawn by an irresistible impulse to the sacred tabernacle. He used to teach this method of prayer to his parishioners: "There is no need for many words in order that we may pray properly. By faith we believe that there, in the sacred tabernacle, the good God is present. We open our hearts to Him. We rejoice that He has admitted us into His presence. This is the best method of prayer." He left nothing undone to stir up the reverence and the love of Catholics toward Christ hidden in the Sacrament of the Eucharist and to urge them to receive Holy Communion. And, by the example of his own piety, he himself showed the way to the rest.

"In order that anyone should be convinced of this," witnesses have reported, "it was enough that they should see him celebrating Mass or even see him genuflecting when he passed in front of the tabernacle."

Pope John XXIII
On the Priesthood

As regards St. Eymard himself, he happened to be in the village of Ars at the beginning of May, and being there, what was more natural than to confer with the holy Cure concerning the trials of the infant Society, and beg him to assault heaven with his prayers. He said to the Cure: "I fear that we have made a mistake in founding this work, and that God is bringing it home to us by not sending recruits to sustain it and enable it to grow. You urged me on to this undertaking that seems so sacred; therefore ask Our Lord to provide for Himself good and numerous adorers of His Divine Sacrament."

To which the saintly Father Vianney answered: "My good friend, you want me to pray to the good Master for you, but you have Him always before you." Three months later, on August 4, 1859, the holy Cure received the reward of his heroic labors and took with him to the throne of the Master he had served so well, the petitions of his friend Father Eymard.

God's answer was not long in coming, for a few weeks after the Cure's death, new recruits came spontaneously to offer themselves for the service of the Eucharist. At once Father Eymard wrote to Father de Cuers: "Thank God with us; He has sent us two good priests, who preach, sing, adore, and obey well. One is from Angers, the other from Moutiers in Savoy. We were not expecting them; they came attracted by the love and grace of the Eucharist. I will bring them both to you. Seeing these two good and devoted priests, Father Champion and I kept repeating: 'How good God is; He wants Marseilles.'"

Fr. Martin Dempsey
Champion of the Blessed Sacrament:
Saint Peter Julian Eymard

All kinds of people travel to St. Maria Goretti because of the wonderful things happening there. Many visitors call and ask, "Will the Blessed Mother appear today?" I tell them I am not sure if she will, but Jesus Christ, her Son, will appear twice. They are amazed and ask how I know. I tell them we celebrate Mass twice a day, 8:00 in the morning and 5:30 in the evening, and that He appears six times on the weekend. Their reply is, "Oh Father, be serious." I am being serious! The real miracle happens on the altar every day. Mary may be appearing somewhere, but Jesus Christ is appearing on the altar. Not only does He appear, He remains in the tabernacle. Every place where there is a Catholic church, Jesus Christ—the Real Presence of God—is there. If all Catholics truly believed that, our churches would be overflowing.

If we knew Jesus was going to appear someplace at a particular time, wouldn't we be there? Have we traveled so far off looking for miracles that we miss the real miracle that happens every day? The Eucharist is the miracle that happens. It truly exists and will continue to exist until Jesus comes again. Just before Jesus ascended to heaven He said, "And behold, I am with you always, until the end of the age." (Mt 28:20). He is with us in many ways; in our Spirit and our heart, in the words of Scripture; and really in His Eucharist. Jesus is present in every Catholic church and tabernacle. He remains with us in His Blessed Sacrament.

Fr. Jack Spaulding
Hope for the Journey

Catholics believe that the Eucharist is a real, unbloody sacrifice that brings into the present time the saving effects of the once-for-all-time crucifixion of Jesus. The work of Christ on the Cross is finished. The crucifixion need never be repeated. But its benefits are applied to me in today's time-frame through the real sacrifice of the Eucharist.

The concept of making Christ's past sacrifice efficacious in the present is not foreign to Evangelicals. That is precisely what Evangelicals believe happens when a person puts his faith in Christ. One day Christ's work on the Cross has not yet benefitted the person, and the next it has been applied through faith. Catholics believe their sacrifice of the Eucharist makes the grace of the Cross available today. Granted, it is a much more physical method.

I remember insisting, as an Evangelical, that sacrifices are no longer needed because of the Cross, yet I had no good explanation for Zechariah 14. I finally came to the conclusion that Zechariah had to be referring to the Eucharist. This is the only logical reason he would write that sacrifices will be done in the Kingdom after the Messiah's coming. When I saw the connection, I got so excited I ran into our living room and gave a "high five" to my thirteen-year-old son. The sacrifice of the Mass is being celebrated every day in Catholic churches, not only in Jerusalem but all over the world. The continuing sacrifices of the Church after Christ's death and Resurrection were foretold in the Old Testament.

David B. Currie
Born Fundamentalist, Born Again Catholic

Feast of St. Dominic
1170-1221

During the ceremony of profession of the nuns of St. Sixtus, there was great excitement and a call for the saint to come out, since the nephew of one of the bishops who was acting with him in this case had just been thrown from his horse and was lying dead in the square outside. The uncle of the boy, hearing the sad news, fell fainting into the arms of a bystander. The body of the young man was brought in, badly mangled from the accident, and laid at the feet of the saint. Dominic ordered them immediately to remove the body to another room. Once more life came back at his request; this time after he had offered the Holy Sacrifice. Bystanders testified that during the Mass they had seen him raised above the ground. There were hundreds of witnesses to the miraculous answer when he spoke to the dead youth and commanded: "Young man, I say to thee arise." The youth rose up joyful and with no sign of injury and was restored to his family. This miracle was instrumental in bringing into the Order two of its most famous sons; they were the brothers, Hyacinth and Ceslaus, and were later to win great renown as the apostles of the North.

Sr. Mary Jean Dorcy, OP
Saint Dominic

In the course of time the Church has introduced various forms of this cult, forms ever growing in beauty and usefulness. Such are, for example, devout and even daily visits to the Blessed Sacrament; solemn processions through towns and villages, especially at Eucharistic Congresses; adoration of the Blessed Sacrament exposed. Sometimes such expositions last only for a short time, sometimes for hours, even forty hours; in certain places they continue, each church taking its turn, the whole year round; and in some cases perpetual adoration is conducted day and night in religious communities, the faithful often taking part.

These devotional practices have contributed greatly to increasing the faith and the supernatural life of the Church on earth, which indeed by this perpetual worship is giving echo to the hymn of praise that the Church triumphant sings everlastingly to God and the Lamb "that was slain." These devotions therefore, which in the course of ages have become universal, the Church has not only approved but has even made her own and commended by her authority. They have their origin in the spirit of the liturgy; and therefore, so long as they are conducted with due seemliness and with faith and devotion that is required by the sacred ritual and the instructions of the Church, they undoubtedly contribute greatly to the living of a liturgical life.

Pope Pius XII
Mediator Dei

Feast of St. Lawrence
Martyr—d. 258

The Pope and the faithful had gathered in the catacombs in the evening of August 6, 258. Being Christians in a cemetery, theirs was an illegal assembly punishable by death. There is every reason to believe that the catacomb Mass that evening was to be offered specifically to strengthen the faithful to endure the new persecution . . . Pope Sixtus was preaching . . . soldiers burst into the crypt. The congregation drew together before them, baring their breasts and extending their necks to signify that they were ready to die to protect the Pope. But Sixtus would have none of that. He came forward and they took him, along with four of his deacons.

Another deacon, Lawrence, cried out: "Father, where are you going without your deacon?" Sixtus replied: "I do not leave you, my son. You shall follow me in three days."

The Vicar of Christ was taken up the nearby stairs and beheaded on the spot, along with the four deacons. For some 1,500 years his name was mentioned in the Canon said by every Catholic priest of the Latin rite, anywhere in the world.

Deacon Lawrence was temporarily spared in order to give the persecuting officials access to the treasure supposedly accumulated by the Roman church. What he actually brought forth before the prefect of Rome was not gold and silver, but a representative group of the poor and needy. . . . The angry prefect commanded that Lawrence be roasted to death on a gridiron. [He] joked with his executioners about turning his body over because "one side is broiled enough."

Warren H. Carroll
The Founding of Christendom, Vol 1

At night she prolonged her vigils, and then, alone, prostrate on her knees before the tabernacle, she gave free course to the transports of her devotion. Going in spirit to the heights of Calvary, she joined her tears to the tears of the Redeemer, and never wearied of offering herself a pure victim to the Eternal Father for the conversion of peoples—the holocaust of her senses by penitence and prayer, and the still better holocaust of her heart by the outpourings of her love. When the hour for Matins came, she lit the lamps, gently awakened her companions, and awaited them in choir to resume prayer with them.

In the daytime she returned to the school of Nazareth, to her functions as Abbess; then to the textile work in which she excelled, as may be judged by what remains to us. She spun, embroidered, made corporals, amices, and albs to distribute among the villages of Umbria; attentive, above all, in clothing as well as consoling Him Whom love has stripped of His glory—Jesus in the Host, Jesus poor and abandoned in His churches. Never idle, her hand at work, her heart in God, by one of those thoughts faith suggests to us, she ennobled the lowliest occupations as well as the highest functions.

Leopold de Cherance, OSFC
St. Clare of Assisi

Thisbread is my *flesh for the life of the world*. The Lord gives His flesh twice: He gives it for the first time and uniquely at the end of His earthly life. He sacrifices himself totally in the form of His flesh in order to redeem the world as a whole. But He further sacrifices Himself unnumbered times, He sacrifices, as it were, piece by piece, particle by particle, of His body in the Host in order to communicate eternal life to each individual also. He has redeemed and saved the person once and for all in Baptism. But the baptized person falls into sin and needs a continuing, continuous redemption. He does not retain the purity that Baptism has given him. The Lord gives this back to him in confession and completes this gift in the Communion that gives him eternal life again. The purity he wins anew through Confession is nothing complete in itself at which one could stand still: rather, it is a making ready, a willingness, an opening for the new life, the new love, and this is given him by the Lord in Communion.

The commandment of the Lord that one eat His flesh, despite its unfathomable profundity, is a wholly unambiguous commandment that allows of no misunderstanding. His word has such a radiant simplicity and clarity that every attempt to twist it or to weaken it, to evade its meaning by taking it symbolically or spiritualizing it, would be an open act of disobedience. As He is God and man at one and the same time, so His bread is wholly divine Spirit and wholly human flesh. And only the one who will eat His human flesh will thereby share in His divine Spirit. But it is only loving faith that grasps this simple unity of the Lord.

Adrienne von Speyr
John

August 13

Feast of St. Hippolytus of Rome
Martyr—170-235

We discover the forerunner liturgy of our current Mass in the *Apostolic Tradition* of St. Hippolytus, written around 225 AD. He composed *Tradition*, a book of Church regulations, "in order that those who have been rightly instructed may hold fast to that tradition that has continued until now."

Hippolytus' model for the Mass reveals a development from St. Justin's time as the Holy Spirit continues to make progress, guiding the Church into all truth as Jesus promised. There is now a Preface introduction and a definite Preface: "The Lord be with you"— "And with your spirit." A Eucharistic prayer and the Words of Institution are given, along with an Epiklesis prayer ("We ask you to send the Holy Spirit upon the offering of your Holy Church") and a doxology, a prayer of praise.

Most interesting is the Eucharistic prayer. Hippolytus was concerned about the informal consecration prayers we find in Justin's *First Apology*, where the celebrant improvises "according to his ability." Hippolytus proposes that the Church at large adopt a formal consecratory prayer and suggests one that extended to apostolic times, he believed. The idea was a good one, and was surely inspired. The prayer quickly came into general use and is our earliest surviving Eucharistic prayer.

Hippolytus' slightly modified "suggestion" is today's Second Eucharistic Prayer. When you hear it recited during daily Mass at your parish, you will hear the clear echo of Christian worship from eighteen centuries past.

Daniel Gallio
Immaculata, January/February 1996

He was totally enamored of God. When in the camp we suffered hunger, cold, and when we slept on the ground or on hay under tents—and it was already a snowy and icy November—and we had no water to drink, and while we hadn't changed our underwear for three months, and while the insects and filth tormented us, Father Maximillian bore it all with joy.

It was at this time that I wrote down his statement that a certain sadness pervades even fervent souls when they realize that in heaven they will no longer be able to show God their love by suffering for him. Brother Pelagius made note of another remark: "The man who avoids suffering doesn't know what happiness is.". . . In the camp we couldn't have Mass, but when he received Communion or distributed it to us, the holiness and union with God that showed in his face was unlike that of any priest I have ever known. He kept trying to teach us that the essence of sanctity consists of our will being one with the will of God. He advised us before we acted to ask the Virgin Mary—whose will is always one with God's—what she would do in the situation and to then proceed as our conscience directed. He prayed a lot with us. . . . He took the entire experience of imprisonment with serenity and submission to God's will. There was only one thing about him that annoyed me: he seemed to repeat too often and too insistently that we would be freed soon and that the Immaculata's help would be involved.

Patricia Treece
A Man for Others

On the eve of the Assumption, 1578, the Prior went to have a look at the prisoner, whom he found kneeling in his cell rapt in prayer. Not perceiving the superior the saint remained motionless; whereupon Father Moldonado, taxing him with disrespect, pushed him rudely; but softened by his gentle excuses, asked of what he was thinking. "Tomorrow will be Our Lady's Assumption," was the reply; "what a joy it would be to say Mass in her honor!" "Not in my time," harshly answered the Prior as he turned away.

The festival brought no consolation to the captive; but towards evening on the following day, Our Lady came to visit him. "Have patience, my son," she said; "thy trial is almost at an end; thou shalt leave thy prison, say Mass, and be glad." During the course of the octave, our Lord, Himself, came with His Blessed Mother and bade His faithful servant be of good cheer; for that He who had enabled Eliseus to divide the waters with the mantle of Elias and so cross the river, would set him free without difficulty. Once more Our Lady appeared to him, showing him in a vision a window of the monastery, from which he could see the river Tagus. She told him he was to descend through that window and put his trust in her.

The Sisters of Notre Dame
Life of Saint John of the Cross

On Sunday, September 3, after Communion, Josefa again saw the Master. He shone with incomparable beauty, and resting His eyes on the nuns who were deep in their thanksgiving, He said with deep feeling: "I am enthroned in hearts that I have Myself prepared. My consecrated ones cannot possibly realize how greatly they relieve the sorrow of My Heart by giving Me entry into theirs. No doubt they are small and miserable, but they belong to no one but Me. Their wretchedness I condone, for all I want is their love. Weakness and worthlessness are of small account; what I want is their trust. These are the souls who draw down on the world mercy and peace; were it not for them, divine justice could hardly be restrained. . . . There is so much sin."

Sr. Josefa Menendez
The Way of Divine Love

Seeing early in my priesthood that marriages break and friends depart when sensitiveness and delicacy are lost, I took various means to preserve that responsiveness. When first ordained and a student at the Catholic University in Washington, I would never go to class without climbing the few stairs to the chapel in Caldwell Hall to make a tiny act of love to Our Lord in the Blessed Sacrament. Later, at the University of Louvain in Belgium, I would make a visit to Our Blessed Lord in every single church I passed on the way to class. When I continued graduate work in Rome and attended the Angelicum and Gregorian, I would visit every church en route from the Trastevere section where I lived.

Later as a teacher at the Catholic University in Washington, I arranged to put a chapel immediately at the entrance of the front door of my home. I tried to be faithful to this practice all during my life, and even now in the apartment in New York where I live, the chapel is between my study and my bedroom. This means that I can never move from one area of my small apartment to another without at least a genuflection and a small ejaculation to Our Lord in the Blessed Sacrament. Even at night, when I am awakened and arise, I always make it a point to drop into the chapel for a few seconds, recalling the Passion, Death and Resurrection of Our Lord, offering a prayer for the priests and religious of the world, and for all who are in spiritual need. Even this autobiography is written in His Presence, that He might inspire others when I am gone to make the hour that makes Life.

Archbishop Fulton J. Sheen
Treasure in Clay

At the Offertory you place in His hands your own gifts, small offerings, indeed, for you have so little to offer. But in His hands these offerings grow, and when He presents them to His Eternal Father they become most acceptable. What are these offerings? The resolution determined upon, to cultivate devotion to the Mass, is always welcome, for the effort to keep a good resolution is a golden gift to Him. Acts of self-denial and self-discipline that hurt in the making are precious gifts. Any victory over self, paid for in the bitter coin of self-discipline, is no cheap gift, but a very welcome one. You come to Mass to offer yourselves, to bring what you have won, to bring also your failures so that through Him they may be turned into victories. No one who uses his imagination to see within the sanctuary the assembled court of heaven can continue to go to Mass empty-handed. Your angel guardian stands beside you. The saint of the day is watching you. Your patron saint is very near.

And as they look at you, they ask: Where is your offering? Have you nothing to give Our Father? Is there no suffering or sorrow you wish to make fruitful? Is there no work you are doing which could sanctify you? Have you not an "act," done joyfully in His Name? Nothing to pick from the week that is gone, but surely there are resolutions you can offer Him for the week that is coming?

Fr. John T. McMahon
Live the Mass

Feast of St. John Eudes
1601-1680

I t was the divinely appointed mission of St. John Eudes to inaugurate in the Church the public worship of the Sacred Heart. That mission could not have been accomplished, however, until he had first established the theological soundness of the devotion, defined its precise object, and provided a suitable liturgical Office and Mass for the proper celebration of the Feast of the Sacred Heart. These tasks he undertook with characteristic courage, zeal and learning. Moreover, the tireless energy he expended in propagating this most tender and salutary devotion not only resulted in spreading far and wide a clearer understanding of its aim and object but also deepened, developed, and spread its regular and formal practice among great multitudes of the faithful.

At long last, the Devotion to the Sacred Heart was firmly established. To this great saint we owe the first public celebration of the Feast of the Sacred Heart in the liturgy of the Church. The heroic sanctity of his own personal life, his zeal for the establishment and propagation of his cherished devotion, his fruitful apostolate in its behalf, his great learning and piety, displayed both in the composition of his liturgical Offices and Masses in honor of the admirable Heart of Mary and the Sacred Heart of Jesus and in his enlightened exposition and defense of the doctrinal foundations of this form of devotion and worship gained for St. John Eudes the honors of the altar as well as high titles of praise and reverence from the Sovereign Pontiffs who declared him Venerable, Blessed and Saint.

Dom Richard Flower, OSB, **Trans.**
The Sacred Heart of Jesus

Feast of St. Bernard
1090-1153

S t. Bernard arrived in the same city two days after the cardinal. "In the morning he caused the bell to ring for Mass," says the chronicler, "and, whether from curiosity to behold the most celebrated man of his day, or from the extraordinary blessing that followed wherever he went, the Albigenses flocked in such great numbers to the church, that the vast nave could scarcely contain them." The servant of God, after the celebration of the holy mysteries, mounted the pulpit to preach the Gospel. . . . He spoke to them with the greatest gentleness, and explained to them the different points of Catholic doctrine that the innovators had rejected or corrupted. Not satisfied with rectifying their doctrinal errors, and enlightening their minds, he applied himself especially to the task of gaining their hearts . . . and this method was the more easy to him, because his gracious words poured forth from an inexhaustible fountain of love.

The people who heard him showed, by their tears, the feeling that he had kindled within them; and the discourse was scarcely finished, when truth triumphed. "Enter, then, into yourselves," said the holy preacher, "return, erring children, into the unity of the Church; and, that we may know who are those who have received the word of salvation, let them raise the right hand to heaven in token of the adhesion to the Catholic faith." At this moment all raised the right hand, and testified, by a shout of joy their return to the bosom of the Church.

M. L'Abbe Ratisbonne
The Life and Times of St. Bernard

Feast of St. Pope Pius X
1835-1914

The Eucharistic Congress in Venice that took place in August 1898, was prompted and carried out by the zeal and energy of the Patriarch, who spared no pains to make it a success.

Each parish was to take its part in the celebration, the whole Congress being carefully organized by the Cardinal himself. "The heart of man," he said, "is inconstant in good; it grows cold and languid if from time to time it is not stirred up to action." Conferences were held and missions were preached in many of the Venetian churches to prepare the people for the great event. The bells of all the towers in the city rang out to announce the beginning of the Congress, which opened with a magnificent procession from the Patriarchal palace to St. Mark's.

"Jesus is our King," he said, "and we delight to honor as our King Him whom the world dishonors and disowns. We, His true subjects, offer our true homage to Christ the King; the intensity of our love shall be greater than the coldness of the world. We meet around the tabernacle where Jesus remains in our midst until the end of time; there faith springs up anew in our hearts, while the fire of His charity—the very fire that He came to cast upon the earth—diffuses itself within us. The object of this Eucharistic Congress is to make reparation to our Lord Jesus Christ for the insults offered to Him in the Blessed Sacrament; to pray that His thoughts may be in our minds, His charity in our institutions, His justice in our laws, His worship in our religion, His life in our lives."

F. A. Forbes
Heroes of the Church: Life of Pius X

The apparition of Our Lady in Knock, Co. Mayo, on August 21, 1879, was seen by fifteen people. Each of the eyewitnesses, ranging in age from six to seventy-five, was cross-examined individually by an ecclesiastical commission and their sworn testimonies confirmed in every detail.

Our Lady spoke no words to the witnesses in Knock. Her message, therefore, lies in the apparition itself and its symbolism, what it represents.

The message of Our Lady of Knock is first and foremost Eucharistic. The central message is about the Mass and its importance. The focal point is not Our Lady but the Lamb on the Altar; Our Lady is positioned to one side, with St. Joseph and St. John, in an attitude of prayer. At the center is the Lamb and the Cross behind it, clearly symbolizing the Mass, the Eucharistic sacrifice of the Lamb of God, Jesus, to the Father, through the power of the Holy Spirit for the sins of the world. The Knock apparition is reminding us, as Irish people, that the Mass should be the center of our lives.

In his homily at Knock on September 30, 1979, Pope John Paul II said: "Mother, in this shrine you gather the people of God of all Ireland and constantly point out to them Christ in the Eucharist."

Ray Burke
The Irish Family Newspaper, February 1995

From the time that she gave birth to her first child in 1973, Marian Carroll began to suffer from various pains and illnesses until finally in 1977 she was diagnosed with multiple sclerosis. By February 1987, she relates: "I had lost the power in both legs. Then in March the bladder and kidneys were giving trouble, and my right arm and hand went. After that my speech was getting bad and my sight wasn't too good, and they also discovered thyroid trouble. I was being treated for epilepsy. I had kidney infections they couldn't get rid of. I had to wear a collar eventually.

"Food had to be cut up very small and the only way I could drink was with a plastic beaker and a straw. Eventually I had to be washed, fed and changed. By 1988 I could only sit in a wheelchair for a few minutes. I was completely disabled. The muscles were wasting in my legs, all there was was the bone and flesh. I had some help, and a nurse coming every day."

Then in September 1989, she was taken to Knock in great pain. "I received Holy Communion from the bishop. It was only three days later that I realized that I had received Holy Communion normally! (I had such difficulty swallowing I needed a drink and I needed help). After receiving Communion I got a very bad pain in both my heels. I remember thinking: I'm due my pain killers and there's a steward behind me; I'll get him to get me a drink. That pain went and looking back, when that pain went, every pain I had in my body went and I never had pain since" (I had never known life without pain since December 1972). (Marion Carroll)

Ray Burke
The Irish Family Newspaper, February 1995

We are at Montmartre, in the Basilica of the Sacred Heart, *consecrated to the contemplation of Christ's love present in the Blessed Sacrament.* We are in the evening of the first of June, the first day of the month particularly dedicated to meditation, to contemplation of Christ's love manifested by His Sacred Heart. Here, day and night, Christians gather in succession to seek "the unsearchable riches of Christ" (cf. Eph 3:8).

We are called not only to meditate on, and contemplate, this mystery of Christ's love; we are called to take part in it. *It is the mystery of the Holy Eucharist, the center of our faith, the center of our worship of Christ's merciful love manifested in his Sacred Heart,* a mystery that is adored here night and day, in this basilica, which thereby becomes one of those centers from which the Lord's love and grace radiate in a mysterious but real way on your city, on your country and on the redeemed world.

We come here to meet the Heart pierced for us, from which water and blood gush. It is the redeeming love that is at the origin of salvation, of our salvation that is at the origin of the Church. Now still, today the living Christ loves us and presents His heart to us as the source of our redemption. At every moment, we are enveloped in the love of this heart "which loves men so much and which is so little loved by them."

Pope John Paul II
Meditation at the Basilica of the Sacred Heart in
Montmartre, June 1, 1980

Feast of St. Louis IX
1214-1270

King Louis of France, who labored perhaps more strenuously than any man in his kingdom and who was one of the best and most glorious sovereigns who ever ruled over France, found time to hear two or three Masses every day!

Some of his courtiers suggested that he was overtaxing himself with so many Masses. The King replied: "If I spent much more time in following the pleasures of the chase, or in entertaining my friends at rich banquets, or in frequenting for several hours each day theaters and places of amusement, you would not complain that I was devoting too much time to pleasure.

"You forget, my good friends, that by hearing Mass I not only secure for myself innumerable blessings, but I confer the most important benefits on my kingdom, many more than I could possibly do in any other way."

Fr. Paul O'Sullivan, OP
The Wonders of the Mass

Our Lord gives me [Columba Marmion] more and more a great confidence in the Holy Sacrifice and in the Divine Office. It seems to me that when I celebrate or when I say the Office, I bear the whole world with me, all the afflicted, the suffering, the poor, and all the interests of Jesus Christ. When I give myself to Jesus Christ, it seems to me almost always that He unites me with Him and then with all His members and that He asks me to do like Him, of Whom it is said: "Surely He hath borne out infirmities and carried out sorrows."

Dom Raymund Thibaut
Abbot Columba Marmion: A Master of the Spiritual Life

Feast of St. Monica
332-387

For on that day when her death was so close, she was not concerned that her body should be sumptuously wrapped or embalmed with spices, nor with any thought of choosing a monument or even for burial in her own country. Of such things she gave us no command, but only desired to be remembered at Thy altar, which she had served without ever missing so much as a day, on which she knew that the Holy Victim was offered, *by whom the handwriting is blotted out of the decree that was contrary to us*, by which offering too the enemy was overcome who, reckoning our sins and seeking what may be laid to our charge, found nothing in Him, in Whom we are conquerors. Who shall restore to Him His innocent blood? Who shall give Him back the price by which He purchased us and so take us from Him? To this sacrament of our redemption Thy handmaid had bound her soul by the bond of faith.

St. Augustine
Confessions of St. Augustine

Feast of St. Augustine
354-430

On the Cross, the Lord effected a great exchange; there the purse that contained the price of our redemption was opened. When His side was opened by the lance of the soldier, there flowed forth from it the price that redeemed the whole world. The faithful and the martyrs were bought by it, and the faith of the martyrs has been tested. Their blood is witness. They have given back what was paid for them, and fulfilled what St. John said, "As Christ laid down his life for us, so should we lay down our lives for the brethren." It is said elsewhere, "You have sat down at a great table. Diligently consider what is set before you because it is necessary for you to prepare the same things." The great table is that at which the Lord of the table is Himself the food. Now no one feeds the guests with his very self, but that is what the Lord Christ does. He is the One who invites, and He is the food and drink. Therefore the martyrs recognized what they ate and drank so that they might give back the same, viz. (their own lives).

St. Augustine
Patrologia Latina, Sermon 329

During Holy Mass, I saw the Infant Jesus in the chalice, and He said to me, *I am dwelling in your heart as you see Me in this chalice.* After Holy Communion, I felt the beating of the heart of Jesus in my own heart. Although I have been aware, for a long time, that Holy Communion continues in me until the next Communion, today—and throughout the whole day—I am adoring Jesus in my heart and asking Him, by His grace, to protect little children from the evil that threatens them. A vivid and even physically felt presence of God continues throughout the day and does not in the least interfere with my duties. (Nos. 1820, 21)

Bl. M. Faustina Kowalska
Divine Mercy in My Soul

s the saint returned thanks to God for these graces with all her power and took delight in considering the extraordinary favors which He had communicated to her it was revealed to her that whenever any one assists at Mass with devotion, occupied with God, who offers Himself in this Sacrament for the whole world, he is truly regarded by the Eternal Father with the tenderness merited by the Sacred Host which is offered to Him and becomes like to one who, coming out of a dark place into the midst of sunlight, finds himself suddenly surrounded by brightness. Then the saint made this inquiry of God: "Is not he who falls into sin deprived of this good, even as one who goes from light into darkness loses the favor of beholding the light?" The Lord replied: "No, for although the sinner hides My Divine light from him, still My goodness will not fail to leave him some ray to guide him to eternal life. This light will increase whenever he hears Mass with devotion or approaches the Sacraments."

Msgr. William J. Doheny, CSC
The Revelations of Saint Gertrude

Behold how Gemma prepared herself for Holy Communion, and with what sentiments of faith, of abandonment, of desire, of love, and above all of humility she approached It. What wonder then that the fruits she gathered from It were not small, as she said and thought, but abundant and precious? And what wonder that our Lord showed such great complacency in the Communions of His Servant? He made her feel His presence, as she herself used to say "strongly, strongly," in her heart during those blessed moments, loading her with consolation that from her soul flowed even into her bodily senses, and beautified her whole being. The Sacred Species themselves often produced on her palate a most delicious sensation. She felt them descending into her interior as if they were a balm, and sometimes also the Divine Lover made her feel the impression and taste of His Precious Blood.

"Yesterday, Feast of the Purification," she said, "after Communion I felt all my mouth full of our Savior's Precious Blood. Oh! How good it was! It did me so much good! And I clasped my arms that it might enter my heart. Oh that you had felt, father, the good it does me to consume Jesus! I felt this (for the first time) in October from Friday at noon until the following Friday; then it left me. This morning it has again returned. It consumes me, and I continually feel that I am about to die. But oh what happiness! Have you ever felt yourself consumed? How delightful it is! The fire of my heart this morning spread as far as my throat. O Eternal Divine Fire! Look, father, if Jesus were to continue to make me feel as at present, I should not last more than a month or two, and who knows?"

Father Germanus, CP
The Life of Gemma Galgani

When Jesus takes the cup on the evening before His death, it is not the cup of wrath but the cup of blessings. It is the cup of a new and everlasting covenant, the cup that unites us with God and with one another in a community of love. Paul writes to the people of Corinth: "The blessing-cup, which we bless, is it not a sharing in the blood of Christ?" (1 Cor 10:15-16).

The immense suffering of humanity can easily be understood as a sign of God's wrath, as a punishment. And we, looking at the horrors that plague our world, are saying, "How can there be a loving God when all this is happening?"

Jesus, however, took upon Himself all this suffering and lifted it up on the cross, not as a curse but as a blessing. That is the mystery of the Eucharist. Jesus died for us so that we may live. He became for us food and drink so that we can be fed for everlasting life. "This cup is the new covenant in My blood poured out for you" (Lk 22:20). The Eucharist is that sacred mystery through which what we lived as a curse, we now live as a blessing. Our suffering can no longer be a divine punishment. Jesus transformed it as the way to new life. His blood, and ours too, now can become martyr's blood—blood that witnesses to a new covenant, a new communion, a new community.

When we lift the cup of our life and share with one another our sufferings and joys in mutual vulnerability, the new covenant can become visible among us. The surprise of it all is that it is often the least among us who reveal to us that our cup is a cup of blessings.

Henri Nouwen
Can You Drink the Cup?

St. Gregory the Great (d. 604), Pope and Doctor of the Church, was another who, fortunately, has left us many writings in which he illustrates his love for the Holy Eucharist and the power of the Holy Sacrifice of the Mass. In his *Homily 37* he relates:

"Not long ago it happened that a man was taken prisoner and carried far away. Now after he had been a long time kept in prison without his wife knowing anything about it, she believed him to be dead, and caused every week, on certain days, the Holy Sacrifice of the Mass to be offered for him. After a long time had elapsed the man returned home, and related to his astonished wife that on certain days of the week the chains that bound him became loose; in this way he succeeded at length in making his escape. Now when his wife inquired on which days of the week this wonder took place, she discovered that the days on which his chains became loose were those upon which the Holy Sacrifice of the Mass was offered for him."

Joan Carroll Cruz
Eucharistic Miracles

As St. Gertrude heard Mass on the Feast of St. Gregory and offered him singular testimonies of veneration and devotion, he appeared to her full of majesty and glory. She thought that he equalled all the saints in merit. He was a Patriarch by the careful and paternal diligence with which he watched night and day over the Church that had been confided to him, a Prophet since in his admirable writings he had discovered the snares and deceits of the ancient enemy and had given advice and remedies against his wiles, so that he was more glorified than any of the Prophets. He equalled the Apostles from his inviolable and faithful attachment to God in prosperity and adversity and by his zeal in the promotion of the Gospel. He resembled the martyrs and confessors by his great bodily austerities and the ardent love which he had for religion and holiness. Above all, he excelled in chastity. As a recompense for his virginal purity, he enjoyed an incomparable glory for every thought, word or work which had been accomplished to preserve the purity of his body and soul or to teach others to preserve the same treasure.

Msgr. William J. Doheny, CSC
The Revelations of St. Gertrude

Nocturnal adoration had begun in Paris, December 6, 1848, chiefly through the instrumentality of Hermann Cohen, the noted convert from Judaism, a former dandy and pianist, pupil of Lizst. In February 1849, it was established in Tours through the zeal of Leon Dupont who was a friend of Cohen and of other apostles of the Eucharist. He did not receive much encouragement from his friends. But nothing could daunt him. In less than two months there were seventy-four adorers. Most of the members were laborers to whom a night of adoration after a hard day's work was a great sacrifice, but they gave themselves eagerly to the work.

All the expenses were borne by Leon Dupont. He went to all his friends and urged them to join, and even stopped strangers on the street and invited them to spend an hour in adoration. He himself often spent several hours in succession, remaining immovable in an attitude of faith and love. Many times he invited Father Eymard, Father Cohen and others to come and preach to the men and stir up their fervor. Sometimes the men would walk miles in order to assist at adoration. From all walks of life they came—officers, law and medical students, laborers, all united as brothers before the Blessed Sacrament.

"When shall we see Our Lord honored day and night in every parish through the Catholic world?" Leon Dupont said. On one occasion he entertained in his house Fathers Cohen, Eymard and Bishop de la Bouillerie, all ardent apostles of the Eucharist. What sentiments of zeal for adoration and reparation were exchanged by all those saintly men! Leon Dupont playfully called the meeting, "a little Eucharistic Congress."

Fr. Hugh F. Blunt, LLD
Witness to the Eucharist

We especially desire, however, that through a more intense participation in the august Sacrament of the altar, a greater devotion be given to the Sacred Heart of Jesus, whose outstanding gift is the Eucharist. For it is in the sacrifice of the Eucharist that our Savior Himself—"always living to make intercession for us" (Heb 7:25)—is immolated and received, whose Heart was opened by the lance of the soldier and from which was poured out on the human race a stream of precious blood and water. Also, it is in this excellent crown, the center as it were of all the sacraments, that "spiritual sweetness is tasted at its source, and the memory of the excelling love is recalled which Christ showed in His passion" (St. Thomas Aquinas). Hence, it is completely fitting that, in the words of St. John Damascene, "we approach it [the Eucharist] with burning desire . . . so that the fire of our desire, having been enkindled from the coals, burns away our sins, and enlighten our hearts, and in the communication of the Divine fire we be equally set on fire and deified."

Pope Paul VI
Investigabiles Divitias Christi

What I and others find in Larry is an ability to reach the poor, the lonely, and those who feel abandoned, because his blindness puts him in touch with what it is to feel powerless. When I celebrate the Eucharist with Larry, I have a sense of offering it with a man who long ago has given everything to Christ. When I watch him hold up the chalice, I have a sense of how much he counts on others, especially on God, for his existence. Larry suffers his blindness redemptively because he uses it to pray and act like Christ: as one totally dependent on the Father, yet reaching out to the poor and the lonely because he knows what powerlessness is.

When the messengers of John the Baptist ask Jesus who He is, He defines Himself as a healer who lets the blind see, the lame walk and the deaf hear (Mt 11:4). John and others also define Jesus as the light (Jn 9:29), the way (Jn 14:6), and the word (Jn 1:1). He heals blindness so people can see His light, the lame so they can walk His way, and the deaf so they can hear His word. In healing us of blindness, lameness, and deafness, He is saying that He wants to heal us of anything that keeps us from knowing Him intimately.

Matthew Linn, sj, and Dennis Linn
Healing Life's Hurts:
Healing Memories through the Five Stages of Forgiveness

D o you remember George, a young friend of mine that you met at Binondo Church? He told me that he would like to enter the seminary and become a priest. He said that the only problem was that he would not be able to memorize a homily, nor learn to give so many of them. After thinking about what he said, I told him that I did not think that there was a problem.

The greatest priest who ever lived would give the same homily every time, over and over, and it was just two lines. St. John Vianney would tell the people every Sunday: "If you only knew how much Jesus loves you in the Blessed Sacrament, you would die of happiness." Then pointing to the tabernacle, he would say, "Jesus is really there."

People came from all over France to hear him talk; and he would say the same thing every Sunday. So profoundly moved to the very depth of his soul at the realization of the love and presence of Jesus in the Blessed Sacrament, that when he pointed to the tabernacle to tell the people that Jesus is really there, he would begin to weep for joy. He would spend hours in prayer before the Blessed Sacrament every day and every night, and hours in the confessional each day hearing confessions. St. John Vianney, the Cure of Ars, was proclaimed by the Church to be the model and patron of all priests.

Msgr. Josefino S. Ramirez
Letters to a Brother Priest

The Birthday of the Blessed Virgin Mary

I t was on the feast of the Nativity of the Blessed Virgin, and the children gathered around the altar for Holy Mass were about six hundred. Six hundred in church on such a day would mean nearly six hundred communicants in any Salesian House. Unfortunately, the only ciborium in the tabernacle was almost empty: it contained from fifteen to twenty wafers at most.

The sacristan knew this; he had even prepared a second ciborium for consecration, but at the last moment, some distraction had made him leave it in the sacristy. He remembered it too late, after the elevation; he could do nothing but await the painful surprise of the Beatus, and his fatherly rebuke after Mass. In fact, at the moment of Communion, when Don Bosco uncovered the ciborium and perceived the misfortune, his expression plainly showed his distress. Grieved at not being able to communicate all his children, he raised his eyes heavenwards in mute supplication, and descended to distribute the Eucharist to the first row of kneeling communicants. But these were followed by others, and these again by others; one row succeeded another, and still the ciborium was not exhausted.

When Don Bosco returned to the altar all the boys had communicated, and the Eucharist still remained at the bottom of the sacred vessel. The sacristan could not understand it.

A. Auffray, SC
Blessed John Bosco

"My dear child, stay close to my Immaculate Heart. Persevere in prayer and in living a good and holy life. Be pure, humble, and charitable. Do not allow the subtle snares of the world to lead you away from my Son and me. I am your loving Mother, the Mother of All. I am the Mediatrix of All Graces, Coredemptrix.

My dear little one, continue to be a soul of prayer and sacrifice. Pray, still, for those intentions that I have confided to you. Love and forgive. Speak only with kind words. Words, my child, that build up not words that tear down. And, as always, love my Son, Jesus, Who is truly with you in the Most Blessed Sacrament of the Altar. Go in peace." (Words of Our Lady, Feast of Our Lady of the Blessed Sacrament, May 13, 1995)

Michael McColgan
Open Your Hearts:
Messages from Our Lord Jesus and His Blessed Mother

Bridget was lying in bed and Mass was being said for her in her room. She understood that the end was drawing near. And she wanted the Holy Sacrifice of the Body and Blood of the Son of God to be offered every morning in her cell. The faith in the Real Presence of Christ in the Sacrament of the Altar had been one of the cornerstones in Bridget's piety. It was this faith that she proclaimed again and again to high and low, to King Magnus as well as to the peasants in Lodose, who with the realism of peasants thought that a piece of bread was nothing but a piece of bread. Had she not herself seen in the consecrated Host as it were the figure of a Lamb, the Lamb that bore the sins of all the world, and in the Lamb as it were a face, that face before which all human souls are one day to stand to be judged?

Johannes Jorgenen
Saint Bridget of Sweden

Dear Fr. Rookey,

How can we thank you for the many blessings received here from your visit? And more to the point, where to begin? After the healing Mass, the elderly gentleman in the wheelchair that got up and walked out with his wife caused quite a stir in the parish. Two years ago he had a stroke and had not walked since. He is a well-known and loved parishioner and his grandson attends our primary school. The morning after the healing service, his grandson (aged almost seven years) stood up in the school assembly and told the whole school: "Jesus made a miracle in our church last night. My Grandad has not walked for two years and last night, when we all prayed, he got up and walked out . . . and that's a miracle." I understand that the headmaster, although a baptized Catholic, did not go to Mass any more, but after that witness he asked the staff about the healing Mass and has said he will come back to the Church. Many others also had their faith renewed that evening. Praise God. (Letter from England)

Heather Parsons
Father Peter Rookey: Man of Miracles

Just imagine that this was the last Mass you would ever offer because of a terminal disease. What surrender and abandonment would you feel at that moment? Try to capture that affection and disposition now at Mass. The last Mass that will be offered for us will be our funeral Mass. Then it will be too late; we will have passed into the light. If there is anything you cannot surrender to the Lord, then you do not possess it; it possesses you. All of us have something that we find difficult or impossible to give. Let us ask the Lord for His grace to give it to Him so He can bless it and then give it back to us.

We come to Mass to unite ourselves to Jesus Christ in His great sacrifice. There is tremendous healing when we offer ourselves and make a sincere effort to be one with Jesus. We hear much about satanism these days. From experience we know that many people who are obsessed with evil have invited it in, or opened themselves to occult activity. The opposite is true for us. The more we open ourselves to Jesus, the more His Holy Spirit can possess and fill us. Each Mass is a golden opportunity to become one with Jesus.

Fr. Robert DeGrandis, SSJ
Healing through the Mass

Feast of St. John Chrysostom
c. 347-407

S t. John Chrysostom, Archbishop of Constantinople, in a
homily on the words of Eucharistic institution at the
Last Supper in Matthew 26, speaks most powerfully on
the reality of the Body and Blood of Christ. No one can read
this text by the great Patriarch of the East and deny for a minute
that he believes in the Real Presence of Christ in the Eucharist.

Imagine the great bishop standing in the cathedral church
of Constantinople before the altar and saying the following:
"How many there are who still say, 'I want to see His shape,
His image, His clothing, His sandals.' Behold, you do see Him,
you touch Him, you eat Him! You want to see His clothing.
He gives Himself to you, not just to be seen but to be touched,
to be eaten, to be received within. Let all of you be ardent,
fervent, enthusiastic. If the Jews stood, shoes on, staff in hand,
and eating in haste, how much more vigilant should you be.
They were about to go to Palestine; you are about to go to
heaven." (*Homily 82* on the Gospel of Matthew)

Fr. Benedict J. Groeschel, cfr, and James Monti
In the Presence of Our Lord:
The History, Theology, & Psychology of Eucharistic Devotion

September 14

Feast of the Triumph of the Cross

On the Feast of the Triumph of the Cross, as St. Gertrude prostrated to reverence the relics, Our Lord said to her: "Consider how I hung upon the Cross from Sext to Vespers and that it is for this I am elevated to such sublime glory. Understand thereby what benefits I will confer on the hearts of those in whom I have reposed for many years." She replied: "Alas Lord, how little pleasure Thou canst have had in my heart!" He answered: "And what pleasure had I in the wood of the Cross? I only honored it because I willed to honor it and so I reward those whom I decide to reward."

During Mass our Lord gave her this instruction: "Consider the example I give to My elect in honoring this Cross. Know that I honored the instruments of My Passion that caused Me suffering more than those things which in My infancy were used for My convenience. If you desire to imitate My example and to give Me glory and further your own salvation you will love your enemies more than your friends. This will advance you marvellously in perfection. Furthermore, if you neglect to do this at first, but afterwards repent and overwhelm your enemies with benefits, you will follow My example in having concealed My Cross for a time, to exalt it triumphantly afterwards.

As the saint ardently desired to have some relics of the wood of the Cross, that our Lord might look on her with more love, He said to her: "If you desire to have relics which will draw My Heart into yours, read My Passion and meditate attentively on every word contained therein and it will be to you a true relic that will merit more graces for you than any other.

Msgr. William J. Doheny, CSC
The Revelations of St. Gertrude

" *I* am the sorrowful Mother of the Eucharist. . . . Jesus in the tabernacle is surrounded by much emptiness, much neglect and much ingratitude. These times were fore-told by me at Fatima, through the voice of the Angel who ap-peared to the children to whom he taught this prayer: 'Most Holy Trinity, Father, Son and Holy Spirit, I adore You pro-foundly and I offer You the most precious Body, Blood, Soul and Divinity of Our Lord Jesus Christ, present in all the taber-nacles of the world, in reparation for the outrages, sacrileges and indifference with which He Himself is surrounded. . . . ' This prayer was taught for these times of yours.

Jesus is surrounded today by an emptiness, which has been brought about especially by you priests who, in your apostolic activity, often go about uselessly and very much on the periph-ery, going after things that are less important and more second-ary and forgetting that the center of your priestly day should be *here*, before the tabernacle, where Jesus is present and is kept especially for you.

He is also surrounded by the *indifference* of many of my chil-dren, who live as if He were not there and, when they enter church for liturgical functions, are not aware of His divine and Real Presence in your midst. Often Jesus in the Eucharist is placed in some isolated corner whereas He should be placed in the center of the church and He should be placed at the center of your ecclesial gatherings, because the church is His temple which has been built first for Him and then for you." (Words of Our Lady, August 8, 1986)

Fr. Stefano Gobbi
To the Priests: Our Lady's Beloved Sons

What happened there on the Cross that day is happening now in the Mass, with this difference: On the Cross the Savior was alone; in the Mass He is with us. Our Lord is now in heaven at the right hand of the Father, making intercession for us. He therefore can never suffer again in His human nature. How then can the Mass be the re-enactment of Calvary? How can Christ renew the Cross? He cannot suffer again in His own human nature that is in heaven enjoying beatitude, but He can suffer again in our human natures. He cannot renew Calvary in His physical body, but He can renew it in His Mystical Body—the Church. The Sacrifice of the Cross can be reenacted provided we give Him our body and our blood, and give it to Him so completely that as His own, He can offer Himself anew to His heavenly Father for the redemption of His Mystical Body, the Church.

So the Christ goes out into the world gathering up other human natures who are willing to be Christs. In order that our sacrifices, our sorrows, our Golgothas, our crucifixions, may not be isolated, disjointed, and unconnected, the Church collects them, harvests them, unifies them, coalesces them, masses them, and this massing of all our sacrifices of our individual human natures is united with the Great Sacrifice of Christ on the Cross in the Mass.

Archbishop Fulton J. Sheen
Calvary and the Mass

S t. John Eudes used to insist that for a fully worthy Communion two eternities would be required, one eternity to prepare and the other to thank Christ for the gift of Himself. . . .

The moment you feel the touch of the host on your tongue, send your guardian angel and your favorite saint and Mary, your Mother, in advance into your heart to make the final last minute preparations in your stead. And when you have returned to your pew, get down to business. We make the following suggestions, merely as guides for your convenience. Build your business time around the worth F-A-T-H-O-M-N. Faith in the Real Presence of Christ truly and substantially in your soul. I believe. Adoration: O Jesus, You are all the mountains and I but a grain of sand. You are all the forests and I but a leaf on a dying tree. You are all the oceans and I but a drop of water. You are Who must be. I am who need not be. Thanks for the goods of nature—the earth, the mountains, the air; our food, our loves, our dreams. Thanks for the goods of grace: for God, for the Church, for our faith—and for this Communion. "O good and gentle Jesus, look down upon me . . ." Here recite the indulgenced prayer before a crucifix. "O Jesus, pardon me my sins, save me from the fires of hell." Mary! Thank her for Christmas, for Calvary and for the Mass. She made them all possible. Needs—of body: health for yourself, your loved ones. Needs—of soul: more charity toward God and your neighbor, grace for your usual weakness, grace to persevere in your resolutions. No more sins!

John N. McCormick, CSSR
John A. Trienen, CSSR
What Is the Mass?

September 18

A swelling had formed on the right knee of Victor Mattei of Osimo and had grown in the course of six years to such an extent that it was finally as large as a loaf of bread and very hard. It was impossible for him to kneel or to walk freely, and he was tortured with incessant pain, which, about a month before his cure, became almost unbearable. The surgeon who was called, realizing that the malady was chronic and that by an incision the sick man would be exposed to great danger, refused to undertake an operation. About the time Mattei despaired of all human aid, the death of Joseph took place. As a last resort the sick man took refuge to supernatural means, trusting to be healed by God because of the merits of the saint, the fame of whose holiness had already spread.

On the morning of September 19, he dragged himself to the Church of St. Francis. The body of the saint lay in state in the sacristy and, not being able to come near because of the great crowd, Victor obtained permission to go to the room in the monastery in which Father Joseph had lived. He devoutly entered and at length came to the private chapel, where the saint had said Holy Mass. He there made an act of lively faith and pressed his knee against the step of the altar that was worn down by the knees of the saint during his long protracted prayers. On touching the step all pain and the swelling disappeared at once, so that no trace of the infirmity remained. The knee was perfectly healed and could be moved like the other, which had never been affected.

Fr. Angelo Pastrovicchi, OMC
Saint Joseph of Cupertino

S t. Paul in 1 Corinthians 11 provides a glimpse of a typical Christian service of around 55 AD. Here the lively community meal, now called the agape meal (love feast), is linked with the solemn Eucharistic memorial (the Lord's Supper), a situation that caused considerable problems. Paul chastises the Corinthians for overeating and not sharing food at the meal, and even for getting drunk. Such gluttony blasphemed the Eucharist held after the meal. Says Paul, "When you come together, it is not the Lord's Supper you eat, for as you eat, each of you goes ahead without waiting for anybody else. One remains hungry, another gets drunk. Don't you have homes to eat and drink in?" Paul is perplexed to anger: "Shall I praise you for this? Certainly not!" The community meal has become unmanageable as more and more Gentiles enter the Church. Change is clearly in order, ironically necessitated by evangelical success.

Paul's letter also testifies to a primitive but very real intuition of the Real Presence. He warns that he who eats and drinks without confessing his sin, and "without recognizing the body of the Lord" in the consecrated bread and wine, "drinks judgment on himself." Clearly, this is no ordinary food.

Daniel Gallio
Immaculata, January/February 1996

Accordingly on January 5, 1644, early in the morning, Jogues knocked at the door of a house of his own Order. When the porter opened he saw before him a wretched man in shabby and grotesque clothes, his head covered by a sailor's cap. On being informed by the stranger that he had news from Canada for the Rector, the porter hastened to inform his Superior, who at the moment was vesting for Mass. On hearing the word, "Canada," he was all attention.

As the rector approached, Jogues handed him the commendatory letters from the Dutch Governor. Without looking at them the rector asked eagerly about the mission and especially about Father Jogues. "Do you know him?" "Very well," replied the stranger. "We have learned," continued the rector, "of his capture by the Iroquois, his captivity and sufferings; but we do not know what fate has befallen him. Is he dead, or is he still alive?" "He is alive, he is free; and it is he, himself, who is addressing you." The rector embraced his ragged and emaciated brother in Christ, tears of emotion filling his eyes.

Conducting Jogues into the assembly room he summoned the community to see and hear the missioner from the Indian country. They kissed his mutilated hands and listened with rapt attention and deep reverence to the briefest mention of his capture, torture and slavery. He was too weak, and too much overcome by emotion, to do more than give the barest outlines of his frightful experiences. The whole community then proceeded to the chapel and there, at the foot of the altar, Jogues still in his sailor garb, fervently thanked God for his return to his brethren and for all the dispensations of Providence in his regard.

Martin J. Scott, SJ
Isaac Jogues: Missioner and Martyr

There, now, I [St. Peter Julian Eymard] have found the whole secret of it: the unconditional gift of self to our Lord. I made this gift and took an oath on it before the Blessed Sacrament at the Consecration; my tears ratified it. At Communion, I placed my heart—in the act of giving itself—in the ciborium that it might itself become a ciborium.

Jesus wants to be my Raphael, my means, my center. *In me manet* ("Abide in me," Jn 6:56), and ("You who have continued with Me," Lk 22:28). I shall renew my gift of self with my every breath. I now feel that I was fleeing from this divine servitude, that I wanted to choose what I should give and to hold fast to my ego.

Totus tuus (My God, You are all mine and I am all Yours); but no pilfering! This morning's meditation is fundamental: I am the servant of Jesus Christ.

Andre Guitton
Peter Julian Eymard

We are never given more than we can carry or bear, and as Simeon helped Jesus carry His cross, so Jesus Himself helps us carry ours. "The Lord is close to the brokenhearted." All trials purify us and lead us into a deeper union with Jesus. We offer Jesus all our suffering for the salvation of souls, even the sufferings we bring upon ourselves.

This is the triumph of the Cross: all suffering has lasting and redeeming value when offered to Jesus Who glorified all human suffering by His holy Cross! Three times He fell on His way to Calvary to teach us never to get discouraged, for here in the Blessed Sacrament He makes a divine success out of all our failures when we humbly surrender them to the redeeming love of His Sacred Heart: "Cling to Him, forsake Him not, thus will your future be great, for in fire, gold is tested, and worthy men in the crucible of humiliation."

Like fire that transforms everything to itself, here in the Blessed Sacrament Jesus transforms everything to good in the fire of His Divine Love, drawing good out of evil, drawing a greater good out of a greater evil, consuming even our very faults and failures (like straw thrown into a burning furnace) and using them to make us more humble and to bring us even closer to His divine Heart.

Fr. Martin Lucia, SSCC
Rosary Meditations from Mother Teresa of Calcutta

My experience of adoration varies. Many times, if not most of the time, I simply jot down in my log-book, "trying to be present with my heart. No obvious movement of the Spirit."

But there are times of anointed presence when I am so aware of the Lord's presence that it even warms my heart. Yet the point of the adoration, I find, is not to experience the Lord's presence, but rather to be present to the One who is present.

What have I found to be the essence of Eucharistic adoration?

Being present with my body, mind, and spirit to the humble, hidden, holy Presence of Mercy itself—Jesus Christ, present Body and Blood, Soul and Divinity.

What is my greatest awareness? My overall awareness is the ultimate and extreme humility of God and a growing awareness of His mercy.

What is my greatest need? I need to let the Lord love me and minister to me, in order that I may love and minister to others.

Why Eucharistic adoration? To become like the Eucharistic presence, the presence of mercy. This echoes my mission statement: Make Mercy present by trust in Jesus.

Thus, Eucharistic celebration and adoration is not a waste of time. It is rather the answer to the questions of our present human condition. It is the answer to the crisis of our times and the counter-sign to our age. The Holy Eucharist is God's merciful, humble, holy presence—the power to renew the earth and bring us to eternal life.

Fr. George W. Kosicki, CSB
Friends of Mercy newsletter

How well Thou knowest, O Lord, how to try souls, and what a tool for purification in Thy hands is suffering! Perhaps Thou hast deigned to accept my interior offering. In spite of inexpressible vexations, trials, and privations of soul and body, I can say a joyful fiat, if by so many crucifying pains I obtain from Thee the fulfillment of my desires and all the graces I have hoped for, and if my sufferings serve souls. I offer all to Thee, beloved Master: dryness, deprivation, solitude of soul, my present lack of religious help, overwhelming bodily miseries.

During these four painful weeks (first attack of the generalized cancer that was to reappear in July and prove fatal after ten months of suffering) a visit from our Lord illuminated my life and my heart. I am at present an exile from the tabernacle, and I hunger for Jesus in the Eucharist. Will I be able to go to Him on Sunday to tell Him my joy in the Resurrection and renew for Him the offering of my trials? I shall spend these holy days in spiritual isolation, in privations, in destitution. Yes, but my beloved Savior is close to my heart, my soul is united to the cross, and I wish only for the fulfillment in me, for me, through me, of the divine will.

Is it not a great honor to be chosen by our Lord to suffer, on the blessed anniversary of His Passion and death on the Cross?

Yes, through all the blows, pains, and sacrifices of life, of soul and body, I want to give God from the deepest recesses of my being complete and joyous assent to His holy and ever beloved will.

Elizabeth Leseur
My Spirit Rejoices

" Come to Me My children and live in My love. Let Me fill you with the fruits of My peace and joy. Let Me touch your hearts so that you can love again.

Today My children I invite you to daily Mass. Start slowly, one extra day, then two extra days, before long you will come everyday. You will hunger for My precious Body and Blood.

My children it is by the Mass that you will learn to live. Because to live you have to suffer. The Mass is a sacrifice, in the Mass you are taught about the suffering that My Son Christ endured. Don't hesitate when suffering comes your way, accept it lovingly in My name and offer it to Me for the conversion of sinners.

Do you not see My children, the Eucharist will change the world. Of all the many gifts I have given you, the Mass and the Eucharist is the greatest. You have the opportunity everyday to attend, if you can come. And if you want to, you can. I will multiply your time if you are *generous with your time with Me*. Today and each day from now, come and receive My Son's precious Body and Blood, the Bread of Life." (Words of God the Father, June 3, 1993)

Matthew Kelly
Words from God

Almighty God took pity upon the sorely-tried saint and granted him a measure of consolation. On greater Church festivals, his trials were temporarily suspended and his spirit seemed more tranquil. The maximum effect took place when he celebrated High Mass. Then his eyes filled with tears and his emotion was so marked that he had difficulty in singing the Preface and the Pater Noster. Signs of God's favor were not altogether lacking. Praying before the crucifix for the conversion of sinners, the saint could not help remembering his own misery and humbly thought: "I pray for others whilst my own soul is in the depth of hell." At once he heard a voice which seemed to come from the figure on the cross: "Your soul is in My Heart."

Father Edmund, CP
Hunter of Souls:
A Study of the Life and Spirit of Saint Paul of the Cross

But she [St. Catherine of Siena] could not hold up those praying hands much longer. She was only thirty-three years old, but her fragile body was now held erect only by the force of an interior flame and this was beginning to flicker. She had said of herself, "Fire is my nature," and this was true; but the fire had ceased to burn brightly and she did not try to kindle it anew. She no longer took a morsel of food or even a drop of water. She lived only upon the Eucharistic Host, just as her soul lived only upon Christ. She still wrote on and on, she still remained accessible to her family and friends, she still went regularly to Mass, though the time came when she could no longer go to St. Peter's, as had been her wont, but only to the oratory in her own house. (This oratory may still be seen. It adjoins the Church of Santa Maria sopra Minerva, where Catherine is buried.)

And, until the last moment, she continued to pray with such intensity that her disciples said afterward they thought not only their hearts but the "very stones" would break. Everything and everyone she had loved was included in these fervent prayers. She had never known fear in her life and she did not know it now in the presence of death, only joy and thanksgiving. "Beloved, You call me and I come. Father, into Your hands I commit my spirit." She made the Sign of the Cross and then she folded her hands and they were still. She lay at rest and her face was radiant, like that of an angel.

Francis Parkinson Keyes
Three Ways of Love

Today there was nocturnal adoration. I could not take part in it because of my poor health, but before I fell asleep I united myself with the sisters who were at adoration. Between four and five o'clock, I was suddenly awakened, and I heard a voice telling me to join those who were adoring at that time. I understood that there was among them a soul who was praying for me.

When I steeped myself in prayer, I was transported in spirit to the chapel, where I saw the Lord Jesus, exposed in the monstrance. In place of the monstrance, I saw the glorious face of the Lord, and He said to me, What you see in reality, these souls see through faith! You see, although there appears to be no trace of life in Me, in reality it is present in its fullness in each and every Host. But for me to be able to act upon a soul, the soul must have faith. O how pleasing to Me is living faith! (Nos. 1419, 20)

Bl. M. Faustina Kowalska
Divine Mercy in My Soul

During the reign of Charles II a number of ruffians forced entrance into the convent of Saint Mary in York. With cries of blasphemy and cursing they began making their way toward the chapel where they planned to sacrilegiously handle the Holy Eucharist. The Superioress with her Sisters hastened to the chapel where the Superioress reverently secured the ciborium from the tabernacle, hid it under her mantle and turned to flee.

At that moment the men pressed into the chapel corridor cutting off escape. The Superioress instructed the Sisters to place the statue of St. Michael before the open door of the chapel as she cried out: "Great God, protect Yourself, for we are no longer able to rescue You!"

The angry cursing mob reached the open door at that point. Suddenly with no natural explanation, the men shrank back. They appeared both astounded and stupefied as they faced the statue of Saint Michael, or, better, perhaps, as Michael faced them. Only seconds passed by when not one of the intending blasphemers was left in the convent.

As a testimony of thanks for the miraculous saving of the Eucharist, and probably outrages to the nuns themselves, Saint Michael's statue was permanently enshrined at the chapel entrance. Each year his feast was marked with great solemnity.

It would seem natural that St. Michael was the special protector, and still is of the Blessed Sacrament.

Fr. Albert J. Herbert, SM
Michael The Archangel: "Life" and Apparitions to Date

If you could see with the eyes of your soul what takes place during the Holy Sacrifice of the Mass! God the Father, sitting on a throne above the priest, watches over His divine Son present upon the altar. All the heavenly choirs of angels are there. If you could hear with the spiritual ears of your soul the melodious tune that the angels are singing during the Holy Sacrifice of the Mass! Michael the Archangel is at the priest's right side, protecting the Host that the priest has just consecrated. When the priest gives the blessing, the angels come out over the people and sprinkle them with graces—the only thing I can compare it with is children's sparkle dust—sprinkling graces upon each one in the congregation. That's what's happening during the Holy Sacrifice of the Mass. Many people say, if there's no one there I'm not going. Jesus and the Father and the heavenly court with the choirs of angels are there. Our Mass is never dull!

Eileen George
Beacon of God's Love: Her Teaching

October 1

Almost as soon as I started school, I was received into the Association of the Holy Angels. I loved the devotional practices this meant, for I took special delight in praying to the angels and particularly to him given me by God to be my companion during my exile on earth. Not long after my first Communion the ribbon for candidates seeking to become Children of Mary replaced that of the Holy Angels. As I had left school before finishing my studies, I was not allowed to be a candidate. I confess this didn't at first worry me, but then I thought that all my sisters had been Children of Mary and I was afraid of being not so fully a child of my heavenly Mother as they were. So I went back to school and pleaded very humbly— which I didn't like doing at all—to be received as a candidate.

The headmistress didn't want to refuse, but she made it a condition that I should return to school two afternoons a week so that it could be seen if I was worthy of being a Child of Mary. This horrified me. Some of the other girls, former pupils like me, had friends among the nuns with whom they could spend these afternoons. But I hadn't. I sat and worked in silence at my sewing and then, when I had finished, as no one took any notice of me, I went to the chapel and climbed up into the tribune. There I remained before the Blessed Sacrament until Daddy came to take me home. There I found my sole comfort: Jesus, my only friend. I could talk only to Him. Talking to other people bored me, even when we spoke about religion. I felt it better to speak to God than about Him.

St. Therese of Lisieux
The Story of a Soul

S he treated her Guardian Angel like a brother—as can be seen in the homely advice she gave to Sister Vincent, still a novice. "When you pass by the chapel and haven't time to stop, tell your Guardian Angel to take your messages to Our Lord in the tabernacle. He will take them and then have time to catch up with you." "I've kept up this practice ever since," declared Sr. Vincent Garros over thirty years later. Certainly Bernadette herself did likewise.

Francis Troche
Saint Bernadette Soubirous

As I knelt to receive Our Blessed Lord in the Holy Eucharist tonight, my Angel said to me, "All who are present, whether receiving Our Lord or not, are to show reverence for the infinite miracle that is happening. God is uniting with human beings. That is a greater miracle than any other you have witnessed. There is no greater miracle on earth or in heaven than this."

I asked if this meant we should kneel. All over the country now, we are told not to kneel during the Consecration, or at all during the Mass for that matter. After Vatican II, the Communion rails were removed and we stood in line to receive the Lord. Now we are not to kneel even in the pews during preparation for the Consecration. We are "encouraged" to stand even during the Consecration itself.

"You are to show reverence in the way you know best," my Angel answered me. I was somewhat confused at this reply.

He said with his wonderful humor, "You stand in line for everything. Are you showing reverence then?"

So the question is not what we do but that we show reverence, and an outward sign of reverence surely helps us ordinary mortals to feel more reverent. Otherwise, why show any respect for anyone or anything if one could always argue, "But I am reverent in my heart" while actions contradict this? But I think with all the arguing over this it is so easy to lose sight of the miracle of which my dear angel spoke: that God should unite in any way, and in such a special way, with us ordinary people!

Patricia Devlin
The Light of Love

October 4

Feast of St. Francis of Assisi
1181-1226

On the feast of St. Francis, our Lord let me [St. Margaret Mary Alacoque] see in prayer this great saint, clad in a garment of light and un-speakable brilliance. He had been raised above the other saints to an extraordinarily high degree of glory, because his life was so like that of the suffering Redeemer who is the life of our souls and the love of our hearts. His glory was the reward of his great love for the Passion of our Lord, a love which rendered him worthy of the sacred stigmata and made him one of the great favorites of Jesus' heart. By a very special favor he had been given great power in applying to the faithful the merits of the Precious Blood, a power which made him in a sense the mediator of this treasure.

After I had seen all this, the Divine Bridegroom, as a token of his love, gave me St. Francis as my soul's guide. He was to lead me through all the pains and sufferings which awaited me.

A. Hamon
Vie de la Bienheureuse Marguerite-Marie

For that reason we draw close to the altar of God. We hear the words of the Lord again, "This is My Body," "This is My Blood," and we realize that His promise is fulfilled in this Eucharist we celebrate. The Lord looks to us with love in our hunger and in our thirst, and He says in this Mass, and in every Mass, "I myself am the Bread of Life. No one who comes to Me shall every be hungry, no one who believes in Me shall thirst again."

Listen again to what He says. "I Myself am the Bread of Life." Jesus is life. In Jesus we celebrate the birthday of life. The Eucharist is given us for life. Not just my life in isolation from others, but rather my life in communion with the life of Christ and in loving communion with every man, woman and child on the face of this earth. We are pro-life because we believe that Jesus, who is life, is present in the gift of the Eucharist. He is present as the Bread of Life, and He is present in His sacrificial death. He offered His life as a ransom, to pay with the price of His blood, that we might have life and have it to the full.

We are pro-life because we have learned from Jesus never to claim to be the master of another's life but to be ready to give our lives, without counting the cost, so that others might live. The "others" of our love's embrace include all those in the womb awaiting their births, all those struggling to survive in this world, and all those at the end of their life's journey.

May the Lord who is life, then, strengthen us in this Eucharist to be faithful disciples and responsible citizens, to be unconditionally pro-life.

Bernard Cardinal Law
Homily at Mass in the Basilica of the Immaculate
Conception, 25th Anniversary of *Roe vs. Wade*

Living the Mass means never wasting suffering but always being good stewards of the trials God gives us. There is hardly anything so tragic in the world as wasted pain. Think of how much suffering there is in hospitals, among the poor and the bereaved! Think how much of that suffering goes to waste. How many, or rather how few, of those lonesome, suffering, abandoned, crucified souls are saying with our Lord at the moment of Consecration: "This is my body, take it."

"Here is my body, take it; here is my blood, take it. Here is my soul, my will, my energy, my strength, my property, my wealth—all that I have. It is Yours. Take it. Consecrate it. Offer it. Offer it with Yourself to the heavenly Father in order that looking down on the great sacrifice, He may see only You, His beloved Son in Whom He is well pleased. As the drop of water is absorbed by the wine at the offertory of the Mass, let my life be absorbed in Your life.

"As Thy great St. Gertrude used to take her life, her heart, her body and soul and mind and all, and drop them into the chalice at the moment of the offertory as a drop of water and pray You to change all into Yourself at the consecration of the Mass—so do I drop my life and all into the chalice of Your Sacred Heart that I may be changed truly into You. Consecrate these trials or my life which would go unrewarded unless united to You. Transubstantiate me, so that like the bread which is now Your body and the wine which is now Your blood, I too may be wholly Yours."

John N. McCormick, CSSR
John A. Treinan, CSSR
What Is the Mass?

October 7

Feast of Our Lady of the Rosary

"**M**y dear child, I ask you to pray every day so that you can grow in the fullness of God's love for you . . . so that you can grow in my love for you. Your prayer makes you stronger against Satan's attacks and against all temptations that come from him. My child, I ask you and all the world to pray, especially the Rosary, every day for the conversion of sinners and to obtain peace in the world— peace which can only come from God. My child, I ask you also to fast strictly, as I have asked in Medjugorje, on Wednesdays and Fridays on bread and water alone. Know that fasting is pertinent to prayer and the graces received from both. Do penance, also, for your sins and the sins of those around you.

Go to Confession frequently and also go to Holy Mass as often as you can. Please, my child, do as I ask and please my heart so much in doing so. I am the Lady of the Rosary. I am the Lady of the Roses. I am the Mother of all mankind. Tell the world of my messages. Do not be afraid, my child. Be strong in the Lord and pray for the Holy Spirit to fill you. Nothing more is needed for peace on earth. Nothing more but God and all that He asks. Again, tell the world of my messages. Tell the world to convert now. The time before the great events is now so very short. Tell my children to pray and repent now. Go in the peace of God. I love you, my child." (Words of Our Lady, May 2, 1991)

Michael McColgan
Open Your Hearts:
Messages from Our Lord Jesus and His Blessed Mother

F r. Frederick Jelly, OP, extends this relationship of the liturgy and the Rosary. He points out that the three Mysteries of the Rosary echo the Eucharist and prepare for it: The Joyful Mysteries contemplate the Real *Presence* of the Lord, the Sorrowful Mysteries resonate with the *sacrifice* of the Lord, and the Glorious Mysteries celebrate the *communion* of God and man. The Rosary is a Eucharistic prayer of intercession.

The point that Father Jelly makes about the relation of the Rosary and Eucharist I find very rich, especially since he chooses the three dimensions of the Eucharist as presence, sacrifice, and communion. Pope John Paul II in his encyclical *Redeemer of Man*, describes the Eucharist with these same three dimensions: "It is at one and the same time a Sacrifice-Sacrament, a Communion-Sacrament, and a Presence-Sacrament." These three dimensions of the Eucharist also reveal some of the grandeur of its mystery. When we contemplate the mysteries of the Rosary we enter into some of this mystery.

Pope John Paul II, in three short talks in 1981, gave his personal testimony to the power of the Rosary. He exhorts us to use it as intercessory prayer. Let these exhortations stand next to the request of our Blessed Mother made at Lourdes and Fatima that we pray the Rosary daily, that we intercede daily for all of "us sinners, now and at the hour of our death."

Fr. George W. Kosicki, CSB
Intercession

I t was probably at almost this same time—very likely August 12, 258, just two days after Lawrence's martyrdom—that another Christian congregation, meeting for Mass in a crypt near the tomb of Sts. Chrysanthus and Daria on the first anniversary of their martyrdom (about which we have little historically reliable information) was trapped by soldiers and buried alive under an avalanche of stones and sand. Later, when it became possible to excavate the site in the Christian Roman empire during the pontificate of Damasus (366-384), the skeletons of the martyrs at this Mass—men, women, and children—were found in their buried crypt, with the priests and deacons still holding the sacred vessels for the Body and Blood of Christ. This scene was on view for pilgrims to the catacombs, through a window in a wall constructed there by Pope Damasus, for more than two hundred years.

Warren H. Carroll
The Founding of Christendom, Vol 1

Don John de Moschera, an officer in the army, had for many years led a life which gave open scandal. One day Don John happened to be passing the Church of St. Anthony. He was told that the throng had gathered in order to hear Fr. Francis Borgia preach. Don John had constantly derided the manner in which the Duke of Gandia had left the world, and he now burst into a violent passion. "Rather," he declared, "would I go straight down to hell this very moment than enter that church! Father Francis is a devil, and so are the other Jesuits who are with him!" These extravagant expressions were repeated to Francis, whose soul at once filled with the tender compassion he felt for all sinners, and more especially for those who declared themselves to be, not only his own personal enemies, but enemies also of the Society.

During eight days he offered the Holy Sacrifice in order to obtain the conversion of so great a sinner. On the morning of the ninth day, as soon as he had finished Mass, he set out in order to call upon Don John at his country-house. On entering the room where Don John was, Francis threw himself at his feet, imploring his forgiveness for any words or deeds by which he might have unconsciously caused so strong an aversion. Completely disarmed, Don John knelt down in his turn, and asked pardon, not only of Francis, but also of God. Francis had the delight of reconciling this obstinate sinner with God by means of a general confession. He began to lead an utterly different life, under the direction of Father Francis. Every week he went to confession and received Holy Communion. . . .

A. M. Clarke
The Life of St. Francis Borgia

When the Church says that Jesus is present in the Holy Eucharist, she is talking about a very special kind of presence. Pope Paul VI referred to the presence of Jesus in the Eucharist as His Sacramental presence "par excellence." By the almighty power of God, a tremendous miracle takes place. The substance of bread and wine is changed into the substance of the Body and Blood of the Risen Christ. While only the appearance of bread and wine remains, this essential change of bread and wine into the Body and Blood of Christ at the Consecration of the Mass is defined as the doctrine of transubstantiation.

Since Jesus is God and God is worthy of adoration, it follows that the Lord, truly present under the appearance of bread and wine, is worthy of adoration in the Holy Eucharist. How great, then, should our reverence be toward the Eucharist.

Private time spent in the presence of the Blessed Sacrament is one of the most effective ways of drawing closer to Jesus. The world is filled with noise. We all need quiet time to gather our thoughts, to speak to God and to listen to Him. If we can do this in the presence of the Blessed Sacrament, we are very fortunate. Our visits should include acts of adoration, thanksgiving, reparation and petition.

Jesus is present in the Most Blessed Sacrament to complete the work which His Father entrusts to Him. He is there to fill our soul with the love which led Him to die on the Cross for us. He is there to take over our hearts and to lead us to the love of God and neighbor. He is there to make us stronger and more resolute in loving Him.

Bishop Thomas V. Daily
Pastoral Letter on the Holy Eucharist

*B*efore the tabernacle. Lord, I want to thank you for Your presence, for recognizing in this house the house of your Father, and for dwelling within it, so as not to be distant and hidden from us with the Father and the Spirit, but rather to remain among us as the way that leads to the Father, as the way by which we will also attain the possession of the Holy Spirit. I want to thank You for being here, veiled in the mystery of the Host, but so fully present that You Yourself teach us to pray and help us to live. You are so fully present that we come to receive from You and take with us what Your presence bestows upon us: the certainty of faith, the love of Your dwelling among us. Lord, You know how weak and distracted we are and how we consider everything else more important than You; but again and again You guide us back to this place where You dwell in order to change us. (Adrienne von Speyr)

Hans Urs von Balthasar
First Glance at Adrienne von Speyr

On October 13, 1989, I was the guest of the Handmaids of the Holy Eucharist for two days in the convent in Akita, and there I witnessed devotion to and adoration of the Blessed Sacrament as I have never seen before. It was also my privilege to meet Sr. Agnes Sasagawa whose hands were covered with gloves to hide the stigmata. She gave me a gift of a blue bag in crochet that she made herself, and which was meant to be the "ark" for my Rosary.

That same morning I met another visitor to the convent. She was a young Japanese lawyer who had come with her mother to give thanks on the anniversary of her miraculous cure by Our Lady of Akita of an illness called Takayasu's syndrome, a disease of unknown etiology, involving major arteries and usually fatal after about five years. She was a most intelligent witness of the disease and of her instant cure. I believed her.

That afternoon the novice mistress of the Congregation, with quiet authority, calmly instructed me: "Go and spend a long time in the chapel with Our Lady of Akita. She is there waiting for you." The weepings had stopped since 1981 and so I did not see the famous statue weep when I was in the chapel, but it is of significance that, as recorded by Fr. Teiji Yasuda, the most copious weeping occurred on March 25, 1979: "There were true streams of tears which covered her face. We never saw them so abundant as at that time." It was on the feast of the Annunciation, the celebration of that day when Mary became the Ark of the Lord. It was the Ark of the Covenant, in the spirit of Rachel, weeping for her children.

Dr. Courtenay Bartholomew
A Scientist Researches Mary: The Ark of the Covenant

The five long years in Lubianka brought this home to me more forcefully than ever. I was deprived of that spiritual food and the reality of that communion. I turned to God in prayer, made frequent acts of spiritual communion throughout the day, but I literally hungered to be able to receive Him once again. Every day I said from memory the prayers of the Mass and sometimes I think these prayers served only to emphasize my sense of deprivation from the Eucharist. In those days of torment and stress, of darkness and humiliation, I knew I desperately needed that source of strength the Bread of Life might have provided—and I could not have it. I prayed to God, I talked to Him and asked for help and strength, I knew that He was with me. All this I had, and yet I could not have Him in my hands, I could not have His sacramental presence. And the difference to me was very real. It was a hunger of the soul as real to me as the bodily hunger I constantly experienced through those years. I have often wondered, in the years since, whether I would have failed as badly, have come so close to despair, if I had somehow had available to me that Bread of Life.

Walter J. Ciszek, SJ
He Leadeth Me

October 15

Feast of St. Teresa of Avila
1515-1582

One day, when I [St. Teresa] had just communicated, I was shown how the most sacred Body of Christ is received by His Father within our soul. So now I understand and have seen how these Divine Persons are there, and how pleasing to God is this offering of His Son, since He delights and rejoices in Him, as we may say, here on earth, for it is not His humanity that is with us in the soul but His Divinity, and it is for that reason that He is so pleasing and acceptable to Him and that He grants us such great favors.

I understood, too, that He accepts this sacrifice even though the priest be in sin, but that the favors that it brings are not communicated to his soul as they are to the souls of those who are in grace. It is not that these gracious influences, which proceed from the communion in which the Father receives this sacrifice, lose any of their power, but that he who is to receive Him is found wanting; just as it is not the fault of the sun that a lump of pitch does not reflect its rays as a piece of crystal does. If I could describe this now, I should be better able to explain myself: it is important to know how it happens, for there are profound interior secrets to be learned when we communicate. It is sad that these bodies of ours prevent us from having the fruition of this.

Msgr. William J. Doheny, CSC
Selected Writings of St. Teresa of Avila

The Blessed Sacrament was exposed, and I [St. Margaret Mary] was experiencing an unusually complete state of recollection . . . when Jesus Christ, my kind Master, appeared to me. He was a blaze of glory—His five wounds shining like five suns, flames issuing from all parts of his human form, especially from His divine breast that was like a furnace. . . . It was at this moment that He revealed to me the wonders of His pure love for mankind: the extravagance to which He'd been led for those who had nothing for Him but ingratitude and indifference.

"This hurts me more," He told me, "than everything I suffered in My passion. Even a little love from them in return—and I should regard all that I have done for them as next to nothing, and look for a way of doing still more. But no; all My eager efforts for their welfare meet with nothing but coldness and dislike. Do Me the kindness, then—you, at least—of making up for all their ingratitude, as far as you can.

"First of all, you are to receive Me in the Holy Eucharist as often as obedience allows. Accept any mortification or humiliation that may result, as a token of My love. Besides this, you are to receive Communion on the first Friday of each month. Then, every Thursday night, I shall give you a share in the fatal sadness which I allowed Myself to feel in the garden of olives; death couldn't be so hard as the agonized state to which this sadness will reduce you. You are to get up between eleven o'clock and midnight, to keep Me company in humble prayer to My Father, exactly as I spent that night in agony."

Vincent Kerns
The Autobiography of St. Margaret Mary

October 17

I n Ignatius' thinking, the reality of Christ's flesh makes martyrdom a necessity. This martyrdom should be approached and experienced as a Eucharist, a participation in the death and resurrection of Christ.

When the Bishop of Antioch thinks of martyrdom in cultic terms, that is, as an act of worship, he thinks of it as a Eucharist. It is a sacrifice offered to God; it is the supreme act of complete and definitive union with Christ and therefore becomes the perfect way of imitating Him. This is why Ignatius cries out as he does in his Letter to the Romans and begs his readers to "let me be the food of beasts, that through them I may find God. I am God's wheat, and the teeth of beasts shall grind me so that I will be a pure bread of Christ."

Matthew J. O'Connell
The Eucharist of the Early Christians

Sometimes as Padre Pio approached the altar, he would tremble. "Why do you tremble like that," Cleonice Morcaldi, a native of San Giovanni Rotondo, once asked him. "Is it because you have to suffer?"

"No," he answered her, "it isn't because of what I have to suffer, but because of what I have to offer. Don't you realize the great mystery of the Mass? We priests are the butchers who slaughter Jesus the victim, to offer Him to our heavenly Father in payment for our sins."

Padre Pio almost always cried throughout the Mass. The same lady asked him why he cried, and he told her: "I don't want to shed small tears. I want to shed a flood of tears. Don't you see the great mystery of the Mass?"

Everyone I spoke to told me that it was impossible to describe what Padre Pio's Mass was like. "His face was transfigured, literally," they told me.

One of his biographers, Maria Winowska, tried to capture something of this when she wrote: "The Capuchin's face that a few moments before had seemed to me jovial and affable was literally transfigured. Fear, joy, sorrow, agony or grief. . . . I could follow the mysterious dialogue on (his) features. Now he protests, shakes his head in denial and waits for the reply. His entire body was frozen in mute supplication.

"Suddenly great tears welled from his eyes, and his shoulders, shaken with sobs, seemed bowed beneath a crushing weight. . . . Between himself and Christ there was no distance.

"I defy those who have been at San Giovanni Rotondo to attend Mass as mere spectators."

John A. Schug, CAP.
Padre Pio

Feast of St. Isaac Jogues
Martyr, 1607-1646

An old man and a woman approached the spot where I [St. Isaac] stood; he commanded his companion to cut off my thumb; she at first drew back, but at last, when ordered to do so three or four times by the old wretch, as if by compulsion she cut off my left thumb where it joins the hand. (She was an Algonquin, that is, one of that nation that dwells near the French, in New France; she had been captured a few months before, and was a Christian. Her name was Jane. Surely it is pleasing to suffer at the hands of those for whom you would die, and for whom you chose to suffer the greatest torment rather than leave them exposed to the cruelty of visible and invisible enemies.)

Then, taking in my other hand the amputated thumb, I offered it to Thee, my true and living God, calling to mind the sacrifice which I had for seven years constantly offered Thee in Thy Church. At last, warned by one of my comrades to desist, since they might otherwise force it into my mouth and compel me to eat it as it was, I flung it from me on the scaffold and left it I know not where.

Rene had his right thumb cut off at the first joint. I must thank the Almighty that it was His will that my right should be untouched, thus enabling me to write this letter to beg my dear fathers and brothers to offer up their Masses, prayers, supplications and entreaties in the holy church of God, to which we know that we are now entitled by a new claim, for she often prays for the afflicted and the captive.

John Gilmary Shea
Perils of the Ocean and Wilderness

Feast of St. Paul of the Cross
1694-1775

For Paul, the chief meaning of Communion was love and its chief effect was love. He did not question the manner or style of going to Communion, which was very different in his day from what it is today, and certainly very different from what it was in the Early Church. But he saw it as a power to intensify love in the heart by union with Jesus and to fill the heart with all the virtues that are needed for love to grow.

Paul wanted those he directed to open their hearts to the totality of the fire of love that he himself found in this Sacrament. He wrote to Sister Colomba Gandolfi, "I beg you and strongly beg you not to omit Communion. Oh my daughter! Never omit this food of eternal life and treat with Him in long thanksgivings in the manner and form in which He will guide you and teach you." Paul saw Communion as real communion, which to him meant love-union with Jesus.

He could become eloquent on the value of Communion and its love-purpose. In the letter to his brothers and sisters he writes, "Oh, my dear ones! I do not speak to you of preparation for Communion, since I know you do all you can. Our dear Jesus could do nothing greater than to give Himself as our food. Therefore let us love this dear Lover, and be greatly devoted to the Most Blessed Sacrament."

Bennet Kelley, CP
Spiritual Direction According to St. Paul of the Cross

The other day I was excitedly talking with a friend about this and he asked where I got the excitement, my zeal, my enthusiasm for God. I thought about this for a few minutes, and I said, I asked for it, I prayed for it. I told him a beautiful little story about St. Girard. St. Girard used to write notes to our Lord in the Blessed Sacrament and he would put them there the night before, and he would knock at the door of the tabernacle, and leave his note, and say: "I'm leaving my note Lord", and the Lord would answer his prayers. I thought WOW, what beautiful trust, faith, love. He knew that all he had to do was ask. He knew that Jesus was there. I thought, I want that. I want what he had. I want that trust and that love and that faith. I began praying, asking St. Girard to pray for me, to intercede for me at the throne of God, that I could have that same kind of trust and faith. My faith has grown tremendously, it has taken off like a shooting star. I don't think God puts any limits on the amount of love He gives or on His graces.

In conclusion I can only say that prayer to the Blessed Sacrament causes action that is filled by the Holy Spirit. It happens in our speech, our attitudes, our heart and our activity. It is by the Spirit that we are able to glorify Jesus, and recognize the importance of prayer in front of the Blessed Sacrament. This prayer reaches the Spirit that in turn feeds our heart with faith and song. It is by the Spirit that we are able to say, Jesus, I thank You for life and everything in it.

Claudia Blache
Perpetual Eucharistic Adoration newsletter, March 1995

Christ puts before us the invitation, "Come, Child, let's you and I fall in love! " Is it so hard to fall in love with the greatest of all lovers? The Son of the King, Jesus Christ, our love, our all! Why does this invitation shake us?

Perhaps you are saying, I accept this invitation, but how are we going to do this? Well, every love affair has a courting stage and your love affair with Jesus must have a courting stage. And how do you do this? By spending time with Jesus before the tabernacle, quiet moments of love, you and Jesus alone. Going daily to the Eucharist and receiving your lover into your heart. This is intimacy. You are loving, you are hugging each other, you are embracing, you are kissing in the Eucharist.

This is all part of the courting stage. How did you fall in love with your wife, with your husband? You spent time with them, maybe every day, at least several times a week. You found out what they like, and what they dislike. And this love grew and grew the more time you spent with each other. Then it led to marriage.

Well, it's the same with the Lord Jesus Christ. We fall in love with Him by spending time with Him. In the quiet moments of the day, just sit and say, "Lord, I put myself in Your presence." And think about Jesus. And if you can't, picture yourself spiritually putting your head on His chest and being soaked in Him.

Eileen George
Beacon of God's Love: Her Teaching

Our Lord wants me [St. Peter Julian Eymard] dedicated entirely to his Eucharistic service; and certainly He is great enough, important enough, to ask for all that I am. But what does this Eucharistic service entail? Two duties for me.

1. Perform my duty as an adorer like any other religious. I owe this service to my Master; and I owe it to myself as the food and life of divine love.

2. Make of the brethren good religious, good adorers . . . to adore and make others adore, to serve and make others serve as perfectly as possible.

Towards the end of my meditation, a beautiful thought came to me, assuredly from the mercy of our Lord. I was asking Him just how He wanted me to serve Him. And then it seemed to me that I heard these words: "Be to Me in My Sacrament what I was to my Father in My Incarnation and My mortal life."

That thought made a vivid impression upon me; I thanked the good Master for it, and I gave myself anew to Him to be entirely His as He was His Father's.

I must be to Jesus what Jesus was to his Father. ("I in them and you in me," Jn 17:23). ("As the Father has loved me, so have I loved you. Abide in my love," Jn 15:9). It is St. Paul's *Vivit vero in me Christus* ("But Christ who lives in me," Gal 2:20).

Andre Guitton
Peter Julian Eymard: Apostle of the Eucharist

Feast of St. Anthony Mary Claret
1807-1870

The following case is mentioned in the process of beatification: Sr. Benigna Sibila Alsina suffered since November 1926 from an ulcer near the stomach. The pain grew worse from day to day and soon became unendurable. This continued for three years. The only remedy was an operation, but on account of the patient's extreme weakness the physicians dared not think of an operation. All earthly means failing the sick religious, her Sisters had recourse to heaven; on May 11, 1930, they began a novena to the Servant of God, Father Claret.

A change took place the following morning. While the community was at Mass the suffering sister felt as if something was being forcibly removed from her stomach. The next moment all pain vanished, she was perfectly well and strong. She could follow the common life and take her meals as in the days of her health. The physicians were greatly astonished and declared the cure to be an evident miracle. It would be an easy matter to add example to example to prove the powerful intercession of the Servant of God. If anyone wishes to experience this powerful intercession, let him pray to St. Anthony with faith and confidence.

Fr. Thomas, CMF
Saint Anthony Mary Claret: A Sketch of His Life and Works

The Lord repeats what He has already said: for the one who acknowledges Him and receives Him as the Living Bread, the life of the Lord will become his own life. Everything the person has looked on as life up to this point was only an animalistic function; its law was the instinct of maintaining life and begetting new life, with a number of ingrafted instincts of enjoyment, of sociability and of activity. But the life the Lord wishes to communicate is a life within faith, love and hope. He Himself is the access to this; in Himself and in the sources through which He gives His life, in the sacraments. What He emphasizes now is no longer, as at the beginning, that He has all life in Himself but that we have all life through Him and in Him alone.

But this life is called the movement to the Father. It is not a static life but a place given in the movement of the Son to the Father, and only the Son can mediate this to us. For He is this movement and this life, and thus He is this movement and this life also in those who believe in Him, love Him and hope in Him. What He has established in them through His presence is transformed immediately into His presence in them. It is as if they accepted a seed into themselves—but a seed that is fully grown as soon as it is accepted.

Adrienne von Speyr
John

The Eucharist that is the gift of the loving Heart of Jesus should always receive special honor and veneration and must find expression in various forms of Eucharistic devotion.

Indeed, since the Eucharistic mystery was instituted out of love, and makes Christ sacramentally present, it is worthy of thanksgiving and worship. And this worship must be prominent in all our encounters with the Blessed Sacrament, both when we visit our churches and when the Sacred Species are taken to the sick and administered to them. Adoration of Christ in this Sacrament of love must also find expression in various forms of Eucharistic devotion: personal prayer before the Blessed Sacrament, hours of adoration, periods of exposition—short, prolonged and annual (Forty Hours)—Eucharistic benediction, Eucharistic processions, Eucharistic Congresses. A particular mention should be made at this point of the Solemnity of the Body and Blood of Christ as an act of public worship rendered to Christ present in the Eucharist, a feast instituted by my predecessor Urban IV in memory of the institution of this great Mystery. All this therefore corresponds to the general principles and particular norms already long in existence but newly formulated during or after the Second Vatican Council.

Pope John Paul II
On the Mystery and Worship of the Holy Eucharist

Today, I experienced a good deal of sorrow because of a certain person, a lay person, that is. On the basis of one true thing, she said many things which were fictitious. And because they were taken to be true and spread around the whole house, when the news reached my ears, my heart felt a twinge of pain. How can one abuse the goodness of others like that? But I resolved not to say a word in my defense and to show even greater kindness toward that person. I became aware, however, that I was not strong enough to bear this calmly, because the matter lingered on for weeks. When I saw the storm building up and the wind beginning to blow sand straight into my eyes, I went before the Blessed Sacrament and said to the Lord, "Lord Jesus, I ask You to give me the strength of Your actual grace, because I feel that I will not manage to survive this struggle. Shield me with Your breast."

Then I heard the words, *Do not fear; I am with you.* When I left the altar, an extraordinary peace and power filled my soul, and the storm that was raging broke against my soul as against a rock; and the foam of the storm fell on those who had raised it. Oh, how good is the Lord, who will reward each one according to his deed! Let every soul beg for the help of actual grace, as sometimes ordinary grace is not enough. (No. 1150)

Bl. M. Faustina Kowalska
Divine Mercy in My Soul

When I left school and went home, I told my family and the members of my church that I was converting to the Catholic Church. On the first night I was home, I talked to my mother and my brother from about 10:00 until 8:00 the next morning. At first my decision was very difficult for them to accept, but we continued to discuss my reasons for becoming Catholic.

By God's grace, these discussions with my staunchly-Protestant family members has borne much good fruit. I am forever grateful that God enabled me to help my mother, my father, and my two brothers (one of whom is now studying for the priesthood at St. Charles Borromeo Seminary, Philadelphia) join the ranks of the Catholic faithful.

The Lord asked me to give up everything and follow Him, no questions asked. But He also has been true to His promise to repay a "hundredfold" those who give up everything for Him. The joy and peace that I now experience, the doctrinal certitude that I now possess, and the tremendous graces that are mine in the sacraments, especially in the Holy Eucharist, are riches far beyond anything I expected.

The pilgrimage was difficult and painful. I had despised for so long the Catholic belief in Mary's intercession. But when I finally gave in to her loving call, bidding me follow Christ her Son wherever He might lead, I knew she was saying to me, "Do whatever he tells you" (Jn 2:5). (Tim Staples)

Patrick Madrid
Surprised by Truth

In 1933, Pius XI proclaimed in Rome a Jubilee Year marking the nineteen hundredth anniversary of the institution of the Eucharist and the death of Jesus on the Cross. And in 1934 the Pope extended this Holy Year to the Universal Church. Marthe [Robin] lived by this rhythm. She had learned in her own body that the reign of Jesus begins, whether one wishes it or not, with the Cross. "When I am raised up, I will draw everything to Myself." Thus she believed more and more that in being a "victim" with Christ she occupied a "post of honor," as she declared in a prayer (which in French is in rhyming verse) on October 22, 1936. Her mission, then, was to pray, to offer up, and to love for the whole world without any limitations.

"No, I know nothing more, I know nothing except to love;
I need love more than air in order to breathe.
Unceasingly I feel my heart beating in my breast,
But I sigh for that divine union
That will bring me to the heavenly abode."

In this stanza, note the theological precision of the poetess: it is divine union that brings about the passage to heaven, not the merits of Marthe. Salvation is gratuitous, a gift from God. And on October 8, 1930, Marthe prayed: "I am the chalice of my God; my mission is to make Him loved by overflowing with love, and therefore I must seize every opportunity of spreading light and truth."

Fr. Raymond Peyret
The Cross and the Joy

The memorial that the Lord bequeathed us is not merely the memory of an event or the portrayal of a great figure; it is the fulfillment of our personal relation to Christ. . . . In the Mass, Christ comes in all His personal reality, bearing His salutary destiny. He comes not just to anyone, but to His own. Here again St. John brings this mystery into particularly sharp focus. God's Son comes from heaven, from the Father, whom He alone knows. He lives from the Father's vitality; everything He has and is, He has and is through the Father. But this intimate bond of love does not stop there. The Father sends His Son to men in order that He may pass on to them the divine life He has received. "As the living Father has sent me, and as I live because of the Father, so he who eats Me, he also shall live because of Me (Jn 6:58).

When He became man, Jesus bridged the gulf between heaven and earth, between the Father and us once and for all. Henceforth He *is* with us in the sense that He belongs to us, is *on our side.* "Emmanuel," the God-who-has-come. Yet in the special manner of the mystery, the Lord spans that gulf anew every time His memorial is celebrated. First, in the readings of the day, we receive word of Him. Then the offerings are prepared and there is a pause. Through the Consecration, He comes to us, the subject of an incomprehensibly dynamic memorial, and gives us His grace-abounding attention. In Communion, He approaches each of us individually and says: "Behold, I stand at the door and knock (Rev 3:30). Insofar as the "door" swings open in genuine faith and love, He enters and gives Himself to the believer for his own.

Romano Guardini
Meditations Before Mass

As Catholics we believe that Christ's death on the cross merited the salvation of the world. His precious blood shed on the cross won for the whole human race all the graces needed for salvation. But we also believe that, the moment Christ died, the Church He founded came into existence. And it is through this Church that the graces of Calvary are communicated to humanity, especially through the sacrament of the Eucharist.

Graces of mercy and expiation. The sacrifice of the Mass, just because it is offered, obtains mercy from God for the remission of the guilt and punishment due to sin. Moreover, these blessings are available through the Mass not only for ourselves but for others, both living still on earth and for the souls in purgatory.

Graces of self-surrender. We do not always think of the Mass as a sacrament. But we should. Every time that Mass is offered, Christ the eternal priest pours out His sacramental graces on the whole of humanity. What kind of graces does He give through the Mass? The graces we need to live sacrificial lives. In practice this means the light and strength we need to surrender our wills to the loving but demanding will of God.

Our cooperation. The graces of the Mass are available. But we must do our part. Three recommendations that go back to apostolic times: We should attend Mass as often as we can. We should participate in the Mass as actively as we can, especially by our daily lives of sacrifice. We should have Masses offered for our own intentions and for others, as the single most powerful source of supernatural blessings available to the human family.

Fr. John A. Hardon, SJ
Retreat with the Lord

As Gertrude reflected on death, she exclaimed to our Lord: "How happy and how honored are they who merit to be consoled and strengthened by Thy saints in their last moments! I am unworthy of this consolation, for I have never honored Thy saints worthily. Therefore I cannot expect consolations from any saint, save from Thee alone, the Sanctifier of all saints." Our Lord replied: "You will not be deprived of this consolation because you expect all from Me. On the contrary, My saints will love and minister to you all the more for it and at the moment when men usually feel most fear and anxiety, I will send My saints to assist you and I will come to you Myself in all the glory and beauty of My Divinity and Humanity." She replied: "And when will thou accomplish Thy promise and bring me from this land of exile to the land of rest?" Our Lord answered: "Will a royal bride complain of the applause of the populace if it only increases the love of her bridegroom for her?" "But Lord," continued the saint, "how can this apply to me, who am the vilest of Thy creatures?" He replied: "Know that I communicate Myself to you entirely in the Sacrament of the Altar, which after this life cannot be. In this union there is more blessedness and delight than in any human love, for that is often vile and transitory, but the sweetness of this union ennobles and dignifies the soul."

Fr. William J. Doheny, CSC
The Revelations of St. Gertrude

On Wednesday, at the elevation of the Host, she besought our Lord for the souls of the faithful in purgatory, that He would free them from their pains by virtue of His admirable ascension. She beheld our Lord descending into purgatory with a golden rod in His hand, which had as many hooks as there had been prayers for their souls. By these He appeared to draw them into a place of repose. She understood by this, that whenever any one prays generally, from a motive of charity, for the souls in purgatory, the greater part of those who, during their lives, have exercised themselves in works of charity, are released.

Msgr. William J. Doheny, CSC
The Revelations of St. Gertrude

November 3

Feast of St. Malachy

1095-1148

The sister of this saint (Malachy) was so worldly-minded that her brother determined not to see her anymore as long as she lived. But although he did not see her in the flesh, he was to see her again in the spirit. After her death, one night he heard a voice telling him that his sister was at the door, complaining that she had had nothing to eat for thirty days. The saint, when he awoke, understood what food it was of which she was in need, for it was exactly thirty days since he had offered the sacrifice of the Living Bread for her. He now again began to give her this benefit, which he had withheld from her. Soon he saw her coming up to the church. But she could not yet enter, as she was still wearing a black garment. He continued to offer the Holy Sacrifice for her every day, and soon saw her a second time, dressed in a lighter garment. Finally, he saw her a third time, clad entirely in white, and surrounded by blessed spirits.

Paul Keppler
The Poor Souls in Purgatory

Q. Tell us what St. Therese, the Little Flower, looks like and what she has said to you.

A. Oh, she's very gentle, very kind, very loving, and the most beautiful of them all. She's the one I feel is really my closest friend. I think of them all as my friends. When I need help or even if I'm making a decision, my little friend, St. Therese, the Little Flower, always seems to come to my aid.

Q. Have you any memorable or special apparitions of her that you can share?

A. I saw during Mass Saint Therese come first from behind the altar and then St. Bernadette. St. Bernadette was small. St. Therese had one rose, huge; lemon-colored with a rim of red— extremely beautiful. They seemed to be sharing among themselves. St. Therese bowed toward the priest.

The Holy Eucharist in enormous light then appeared. I saw them, the Holy Souls, in a gray cloud, all raising their hands to the Holy Eucharist. Then little drops of blood began to stream down the center of the Holy Eucharist.

The clouds began to turn from gray to white and the hands of the souls reaching from the clouds grew calm. From this I understood these souls were raised to a higher level of Purgatory, but not fully released on this occasion.

Thomas W. Petrisko
The Sorrow, The Sacrifice, and The Triumph:
Prophecies of Christina Gallagher

" Dear children, today, I invite you and your family to continue to be witnesses of living my messages. Share my messages with others who live in darkness. Pray for your own conversion and for the conversion of the world.

Dear children, abandon yourselves completely to doing the will of God. Live the Ten Commandments, for these are the guidelines given by God to His servant Moses. If you follow and live by the Ten Commandments, you will learn to live without fear.

I invite you to spend more time in prayer and less time talking about prayer. Spend time with my Son in the Blessed Sacrament and tell Him all your concerns. Trust in the Presence of my Son in the Blessed Sacrament. The more you visit the Blessed Sacrament, the more your lives will begin to change. You will hunger for and seek holiness, instead of sin.

My little ones, open your hearts and listen to my motherly teaching and follow the path that leads to holiness and purity of heart.

Pray for the poor souls in purgatory and offer up your Masses for their intention, for they so long to be in heaven.

My children, attend daily Mass whenever possible. Invite your children to spend time before the Blessed Sacrament and help them to know my Son. Many parents attend daily Mass and spend time with my Son, but they do not bring their children. Teach your children about God, before it's too late! Pray together as a family. Thank you for listening to my message."
(Words of Our Lady)

Janie Garza
I Am Your Mother Come from Heaven to Love You

The suffering souls never ceased to claim her prayers, but their deliverance cost her the pains of a continual purgatory. For souls she would drag herself to the cemetery. Her visits took place on forty consecutive days. She always made them, whatever the season, in spite of sun, rain, cold, mud; and recited over every grave three times, "Eternal rest . . ." and a prayer. She prayed especially for the souls of priests.

One day, while she was assisting at Mass for the sake of some soul, she suffered untold anguish. Cardinal Pedicini said the second Mass and at the *Gloria* the Beata saw the soul delivered and entering heaven; she felt ready to die for joy at this ravishing sight. To souls delivered from purgatory she recommended the interests of the Church and of the Pope, "the Christ on earth," as she called him, after Catherine of Siena.

Albert Bessieres, SJ
Wife, Mother and Mystic: Blessed Anna-Maria Taigi

I n the first centuries there was no Church law obliging all the faithful to assist at Mass. This was rather taken as self-evident. When in the year 303 the priest Saturnius with his little community was arrested, the proconsul of Carthage asked the lector Emeritus, in whose house the Mass had been celebrated: "Was the meeting held in your house despite the imperial prohibition?" To this Emeritus replied: "Yes, it was in my house that we celebrated the Lord's feast."—"Why did you let the people in?"—"Because they are my brothers, and I could not close my doors to them."—"But you should have."—"I could not, for we could not continue to exist without the Lord's feast."

With the exception of those who were doing penance, all who were present at Mass could receive Holy Communion. As we have already seen from Justin's *First Apology*, the deacons carried the Blessed Sacrament to the homes of those who were absent. The faithful, moreover, could reserve the consecrated hosts in their homes, and on days when no Mass was offered, or when they were prevented from going to church, they gave Communion to themselves.

Ludwig Hertling, SJ
Engelbert Kirschbaum, SJ
The Roman Catacombs and Their Martyrs

Devotion to the most Blessed Sacrament took deep root in St. Ignatius' soul from the earliest days of his "conversion" in the paternal castle of Loyola. Soon he began to recommend it earnestly to his fellow townsmen of Azpeitia.

During the providential sojourn at Manresa, before finding means to embark at Barcelona for the Holy Land, he heard Mass every day with great fervor and tenderness of soul. Certain it is that Our Lord rewarded his devotion with a very special grace. According to Father Ribadeneira: "One day, in the church of that monastery (Santo Domingo), he was hearing Mass with deep reverence and devotion. At the moment when the Host was raised and shown to the people, he saw clearly with the eyes of the soul in what way Our Lord, Jesus Christ, true God and true Man, is truly hidden in that divine mystery beneath that veil and species of bread."

Through this divine favor, doubtless, devotion to the Adorable Sacrament of the altar increased greatly in St. Ignatius' soul. The supernatural knowledge granted him of the way in which Our Lord, Jesus Christ, is really and truly present in the consecrated Host kindled more and more ardently in his breast the longing to unite himself with Him in Holy Communion as often and as intimately as possible. The fact is that, despite the almost universal custom of the times, we find Ignatius already confessing and communicating every week, "which for that age," says Fr. Gabriel Alvarez, SJ, at the beginning of the seventeenth century, "meant more than every day means now."

P. Justo Beguiriztain, SJ
The Eucharistic Apostolate of St. Ignatius of Loyola

During an outdoor summer morning Mass in the early 1970s, my wife and I were standing around the altar with about 150 people. After distributing communion, Father Frank asked us to lay hands on one another and pray for each other's healing.

In a little while, a man was excitedly moving his arm up and down and clenching his fist. I was deeply moved as I witnessed the event, especially as I saw his tears. I later discovered that he had badly damaged his hand many years earlier. After prayer he achieved almost full mobility with no pain. There were many healings after Mass that morning. It was a powerful witness to Christ's love for His people. (Deacon Allan, Massachusetts)

Fr. Robert DeGrandis, ssj, with Linda Schubert
Praying for Miracles

I n the city of Lisbon, a lady lay dying of a mortal illness. The physicians held out no hope of recovery. She was suffering from a malignant cancer that had reached such extremes that an operation was impossible.

Her confessor suggested a Mass should be offered for her complete cure. The dying lady gladly accepted the counsel. The Mass was offered in honor of St. Dominic, and by its infinite efficacy the sick lady made a speedy recovery, much to the joy of her friends and to the surprise of her medical advisers.

Fr. Paul O'Sullivan, OP
The Wonders of the Mass

This morning, five unemployed men came to the gate and insisted on being let in. When Sister N. had argued with them for quite awhile and could not make them go away, she then came to the chapel to find Mother (Irene), who told me to go. When I was still a good way from the gate I could hear them banging loudly. At first, I was overcome with doubt and fear and I did not know whether to open the gate or, like Sister N., to answer them through the little window. But suddenly I heard a voice in my soul saying, *Go and open the gate and talk to them as sweetly as you talk to Me.*

I opened the gate at once and approached the most menacing of them and began to speak to them with such sweetness and calm that they did not know what to do with themselves. And they too began to speak gently and said, "Well, it's too bad that the convent can't give us work." And they went away peacefully. I felt clearly that Jesus, whom I had received in Holy Communion just an hour before, had worked in their hearts through me. Oh, how good it is to act under God's inspiration! (No. 1377)

Bl. M. Faustina Kowalska
Divine Mercy in My Soul

God is so good to me. I [Columba Marmion] live now on my daily Communion. All the morning I walk in the strength of that divine food, and from the afternoon I live on the thought of the following Communion, for It strengthens us according to our desires and preparation. Our Lord has promised that "he who eateth Me shall live by Me." His life becomes ours, the source of all our activity.

Fr. Raymund Thibaut
Abbot Columba Marmion

Feast of St. Frances Xavier Cabrini
1850-1917

Not only did she [Mother Cabrini] prescribe a daily hour of meditation, but she urged also that two hours in the morning and two in the evening be devoted intensively to community prayer in addition to the other pious practices of the day. Ardent in her own love for the Sacred Heart of Jesus, Mother programmed the sisters to take turns each hour for the adoration of the Blessed Sacrament and to have a one-hour exposition of the Blessed Sacrament each Friday and each day during the novena to the Sacred Heart. From the inception of the Institute in 1880, she encouraged both the sisters and the children to receive Holy Communion daily.

At the Holy Table the presence of the sacramental devotion of the Sacred Heart so elevated her spirit that she seemed to be in ecstasy. She said to the sisters, "We should traverse the whole world to make Jesus Christ known and loved; and if we cannot yet do that because we have not the wings of total virtue, we can at least pray and suffer for those poor unfortunate souls who, had they received the gifts that we have received, would have responded to them more faithfully. Reflect on this; and, when you are before the tabernacle where Jesus is suffering for us, meditate, and then return, all changed for the better. A God Who loves us so much! Can we not love Him with all our souls, no matter what the sacrifice?"

Mother Saverio De Maria, MSC
Mother Frances Xavier Cabrini

S tanislaus was cheerful during his illness, not because he hoped that he would escape from his hard life, but because he thought he was to be with God so soon. He called Bilinski to his bedside and said: "Go to the Church and ask the Fathers to bring the Blessed Sacrament to me, that I may receive Communion before I die."

Stanislaus entreated them to help him, but it was useless. They refused to do anything. At last he said no more, but turned to his friends in heaven. Full of faith and trust, he told his sorrow to St. Barbara. It was said that she had special charge to help those who were dying. "Do not let me die alone," he prayed. "Let some one bring our dear Lord to me."

It was night. Bilinski kept a vigil by the bed, for though he told the boy he was not dying, he really thought he could not live till morning. The house was still, and the watchman's voice, as he called the hours in the street, was the only sound to be heard. Suddenly Stanislaus opened his eyes and knelt in bed. Bilinski sprang forward, thinking that he would fall.

"Kneel down!" said Stanislaus, waving him back. "Don't you see that Our Lord is here?" In reply to his prayer, as he told a friend, St. Barbara had come, and with her two angels bearing the Blessed Sacrament. Three times, as in the Mass, Stanislaus said aloud, "Lord, I am not worthy," and then with great love he added: "Oh God of my heart," and received Communion. Bilinski watched him in amazement.

Stanislaus then lay down in peace, quite ready now to die.

Sigmund H. Uminski
No Greater Love: A Story of Saint Stanislaus Kostka

In the early days the Franciscan brotherhood was a community of laymen. But it was not long before the Order attracted men who were in priest's orders, with whom Francis pleaded that they should never forget how great was the honor and privilege that had been bestowed upon them. Writing in later years to the priest friars, he poured out his concern that they should treat the Sacrament with the greatest possible respect:

"Kissing your feet with all the love that I am capable of" (he wrote), "I beg you to show the greatest possible reverence and honor for the most holy Body and Blood of our Lord Jesus Christ, through whom all things, whether on earth or in heaven, have been brought to peace and reconciled with Almighty God. And I implore all my friars who are priests now or who will be priests in the future, all those who want to be priests of the Most High, to be free from all earthly affection when they say Mass, and offer single-mindedly and with reverence the true sacrifice of the most holy Body and Blood of our Lord Jesus Christ with a holy and pure intention, not for any earthly gain or through human respect or love for any human being, not serving to the eye as pleasers of men. With the help of God's grace, their whole attention should be fixed on Him, with a will to please the most high Lord alone, because it is He alone who accomplished this marvel in His own way."

John R. H. Moorman
The Spirituality of St. Francis of Assisi:
Richest of Poor Men

Devotion to the Holy Eucharist became intense and widespread during the thirteenth century. For Gertrude, appreciation of the sacrament was of course inseparable from her appreciation of the Sacrifice of the Mass. She was taught by Christ that no number of individual prayers and penances can approach in value the offering of His own Body and Blood to his Eternal Father. It is like gold, which united to the silver of humanity forms a precious amalgam. Once, when after having planned to abstain from Communion, Gertrude was so drawn by the grace of God that she received the Blessed Sacrament. Christ said to her: "Today by your own will you were going to render me only the service of one who brings to his master mortar, bricks, and straw; but in My love I have chosen you and placed you among the joyful banqueters who feast at My table."

Sr. Mary Jeremy, OP
Scholars and Mystics

November 17

lthough they could not communicate with her verbally, the Indians loved Mother Philippine. They named her "The Woman Who Prays Always," for she spent much of her time praying in front of the Blessed Sacrament for the success of their mission.

Mother Philippine was recalled to St. Charles after only a year. Although she went willingly in obedience to her superiors, she felt the loss of her Indian children keenly. In a letter to a priest friend she wrote, "I live in solitude and am able to employ all my time in going over the past and in preparing for death; but I cannot put away the thought of the Indians, and in my ambition I fly to the Rockies."

During the last ten years of her life, Philippine spent most of her time praying in front of the Blessed Sacrament for the Church, her society, and its missions. She died peacefully on November 18, 1852. Many years before, she and Father de Smet had made a pact that the first of them to die would obtain a particular favor for the other. Immediately after her death, Father de Smet received the favor.

Ann Ball
Modern Saints: Their Lives and Faces, Book I

One of the most important events during Mass is healing; moral, spiritual and bodily healing. Sin is the destruction of something already existing or a hindrance to something that ought to exist. Anything that destroys friendship, joy, love, trust, hope, faith or the development of these values, is sin. Where there is sin, man will be wounded, ill or unprepared for the life for which he was created.

It is necessary to emphasize our human powerlessness in the struggle against individual sin and collective evil, destruction, annihilation and wounding. But to eradicate this incapacity, the Christian taking part in the celebration of the Eucharist acquires great personal, inner healing, which is often accompanied by physical relief. . . .

We should not leave the church without being healed in our inner selves, without having been freed from sin, or without being ready to act differently. On leaving the church, we are also called upon to be bearers of this gift of healing. This does not mean we are all expected to perform amazing miracles, but rather we should perform those miracles that derive from love. Love is the healing force, since what we need most of all is inner healing. Speaking words of hope and encouragement to a person, giving valid advice, knowing how to come to terms with people to help them, this is what healing means. Just as an evil word can take away joy . . . and kill the spirit and bring darkness, so a good word based on the Word of God has exactly the opposite effect. Man becomes wounded when a fellow creature does not offer himself; but he becomes cured when a person offers himself to him, and he in turn offers himself.

Fr. Slavko Barbaric
Celebrate Mass with Your Heart

Now indeed did my soul, like that of the Psalmist, faint in the courts of the Lord. The very pace and movement of the heart were altered with desire for its absent Lord. Not the heart only, but the whole body through which the heart's pulse flowed, was penetrated with the sense of exile and of longing for Him of Whom it had been told. The ears were impatient to hear the sound of His voice saying through the lips of His appointed priest, "Arise and go in peace; thy sins are forgiven thee." The eyes cared to look upon naught else if they could not behold Him in the Holy Eucharist. The very sense of touch craved to feel the trickling water of Baptism. The tongue was dry and the stomach empty with hunger to receive substantially the Bread of Life. Where, O Lord, cried out the bodily organs in unison, can we, even we, be united with Thee?

In My Church, came the gracious reply, you will find Me indeed. There you will be united with Me as flesh of My flesh and bone of My bone, for the Church is My Body and the temple of My Spirit. Speaking to My son Paul after he had caused Stephen to be martyred, I told him that it was none other than I Whom he persecuted. When he was bound in chains for My sake, he sensed that he had in effect become a member of My Body, for he testified, "I live, yet not I, but Christ liveth in me."

Fr. Avery Dulles, SJ
A Testimonial to Grace

I attended my prayer group and Father Rookey was there to celebrate Mass. Because I wasn't able to walk, Communion was brought to me. At the end of Mass, Father prayed over me and many others. Leaving the prayer group, I wasn't able to walk normally, but I declined the use of a wheelchair. I persevered while inching toward the car.

I had the chance to attend Mass on Monday, August 22, 1994. Dad drove Mom and I along with with our neighbor to 5:00 PM Mass at Immaculate Conception Church in Chicago. When I entered the church, I knew I wanted to be as close to the tabernacle as possible. I began praying fervently as I pulled myself from pew to pew. My fervency increased as Mass built up to the Consecration which is the most powerful part of the Mass. My prayer was simple. I said, "Lord, if you will it, I can walk out of Church. Only You can heal me." At the same time, I thanked Jesus.

During the Consecration, the pain left. When it came time to receive Holy Communion, I made my way slowly to the priest. As soon as the priest gave me Jesus, I began walking back to my pew. I walked out of Church as though there had never been a problem. After getting out of the car in the garage, I told Mom what had happened, and to prove it, raced her to the back door. I told her I was healed after receiving Holy Communion and she was speechless. She and our neighbor saw me walk because I had received Holy Communion first. I've been walking everywhere without pain. Jesus is present in the Holy Eucharist! (Irene Hand)

Margaret M. Trosclair, SOSM
Father Peter Mary Rookey, OSM:
Do You Believe that Jesus Can Heal You?

Whoever eats My flesh and drinks My blood remains in Me and I in him. In this mutual indwelling of man and the Lord, everything that has been said hitherto is summarized and yet once again reversed. For it is not only He Who communicates his Body and his Blood to us, Who lives now in us, but we live in Him. This means not only that He has power over us and that we are made available to Him from now on through His life in us but also that He grants us a place within His own life, that He holds us in Himself.

Not only in order to help us when we need this, not only in order to be available to us when this is urgent, but in order Himself to make use of us, when He needs this and yearns for it. Not only does the Lord obligate Himself in our regard: He obligates us, too, in His own regard. So much does He reckon with the mutuality of love that He makes use of us when He needs us for Himself; but, for Himself, He needs us in others. In us and through us, He lives His life of the Eucharist and makes the gift of Himself through us to others. Our dwelling in Him and His dwelling in us penetrates everything, the customary everyday life, joy and suffering, anxiety and abandonment. This will perhaps be more clearly visible to us in difficult moments; for our relationship to the Lord is something of which we are less clearly conscious when everything goes well.

Adrienne von Speyr
John

" **B**eloved sons, by a miracle of love which you will be able to understand only in paradise, *Jesus has given you the gift of remaining always in your midst in the Eucharist.*

In the tabernacle, under the veil of the consecrated bread, there is kept the same Jesus Whom I was the first to see after the miracle of His resurrection; the same Jesus Who, in the splendor of His divinity, appeared to the eleven apostles, to many disciples, to the weeping Magdalen, to the holy women who had followed Him all the way to the sepulchre.

In the tabernacle, hidden beneath the Eucharistic veil, the same risen Jesus is present Who appeared again to more than five hundred disciples and who struck with a bolt of light Saul, the persecutor, on the road to Damascus. He is the same Jesus Who is sitting at the right hand of the Father, in the splendor of His glorified body and of His divinity, even though, for love of you, He hides Himself under the white appearance of the consecrated bread.

Beloved sons, today you must believe more in His presence among you; you must spread, with courage and with force, your priestly invitation for a return of all to a strong and witnessed faith in the Real Presence of Jesus Christ in the Eucharist. You must orientate the whole Church so that she will find herself before the tabernacle, with your heavenly Mother, in an act of perennial reparation, of continual adoration and of unceasing prayer. Your priestly prayer must become wholly a Eucharistic prayer." (Words of Our Lady, August 21, 1987)

Fr. Stefano Gobbi
To the Priests: Our Lady's Beloved Sons

What is the precise meaning of Eucharistic contemplation? In itself, it is really the ability or better, the gift, of establishing a heart-to-heart contact with Jesus really present in the Host and, through him, of raising oneself to the Father in the Holy Spirit. All of this is done, as far as possible, in a state of outer and inner silence. Silence is the dearest spouse of contemplation; it protects it, as Joseph protected Mary. To contemplate is to intuitively fix the mind on the divine reality (this could be God himself, or one of his attributes, or a mystery in Christ's life) and relish His presence. In meditation the search for truth prevails while, in contemplation, *delight* in the found truth prevails.

Great spiritual masters have given us definitions of contemplation: "A free, penetrating and still gaze" (Hugh of St. Victor), or: "A loving look at God" (St. Bonaventure). In the parish of Ars there was once a peasant who used to pass hours in church, immobile, looking at the tabernacle, and when the Saint Curate of Ars asked him what he was doing there every day like that, he replied: "Nothing, I look at him and he looks at me!" This tells us that Christian contemplation is never a one-way gaze and neither is it directed at the "Nothing" (as in certain Oriental religions, in particular Buddhism). It is always the meeting of two looks; our look at God and God's look at us. If, at times, our gaze weakens, God's never does. Sometimes Eucharistic contemplation just means keeping Jesus company, being there under His gaze, giving Him the joy of contemplating us, too. Although we are but useless creatures and sinners, we are still the fruit of His passion for whom He gave His life.

Fr. Raniero Cantalamessa
The Eucharist: Our Sanctification

This crazy world of ours is spinning right out of control and sometimes we spin with it. We need to stop spinning and come in to the quiet that Jesus offers in His Blessed Sacrament. He will give us His grace and strength if we allow Him. He wants to heal, forgive and encourage us. He wants to give us consolation, hope, strength and courage. We need to go to Him and ask Him because He will not impose Himself upon us. Since we are human we probably need to ask Him repeatedly before His message will sink into our heads and our hearts. Jesus knows that and therefore remains with us as He promised He would.

Every equation has two parts. The first part of the Eucharistic equation is the Real Presence of Jesus; the second part is our presence. What does it mean to be really present? Jesus is really present under the species of bread and wine. It is not merely a piece of bread and a cup of wine; it is Jesus' Body and Blood, Soul and Divinity. How are we really present? I always pray that the Lord will help me to be as really present to Him as He is to me. One of the prayers I use, which says a great deal about being really present, goes like this:

Lord, Jesus, as I kneel before Your hidden presence, help me respond to Your graces so that I may be as really present to You, as You are to me, in the most Blessed Sacrament of Your love and mercy. Allow Your radiant presence to re-ignite the fire of Your Spirit within me, so that I may be Your Sacrament of love and mercy to all. Amen.

Fr. Jack Spaulding
Hope for the Journey

One of the most thrilling, beautiful and heroic scenes that I have ever been privileged to witness is that of the consecration of a young lady to Christ—the scene of a nun's religious profession. The entire consecration is spread between two ceremonies; between the two is interposed the period of her novitiate. She enters the chapel for the first time clothed as a lovely bride, white-robed, veiled, carrying a gorgeous bouquet in her arms. She comes forth for the second time a somber nun, clothed in black, her body entirely garmented except for her face. She has almost lost her identity, even to the extent of changing her name.

Now she is called Sister.

But the sister of whom? The sister of Him Who is called the First-born of all the brethren, our Brother, Jesus Christ. The human being has suffered a mystical death; there is born of that act of consecration a new being, a spouse and lover of the divine Christ.

This act of consecration of a nun, this transformation usually takes place during Holy Mass. It is a sacrifice within a sacrifice: a small Calvary erected side by side with the mystic Calvary of Christ. This act of consecration and change, this transformation takes place at Mass because it is through the Mass that each of us can and must be changed into the likeness of Christ. Through the Mass we must put on Christ that we may be able to say: "I live, now not I, but Christ lives in me." And this transformation of us into Christ can be effected only by suffering and by sacrifice.

John N. McCormick, CSSR
John A. Treinan, CSSR
What Is the Mass?

Once I [St. Teresa] was in a college of the Company of Jesus, suffering severely in soul and body, as I have said I sometimes used to, and still do, to such an extent that I was hardly capable of thinking a single good thought. On that night a brother of that house of the Company had died (this was Alonso de Henao, who had come from the Jesuit College at Alcala and died on April 11, 1557); and, while I was commending him to God as well as I was able, and hearing a Mass that was being said for him by another Father of the Company, I became deeply recollected and saw him ascending to Heaven in great glory, and the Lord ascending with him. I understood that it was by a special favor that His Majesty bore him company.

E. Allison Peers
The Autobiography of St. Teresa of Avila

To be so in love with Jesus, our Eucharistic King, can give a person much pain. I preach in the United States and outside it, and wherever I go I see irreverences every day. A priest said to me, "I can't believe you are so sensitive about the Eucharist." And all I could say was, "My God, you're a priest." He said this because something happened at the altar, and I began to cry. My heart was broken. But this sensitivity should be in each and every one of us and it doesn't come over night. It doesn't come through a magic wand. It comes from practicing your faith every day of your life.

When I hunger for Him so much, it tells Him how much I love Him. That's what I want for you. I don't care if you move mountains. I don't care if you heal the people. I don't care if you speak many languages through the Spirit. I don't care if you fall down in the Spirit. I want you to be excited about coming and receiving Him. I want you, if you do wake up at night, not to grumble, "O Lord, let me sleep." It's o.k. to say that, but let your heart beat fast because you're going to Mass that morning. I want you to be so in love with Jesus, that your whole world will change. I want you to radiate love for your Eucharistic King.

Eileen George
Beacon of God's Love: Her Teaching

Feast of St. Catherine Laboure
1806-1876

S ister Laboure was given "another great grace," during the whole time of her novitiate: the visible presence of Our Lord in the Blessed Sacrament. She does not say whether this vision was a constant thing, that is, vouchsafed each time she entered the chapel, whether it was only during Mass, or during a certain portion of the Mass. She says only that she "saw Our Lord in the Most Holy Sacrament." She continues: "I saw Him during the whole time of my seminary, except when I doubted; the next time, I saw nothing, because I had wished to penetrate the mystery, and, believing myself deceived, had doubted."

Joseph I. Dirvin, CM
Saint Catherine Laboure of the Miraculous Medal

Perhaps we feel like someone in the crowd when Jesus healed the woman with the flow of blood (Lk 8:43-48). Why did she find healing when she pressed against Jesus yet most others in the pressing crowd probably didn't find healing? The woman differed from the crowd because she brought not just her pain but a high expectancy that touching Christ would make a difference. She was not just a spectator in a pew but a person hungering for healing and expecting it.

Unlike the healed woman perhaps we have found ourselves to be little more than spectators in a pew with little happening besides our watch advancing an hour. But when we come with our pain making us hungry for healing and expecting it, we touch Christ and hear, "Your faith has made you whole, go in peace." Besides bringing the pain of past years like Agnes Sanford or the sharp pain of present situations like the Indian woman who lost her husband, we can also bring the pain experienced at the Eucharist itself. "Eucharist" means "giving thanks." To discover what the Lord wants to heal at the Eucharist, we just ask. "For what is it most difficult to give thanks?"

Matthew Linn, SJ, and Dennis Linn
Healing Life's Hurts:
Healing Memories through the Five Stages of Forgiveness

To be able to become bread! To be able to nourish the whole world with His Flesh and Blood! I am terribly selfish and fearful when faced with suffering, but if I could become bread to save all humanity, I would do it. If I could become bread to feed all the poor, I should throw myself into the fire at once.

No, the Eucharist is not something strange: It is the most logical thing in the world, it is the story of the greatest love ever lived in this world, by a man called Jesus.

When I gaze on this bread, when I take up this bread into my hands, I gaze on and take up the passion and death of Christ for humanity. This bread is the memorial of His death for us. This bread is the trumpet call of the Resurrection, through which we, too, shall one day be able to rise.

This bread is the living summary of all God's love for man. From Genesis to the prophets, from Exodus to the Apocalypse, everything is yearning towards this terrible mystery of God's tragic love for man. God, who made Himself present in the first covenant and yet more present in the Incarnation, becomes still more present in this mystery of the bread of life.

Carlo Carretto
The God Who Comes

Jeanne Tulasne was cured of Pott's disease of two years duration. During the Procession of the Blessed Sacrament, Jeanne Tulasne rose to her feet and her spinal deformity disappeared suddenly and painlessly, leaving no traces other than three depressions.

Marie Antoinette Riviere was cured of gastro-intestinal ulcerations, which had existed for five years and had caused numerous hemorrhages. The cure was effected at Lourdes in two stages. In the morning, after having received Holy Communion, she drank a cup of milk mixed with the miraculous water; she immediately experienced a fierce burning pain in the abdomen, then all her sufferings suddenly left her; she remained, however, in a state of complete exhaustion. In the afternoon, during the Procession of the Blessed Sacrament, she felt a warmth pervading her limbs and her strength returning; and she felt herself able to walk. Her health has not failed since that time.

Dr. F. DeGrandmaison De Bruno
Twenty Cures at Lourdes

September 29 (Mass at the Chapel of the Companions). Always this nagging fear that He won't come. There are four of us this evening. During the Mass, before the Consecration, He speaks to me gently, as if to reassure me.

—*I'm like a raincoat.*

—What a strange notion, Lord.

But I wait. If this is really from Him, He will explain it to me.

After the Consecration:

—*You put Me on like a raincoat.*

—Go on.

—*I am the raincoat. You feel Me. The lining is pleasant to the touch. The storms, the wind, the rain will come and drench the raincoat, but not you. Do you understand? I protect you.*

—The wind, the storm, the rain . . . all these are our human and material difficulties?

—*Yes. I don't take them away. I protect you. First live in me.*

Nicole Gausseron
The Little Notebook

December 3

Feast of St. Francis Xavier
1506-1552

A much longer ecstasy was experienced by St. Francis Xavier during the time when he was a missionary in India. He was scheduled one day to transact some business with the Viceroy. When St. Francis' young assistant, Andrew, was sent to remind him of the time, he found the saint sitting on a low stool before the tabernacle, his face tilted upward and his hands folded across his chest. Hesitating to disturb him, Andrew finally whispered his message, but St. Francis did not respond. Two hours later he was found in the same position, but this time Andrew was successful in rousing him. When St. Francis learned how long he had been in ecstasy, he at once prepared for his appointment. But hardly had he left his dwelling when, walking down the street, he once again fell into a rapture. He stood motionless in the street until nightfall, when he emerged from his ecstasy and returned to his home. "My son," he said to Andrew, "we must visit the Viceroy another day. This day God has willed for Himself alone."

Joan Carroll Cruz
Eucharistic Miracles

I would also like to repeat my invitation to you to make adoration of the Blessed Sacrament a habitual practice in all Christian communities, in accordance with the Church's spirit and liturgical norms.

This worship extends and prepares in the best possible way the meeting with Christ in the Sacrifice and Eucharistic Banquet. It is an expression of the whole Christian community's love and worship of its Lord. Priestly, religious, and missionary vocations will stem from this meeting with Christ in the tabernacle, and will bring the light of the Gospel to the ends of the earth; in this crucible of the "Love of loves," will be forged the apostolic spirit of lay Christians, witnesses to Christ amid temporal realities; in the intimacy of the tabernacle, the values that must reign in homes will receive new strength to make the family a meeting place with God, a center that radiates faith, a school of Christian life. In the Bread which came down from heaven, the family will be able to find the support that will keep it united in the face of today's threats and will preserve it as a bastion of life, steadfast against the culture of death.

Pope John Paul II
Message to Archbishop Vallejo of Seville, June 5, 1994

Father Cholenc said to Father Fremin: "I believe that the longer period of probation for First Holy Communion, that we usually demand among the Iroquois, should be shortened for Kateri Tekakwitha."

"You are right, Father," the Superior replied, "not only is her conduct irreproachable; but in her devotion and the enthusiasm with which she enters into the life of the mission, she is already outstripping our other Christians."

"I shall tell her that she may receive our Lord on Christmas day," said Father Cholenec. "She will have been here little more than two months; but she is too well disposed to be deprived of this grace."

For Kateri this first Christmas in Canada was the fulfillment of the story of Bethlehem that Father Boniface had told in the Mohawk Valley while she, a pagan, was looking in rapture at the Christmas crib. This was the Christ Child alive, and He had come into her heart! We cannot pry into the soul of Kateri, enfolded in the mystery, the wonderment, the reality of that first meeting. We cannot capture those moments of interchange, but in the words of Father Cholenec: "All that we can say is that from that day forward she appeared different to us, because she remained so full of God and of love for Him." And this same biographer . . . gives the assurance that in the frequent Communions that followed, her first fervor did not abate. This was so evident to all in the village that at a time of general Communion the most devout women tried to find a place near her, maintaining that the mere sight of her inspired them and provided an excellent preparation for receiving the Sacrament.

Marie Cecilia Buehrle
Kateri of the Mohawks

Mother Angelica from Birmingham, Alabama, the Franciscan nun who founded the first Catholic satellite television network, is widely known for her wit and wisdom. I had given a retreat to priests in Birmingham with Fr. Harold Cohen from New Orleans. Mother had heard about me and invited me to her monastery to make a retreat.

I thought that this would be a good time to learn more about healing, so I arrived with all kinds of books on healing written by recognized experts. I thought I'd learn from them why people aren't healed, and then when they ask me, I'd be able to give them an answer off the tip of my tongue.

On the first day, I read the first chapter of a book, and the next morning I couldn't remember anything. For several days, I couldn't remember anything I'd read.

Finally, one day, Mother Angelica took me by the hand and brought me into the chapel. She pointed up at the monstrance where the Eucharist was exposed and she said to me, "If Jesus wanted you to be somebody else, he would have made you somebody else. He made you to be Briege McKenna—and," she said, still pointing to the Lord, "there's the teacher. Don't be trying to copy other people's styles. Come to Jesus and let Him teach you."

That day I made a commitment to spend two or three hours a day in personal prayer. Then the Lord started to teach me that I didn't have to answer all the questions. Not everybody was going to be healed physically, but that wasn't my business. My business was not to defend Him, but to proclaim Him.

Sr. Briege McKenna, OSC
Miracles Do Happen

S t. Ambrose, the towering Archbishop of Milan, did much to define and stabilize the liturgy of the Church, especially the presentation of the Sacraments. He very clearly indicates the belief of the Early Church that the bread is transformed or transfigured—it is no longer bread but really the Body of Christ. He clearly states that because Christ has divine power, by reason of His blessing, "the nature of the elements" itself is changed (*De Mysteriis*, no. 52). In his book *De Fide* (*On the Faith*) published around 380, commenting on John 6:55, he writes: "'For my Flesh truly is food and my Blood truly is drink.' You hear of flesh, you hear of blood, and you are aware of the Sacraments of the Lord's death. . . . For as often as we receive the Sacraments, which, through the Mystery of the sacred prayer, are transfigured into Flesh and Blood, 'we announce the death of the Lord.'"

Fr. Benedict J. Groeschel, CFR, and James Monti
In the Presence of Our Lord:
The History, Theology, & Psychology of Eucharistic Devotion

December 8

Feast of the Immaculate Conception

We think of Moses who saw the burning bush. As he drew close, he heard the voice of God coming from the bush saying, "Moses, take the shoes off your feet. This is holy ground." Today is the date of the Immaculate Conception, the eighth of December. . . . Mary was made immaculate, conceived without any trace of sin because she was going to be the co-creator of the humanity of Christ. She was going to be, as God the Father was the Creator, the re-creator of the human race with Christ. She was going to be the tabernacle in which Christ would be conceived.

We can not now, of course, be conceived without original sin. But the more we can purify ourselves through the Sacrament of Penance, through our own penances, through trying to observe the Commandments and keeping close to Christ, then the more fitting we become as tabernacles of the Eucharist.

All of this requires an effort, perhaps for some an unaccustomed effort. St. Augustine tells us the reward. He was still in process of conversion from a highly profligate, promiscuous life. Then he went into a Catholic community to worship in the Eucharistic sacrifice. He said to a Catholic friend:

"How I wept, deeply moved by your hymns, songs and the voices that echoed through your Church! What emotion I experienced in them! Those sounds flowed into my ears, distilling the truth in my heart. A feeling of devotion surged within me, and tears streamed down my face—tears that did me good."

May that be our experience in this Holy Sacrifice of the Mass.

John Cardinal O'Connor
Excerpt from a homily in St. Patrick's Cathedral,
December 8, 1996

"When I went back into the church," says de Bussierre in his deposition, "I could not at first see Ratisbonne where I had left him. I soon discovered him kneeling, deeply absorbed in prayer, before the Chapel of the Archangels Michael and Raphael. I shook him by the shoulders several times before he seemed to realize my presence. At last he lifted his face streaming with tears.

"I have seen Her, I have seen Her!" he exclaimed. "I had only been in the church a few moments when I began to feel agitated. I looked up and the whole interior seemed veiled in shadow, one chapel only had concentrated all the light, and in the midst of this radiance I saw standing on the altar, clothed with splendor, full of majesty and sweetness, the Virgin Mary, just as she is represented on my [Miraculous] medal. An irresistible force drew me towards her. She made a sign with her hand for me to kneel down; she spoke not a word, but I understood all."

By the light that streamed from Mary's hands Alphonse had indeed understood all, and now longed for Baptism, "and truth had revealed itself to him so fully," says Father Roothan, "that he quickly grasped and completely absorbed all that was taught him.

"What?" he exclaimed, when it was suggested he should wait a while for his baptism; "the Jews were baptized as soon as they had heard the Apostles, and you want to keep me waiting when I have heard the Queen of the Apostles?" When asked to whom he believed he owed his conversion, he answered: "To the Blessed Virgin, who obtained it from God, and to the prayers of my brother. . . ."

L. M. Leggatt, Trans.
A Nineteenth Century Miracle: The Brothers Ratisbonne

O n Monday, May 28, transferred Feast of St. Madeleine Sophie, a day of great solemnity in all convents of the Sacred Heart, Our Lord was about to crown her faithful service by adding to the signal graces of the last days one which became a veritable foretaste of heaven.

"After Holy Communion," wrote Josefa, "it seemed to me that heaven itself was in my soul. Suddenly I saw Jesus in all His beauty . . . with His Heart resplendent and shining as a very sun. It was surmounted by a cross of fire. . . . He said: 'She that eats My Flesh possesses God, Author of Life . . . and of Life Eternal . . . That is how this soul becomes My heaven. Nothing can compare with her in beauty. The angels are in admiration and as God is within that soul, they fall down in adoration. . . . O soul, didst thou but know thy dignity. . . . Your soul, Josefa, is My heaven and every time you receive Me in Holy Communion My grace augments both your dignity and your beauty."

Josefa could do nothing but humble herself at her Master's feet and confess her sins, her miseries and weakness, knowing herself unworthy of the infinite Sanctity that, descending to her nothingness, went to the length of making her in reality His heavenly place of repose. "Lord," she said, "I give Thee my heart, my life, my liberty . . . all.

"I desire nothing else," He answered. "What does all the rest matter? . . . Your sins? Why, I can wipe them out . . . Your miseries? I consume them . . . Your weakness? I will be its support . . . Let us remain united."

Sr. Josefa Menendez
The Way of Divine Love

There are few advantages to being a chairperson. Usually, it is just a lot of hard work. Sometimes, however, there is a benefit to it. As chairperson of the Guadalupe Foundation, I got a free ticket to Mexico.

I am writing you from the Shrine. It's magnificent. During my Holy Hour I was thinking. What is better: The visit Our Lady gave to Juan Diego, or one hour in the Presence of Jesus in the Blessed Sacrament?

Roses bloomed in the snow. A poor garment is imprinted with an image of Our Blessed Mother. It has lasted for centuries and no scientist can figure out how the image is on the cloth. She is the woman clothed with the sun. The sun is symbolic of her Eucharistic Son. Both hearts beat as one.

Look at her request to the Bishop. Build a chapel. Who is in the chapel? Her Eucharistic Son! Mary brings all of her children to the Eucharist.

During our Holy Hour of prayer there is always the beauty of Guadalupe. No matter how cold our heart, the roses of holiness bloom. The fragrance of sanctity will last for all eternity. Each moment we spend in His presence we grow, we bloom, we blossom like the roses in the snow.

Msgr. Josefino S. Ramirez
Letters to a Brother Priest

December 12
Feast of Our Lady of Guadalupe

"My dear children, gaze upon my image with love. I come to you as a loving and merciful Mother: a Mother who wishes to comfort you in your times of sorrow, a Mother who wishes to remedy your ills and your pains. My children, do not think that I do not hear you calling my name. Do not think, my children, that I do not see the tears you shed.

My children, I come to you now with love and with an urgent message from Heaven. Look upon my Image of Our Lady of Guadalupe. See my loving gaze as I looked down upon Juan Diego, as I look now upon all of you. My children, pray the Rosary from your hearts. Pray with love and with sincerity. Come to me now . . . ask for the mercy of my Son to come down upon each one of you. I love you all, my dear children. Come and look upon your Mother who comes to you with love, who comes to assuage and comfort, who comes in these darkened times to lead you all, by the hand, back to my Son, Our Lord and Savior, Jesus Christ. Celebrate the Mass with love and with repentance for your sins. Open your hearts to my Son, Who is present in the Eucharist and Who wishes to fill you with His light and thus transform each one of you into vessels of love, of light, and of mercy for the world. Go, my children, when you leave here tonight and spread my message and the light of my Son. I love you all and I, your Mother, am with you. Go, my children, in the peace of God." (Words of Our Lady, April 1, 1992)

Michael McColgan
Open Your Hearts:
Messages from Our Lord Jesus and His Blessed Mother

In December of 1975, my wife, Patricia, bought me a book entitled *Something More* by Catherine Marshall, as one of my Christmas gifts. I started to read it during the holidays and planned to finish the book while on a business trip from Florida to Chicago in January 1976.

I was thousands of feet above the ground when I began the chapter on "The Holy Spirit." As I read about the Third Person of the Trinity, He chose to come into my life—virtually out of the pages of this book. Tears started to run out of my eyes like a river. I started praying. I was overcome by a power that was much greater than I am.

It was not until much later that I understood these tears to be not of sadness but rather of purification. I had been brought up and raised a Catholic, but had never experienced any personal relationship with God.

I was still on the plane when I heard a voice in the form of a beautiful soft whisper ask me if I would go to Mass every day for the rest of my life. I was confused; I did not know who originated the question. "Are you God?" I posed mentally. After a long silence and some deliberation on my part, I concluded that the prompting was not coming from my own imagination, and I responded in the affirmative. "Yes, Lord, I will go to Mass every day for the rest of my life."

Since then, my life has never been the same. Over the years, as I have thought about this question, I have come to see God was asking me if I would be willing to make a sincere commitment to Him, every day, for the rest of my life. (Ferdinand G. Mahfood)

Robert Baram, Ed.
Spiritual Journeys

December 14

Feast of St. John of the Cross
1542-1591

H is Mass had become so wonderful a transport of love as to entail an almost daily ecstasy. One day after receiving the Precious Blood, he remained motionless with the chalice in his hands, unable to go on with the Mass. He quitted the altar like one in a trance, seeking the solitude of the sacristy to entertain his divine Guest. Whereupon a woman, well known for her holiness and almsgiving, said aloud: "Call the angels, who alone can finish this Mass with the devotion of the saintly man who is at present unable to do so." But his brethren gently brought him back to the altar, where they helped him to complete the Holy Sacrifice.

The Sisters of Notre Dame
Life of Saint John of the Cross

If we take a close look at what contemporary men and women expect from priests, we will see that, in the end, they have but one great expectation: *they are thirsting for Christ.* Everything else—their economic, social, and political needs—can be met by any number of other people. From the priest they ask for Christ! And from him they have the right to receive Christ, above all through the proclamation of the word. As the Council teaches, priests "have as their primary duty the proclamation of the Gospel of God to all" (*Presbyterorum Ordinis*, no. 4). But this proclamation seeks to have man encounter Jesus, especially in the mystery of the Eucharist, the living heart of the Church and of priestly life. The priest has a mysterious, awesome power over the Eucharistic Body of Christ. By reason of this power he becomes the steward of the greatest treasure of the Redemption, for he gives people the Redeemer in person. Celebrating the Eucharist is the most sublime and most sacred function of every priest. As for me, from the very first years of my priesthood, the celebration of the Eucharist has been not only my most sacred duty, but above all my soul's deepest need.

Pope John Paul II
Gift and Mystery:
On the Fiftieth Anniversary of My Priestly Ordination

I t was Christmas morning, December 25, 1975. As I marched in procession with my altar boys and the lay leaders of the congregation, I looked around the church and my spirits fell. The pews were less than a quarter full and looked very sparse. On numerous occasions, bingo, a concert, or other social events had almost filled the church. Now, for worship on Christmas morning, the church was almost empty.

All the ways I had tried to draw my congregation to Christ had failed. The material goods and services had not done it, nor had my prayers. As I proceeded up the center aisle on my way to the altar, I looked up at the tabernacle and prayed, "O Jesus, Master, I don't know what else to try. What else can I do to bring them to a spiritual renewal, to bring them to You?"

The answer immediately filled my waiting heart: "Ralph, why not try simple, pure Me?" The answer was like a lightning bolt through a dark cloud! The truth was illuminated. All the humanistic means I had employed to draw more people to Christ passed through my mind, a list of natural methods I'd used to bring people to the supernatural. Now God's words filled my heart. Why not go straight to Christ? That was it. My answer was there.

At that moment, God awakened my priestly heart to the powerful potential of a new ministry of Christ alone. When I called out to God from the depth of my sincere need, He heard my prayer. He was ready to fill my brokenness with Himself, but He would not be the Christ about Whom I'd studied in seminaries. He was the Christ Who, in His Own Divine Providence, fills and directs us with His Holy Spirit.

Fr. Ralph A. DiOrio
The Man Beneath the Gift: The Story of My Life

There are many approaches by which God can lead souls to the Catholic Faith. Mine was only one, and perhaps not the best. Some time passed before I again crossed the threshold of a Catholic church, and a great deal longer before I acquired an appreciation of the exceptional beauty of Catholic ecclesiastical ceremonies. In my senior year at college I began attending High Mass regularly on Sundays, and gradually mastered the complexities of the Roman Missal. Better still, I came to understand the action of the Mass, apart from which its trappings are meaningless and even, to some, distasteful.

That year I assisted with great devotion at nearly all the special Lenten services, and was deeply moved by the chanting of Tenebrae. The most thrilling experience of the year was perhaps Holy Saturday, when I rose at 5:30 in the morning to witness in full the blessing of the New Fire, of the Paschal Candle, and of the Baptismal Font, together with the recitation of the Prophecies, the celebration of Holy Mass, and the singing of Vespers. These observances, however, were scarcely instrumental in causing my conversion, for I was already at that time a Catholic in opinion. Only the decisive act of faith was wanting.

Fr. Avery Dulles, SJ
A Testimonial to Grace

I t was the eve of Christmas when the vessel set sail for France, and on Christmas day, 1643, the holy missioner again found himself on his native soil, on the coast of Lower Brittany, near Saint-Pol de Leon. His first object after landing and thanking God for his return, was to hear Mass and receive Holy Communion, of which for over a year he had been deprived. He inquired where the church was at the first cottage he came to. The good people, thinking he was a pious pilgrim and being impressed by his devout bearing, on hearing that he wished to receive Holy Communion, loaned him a hat and cloak that he might be suitably attired. As it was the great festival of Christmas they were in holiday dress, prepared to attend the celebration of Mass. Their guest was invited to accompany them and to return afterwards for breakfast.

His emotions on entering the church, and beholding the pious Catholic folk at their devotions, almost overcame him. What a contrast to the scenes he had been witnessing the past year and a half! But his sentiments when he advanced to the altar to receive His Lord in Holy Communion were the culmination of spiritual joy. "At that moment," he said afterwards, "I seemed to begin once more to live and to enjoy all the happiness of my deliverance."

Martin J. Scott, SJ
Isaac Jogues: Missioner and Martyr

Fr. Charles Banet is a seventy-three year old priest who has suffered from a blood disease he has had for many years. Recently diagnosed with prostate cancer, he was told one afternoon that he'd have to discontinue radiation therapy because his blood platelet count was alarmingly low. It unnerved him to think that he had no other options which meant he probably only had a short time to live. Back home in Holy Rosary rectory he asked Fr. Robert DeGrandis, with whom he lived, and Annie Ross Fitch, who was visiting, to pray over him. He had seen a lot of marvelous healings take place in Holy Rosary and thought he'd ask for prayers for himself. Annie inquired if he had said Mass yet that day. When he said he hadn't, she suggested that when he say Mass, he ask Jesus to give him a transfusion of His Blood. So he did just that. When he was about to drink the Precious Blood he said, "Jesus. . . I want . . . if you can afford it . . . I'd like a transfusion of Your Blood in anticipation of the evaluation they're going to make of my blood tomorrow. "

The next day Fr. Banet went for another blood test and they told him that his blood tested perfect. "I guess it ought to be because it's Jesus' Blood" he said spontaneously, to which they kind of laughed then dropped that line of thinking. This was the first blood test in many years which tested perfect. Today Fr. Banet is completely healthy and cancer free and no medical explanation was ever given for the healing of his blood. Fr. Banet has been a priest for forty-seven years in the same order, the Missionaries of the Most Precious Blood.

The Mercy Foundation
From the documentary film, *Living Presence*

O ne of the things that I always suggest to priests when I give a priest retreat is that they take the words of Consecration very, very seriously. When you hold up the Host and pronounce the words of Consecration, "This is My Body," I plead with the priests not only to believe that it's really the Body of Jesus Christ, but that they should also feel that it is their body that they are offering to the people whom they are sent to serve. And I'd suggest that perhaps you could benefit in the same way when you revere the Eucharist and you hear the words, "This is My Body, this is My Blood." Yes, it is the Body and Blood of Jesus Christ and it is the Body of Jesus that we offer to the people, but if we are disciples of Jesus, we will also recall what He said after He pronounced the words. He said, "Do this in memory of Me," and I think Jesus would want us not only to repeat the Consecration to bring His Body and Blood on the altar. I think Jesus would want us to also do as He did, offer our own bodies and blood for the salvation of all.

I come back to the example that we all saw so beautifully in Frank Scardina. I think Frank got that message. He loved the Eucharist, but he also was willing to put himself in that same position so that as the Body and Blood of Christ was present on the altar, his body and blood was also offered to the Lord and to each one of us. The Mass must never end. Each one of us has to go forth from this place and lift Jesus higher so that the whole world can be converted to love the Body and Blood of Jesus.

Bishop Raymond Goedert
Homily given during Mass for "Lift Jesus Higher"
Catholic Charismatic Conference, June 1, 1997

When Peggie O'Neill's son ran away from home, she recalls, "I promised Our Lord to make a Holy Hour every day," and the concerned mother kept her pledge, frequently in the chapel at Philadelphia's St. Charles Borromeo Seminary. After three years, her son called at last: He wanted to come home. But Peggie O'Neill's Holy Hours didn't stop. Her concern for other young men grew as she continued daily prayer at the seminary chapel. As time went by, she noticed the dwindling class size at the seminary. Fewer young men were discerning a call to the priesthood . . .

O'Neill thought that the form of prayer she used to intercede for her son might also bear good fruit for vocations and for blessings on the lives priests in the Philadelphia archdiocese. She recruited two seminarians to participate in these first Holy Hours in the fall of 1982. The result? "From 1982 to 1983, the class entering St. Charles Seminary rose from four members to seventeen," O'Neill recounted. That same year, the local Augustinian friary saw the number of their aspirants increase from four to eight.

In 1983, with the support of John Cardinal Krol of Philadelphia, a weekly Holy Hour for vocations began at St. Charles Borromeo Seminary. . . . Today, at least 5,000 people are part of this movement called "Prayer Power." They meet regularly . . . in Philadelphia . . . [and] the dioceses of Allentown, Pennsylvania, and Wilmington, Delaware. A certain number of hours are set aside at a seminary chapel or a parish church, and prayer-team members come for thirty minutes or an hour of private and communal prayer in the presence of the Blessed Sacrament.

Charles Wood
Catholic Digest, September 1996

It seems that there is a special relationship between food and Jesus. Jesus is the spiritual food we all greatly need. That is why we are so moved by the account of the Last Supper, when Jesus gave his disciples the Bread of Life. That is why the Eucharist is the center of our faith and the high point of our worship.

I learned to take advantage of the relationship between Jesus and food. I'd take the microphone while my patrons were eating and say, "Dear brothers and sisters, I want to thank the one who allowed this meal to be possible for you. His name is Jesus." (Everyone would clap.) "Is there anyone here tonight who wants to give his life to Jesus?" Sometimes only a few people would respond, but at other times table after table of men and women would stand up and join me in a prayer of surrender. Many of the people who responded to my preaching were Catholics. I began to see ever more clearly that my mission in life was to win souls for the Lord as a Catholic evangelist. . . .

We have been created, baptized, and blessed in abundance so we can win souls for the kingdom of our Lord Jesus Christ. The money we've made, the things we've done as artists, craftsmen, writers, or anything else won't matter when we get to heaven. What God is interested in is whether we have given His love to others. At judgment, God is going to ask you a question: "Did you reach out to the poor, the hungry, the naked, the lonely with My love? What did you do to feed their empty stomachs and their empty spirits? Did you tell others about how I could help them?"

How will you answer?

Charlie Osburn
The Charlie Osburn Story

Jesus needs. Christmas is the birthday of the Lord. And who is this tough guy who comes to be crucified, to sit in our tabernacles? Is He not the Lover, the One prowling the world, looking for those "permanent relationships" of which we speak? So great a need does He have that He gives Himself permanently in Holy Communion, and is always present in our homes and on the street.

Before I began this work with gangsters in the projects and heard in real words the call of Christ, I thought of Him as powerful, a magician able to read minds and see into the future. He was the one who controls life and death, the one in control. I did not think that He was the one in need. Need for you and me, need for gangsters and murderers. I did not think that our response to Him mattered that much. How could a powerful God Person need us so much? Is He human? Does He love? Does He feel heat and cold? Does He need you and me, the waitress and the soldier, the politician, the gangster and his girl, the business woman and the working man, the Bulls and Bears and, finally, the golfers? Who is the Babe in His Mother's arms in Bethlehem and in Jerusalem? And who is this Mother, loving Him so much and loving us as well? Is He that much different than any other lover . . . or is He more so?

Bro. Bill Tomes
Brothers and Sisters of Love newsletter, January, 1996

When I arrived at Midnight Mass, from the very beginning I steeped myself in deep recollection, during which time I saw the stable of Bethlehem filled with great radiance. The Blessed Virgin, all lost in the deepest of love, was wrapping Jesus in swaddling clothes, but St. Joseph was still asleep. Only after the Mother of God put Jesus in the manger, did the light of God awaken Joseph, who also prayed. But after a while, I was left alone with the Infant Jesus who stretched out His little hands to me, and I understood that I was to take Him in my arms. Jesus pressed His head against my heart and gave me to know, by His profound gaze, how good He found it to be next to my heart. At that moment Jesus disappeared and the bell was ringing for Holy Communion. (No. 1442)

Bl. M. Faustina Kowalska
Divine Mercy in My Soul

When we receive Holy Communion, as we have noted so often, it is a two-way participation. This is what can be so easily forgotten. It can become so very mechanical. I say what I have said before. There can be a crowd, particularly in the cathedral, with many people standing through the entire Mass. Sometimes we have to jostle and push our way to get up to receive Holy Communion or to the center of the aisle or wherever it may be. It is so easy to be distracted. We feel too hot. We feel too cold. But what are we doing?

We are not only about to receive the Body and Blood of Jesus, but I emphasize and re-emphasize Jesus receives us. Jesus absorbs us into Himself. Jesus divinizes us. Jesus burns away, in the fire of His love, the differences between us, the differences between husband and wife, brother and sister, parent and children. We are all fused into Jesus. He lifts us up into His divinity. This is what receiving Holy Communion is.

May I remind myself with all of us here that when we pray, "The Mass is ended. Let us go in peace and love to serve the Lord," we serve the Lord through serving others, through loving others. Christmas is Christ's Mass. If we can, we still give gifts, however trifling; it is wonderful because they suggest some kind of sacrifice, or they should. We want to give ourselves to others with the gift. We want to give ourselves to those made in the image of Christ.

Wherever you are for Mass on Christmas, this is Christ's Mass. You are suffering and dying with Christ. One day, please God, you and I will rise with Christ.

John Cardinal O'Connor
Homily in St. Patrick's Cathedral, December 22, 1996

December 26

Feast of St. Stephen
The First Martyr, d. 34

"Thursday the 26th, St. Stephen's Day. I [St. Paul of the Cross] was in particular uplifting of soul, especially at Holy Communion; I wanted to go and die a martyr's death in a place where the adorable mystery of the Most Blessed Sacrament is denied. This wish has been given to me for some time past by the Infinite Goodness, but today I had it in a special manner; I had the desire for the conversion of heretics, especially in England and the neighboring kingdoms, and I offered a special prayer for that at Holy Communion . . ."

Fr. Father Edmund, CP
Hunter of Souls:
A Study of the Life and Spirit of Saint Paul of the Cross

I t is, therefore, not surprising, that the central devotion of her [St. Gertrude's] life, too, should be intimately linked up with the Liturgy. Like St. Margaret Mary, she receives the great revelation of the Sacred Heart on the Feast of St. John, not, however, as the modern Saint at the time of private prayer, but at Matins. The Apostle appears to her and invites her to come with him, that they may rest together on the Breast of the Lord. Then, taking her up with him, he presents her to Jesus and places her on His right side, reposing himself on the left. This he does, as he explains, so that she may drink more easily the consolations flowing from His Divine Heart, for it was the right side that was pierced by the lance. Then, as the beating of the Divine Heart fills her with ineffable joy, she asks St. John why he had written nothing about it in his Gospel, and he replies: "It was my mission to instruct the Church in her earliest age in the mysteries of the Uncreated Word, so far as they may be comprehended. But I did not speak about the sweetness of the Divine Heart-beats until these later ages, so that the world that has grown cold may be rekindled by the knowledge of these mysteries."

H. C. Graef
The Way of the Mystics

While I was going to receive Holy Communion, I saw the Holy Family where the priest was giving Communion. St. Joseph and Mary were kneeling and Jesus was giving Communion.

The way that I saw Jesus giving Communion (or the way that each individual would receive Him), as they came up to receive Him, He would embrace each individual. The altar was crowded with angels who were prostrated before Jesus. Later, after Mass, I went before the Blessed Sacrament to give thanks.

Janie: Dear Jesus, I saw You, Most Holy Mary, and St. Joseph. I am so happy.

Jesus: That was a gift for you, so that you understand the importance of the Holy Family in your life. Consecrate your family to the Holy Family every day, and you will have peace in your family. Through consecrating your family to the Holy Family, you will be protected from daily temptation. My child?

Janie: Yes, my Jesus.

Jesus: Did you notice how much holiness your heart felt as you gazed upon the Holy Family?

Janie: Yes, my Jesus, oh yes!

Jesus: When you consecrate your family to the intercession of the Holy Family, you will live in holiness.

Janie Garza
I Am Your Mother Come from Heaven to Love You

This sad year is over! I ended it on my knees in my little oratory, offering myself to God with all my soul, confiding to Him those I love and the Church.

May this be a good year for souls and for me; may at least one heart know and love Jesus Christ through me. For that it would be well worthwhile to live and suffer and wait.

I went to Communion on Christmas Eve and on Christmas Day, and drew strength and peace from that blessed contact with the Savior. And yet now I suffer from great physical exhaustion; and longing for the things I lack—candor, recollectedness, and Christian action—is causing me pain. In spite of my resolves I have allowed my peace to be troubled a little by certain offenses and excitements.

My God, I thirst (cf. Jn 19:28); grant me Thy peace and this infinite joy that Thou sometimes dost grant me, this beautiful light that enlightens and transforms all. To possess even a glimmer of it is already a small portion of Heaven, and it is for this reason, no doubt, that Thou dost give it all the more infrequently as the soul loves Thee more deeply and progresses further in Thy way.

Elizabeth Leseur
My Spirit Rejoices

When you come into church, genuflect or make a profound bow, and say, "O Jesus, it's good to be here." Talk to Him; don't ignore Him. I know we don't do it willfully. Pour out your heart to Him. There's nothing that we have, illness, trials or tribulations, that He can't remedy. So pour out your love to Him. Is it so difficult to love Him? Why? A cat gets more love than the Lord Jesus Christ. My dogs get more love than the Lord Jesus Christ, and it breaks my heart. The clothes we wear probably get more attention than the Lord Jesus Christ. What are we all about? Are we all about rubies and diamonds and coats and cars and furniture, or are we all about Jesus? Let's look within ourselves. He loves us so much. Even if we ignore Him, He pursues us by grace. What a lover. I tell you one thing, you've never been kissed, until you've been kissed by the Lord. You've never been loved until you've been loved by the Lord. Now is the hour. Fall in love with Jesus. Praise the Lord Jesus Christ.

Eileen George
Beacon of God's Love: Her Teaching

"Let yours be a continual prayer of adoration and of intercession, of thanksgiving and of reparation. Let yours be a prayer that is united to the heavenly song of the angels and the saints, to the ardent supplications of the souls who are still being purified in purgatory. Let yours be a prayer that brings together the voices of all humanity that should prostrate itself before every tabernacle of the earth, in an act of continual gratitude and of daily thanksgiving.

Because in the Eucharist Jesus Christ is really present, He remains ever with you and this presence of His will become increasingly stronger, will shine over the earth like a sun and will mark the beginning of a new era. The coming of the glorious reign of Christ will coincide with the greatest splendor of the Eucharist. Christ will restore His glorious reign in the universal triumph of His Eucharistic reign, which will unfold in all its power and will have the capacity to change hearts, souls, individuals, families, society and the very structure of the world.

When He will have restored his Eucharistic reign, Jesus will lead you to take joy in this habitual presence of His, which you will feel in a new and extraordinary way and which will lead you to the experience of a second, renewed and more beautiful earthly paradise." (Words of Our Lady, August 21, 1987)

Fr. Stefano Gobbi
To the Priests: Our Lady's Beloved Sons

Selected Bibliography

Angelica, Mother M. *The Mass in My Life*. Birmingham, AL: Our Lady of the Angels Monastery, EWTN, 1976.

Angot Des Rotours, J. *Saint Alphonsus Liguori*. New York: Benziger Brothers, 1916.

Antoine de Porrentruy, Louis. *The Saint of the Eucharist: Saint Paschal Baylon, Patron of Eucharistic Associations*. New Edition. London: R. & T. Washbourne, Ltd., 1908.

Aradi, Zsolt. *The Book Of Miracles*. New York, NY: Farrar, Straus and Cudahy, 1956.

Autobiography of St. Therese of Lisieux: The Story of A Soul. Garden City, NY: Image Books, A Division of Doubleday & Company, Inc., 1957.

Baldwin, Anne B. *Catherine of Siena: A Biography*. Huntington, IN: Our Sunday Visitor Publishing Division, 1987.

Ball, Ann. *Modern Saints: Their Lives and Faces*, Book One and Book Two. Rockford, IL: Tan Books and Publishers, Inc., 1983.

Baram, Robert, ed. *Spiritual Journeys Toward the Fullness of Faith*. Boston, MA: St. Paul Books and Media, 1988.

Barbaric, Slavko, OFM. *Celebrate Mass with Your Heart*. Milford, OH: Faith Publishing, 1994.

Bartholomew, Professor Courtenay, M.D. *A Scientist Researches Mary: The Ark of the Covenant*. Asbury, NJ: The 101 Foundation, 1995.

Beguiriztain, P. Justo, SJ. *The Eucharistic Apostolate of St. Ignatius of Loyola*, trans. John H. Collins, SJ. Brighton, MA: Cenacle Convent, 1944.

Bessieres, Albert, SJ. *Wife, Mother And Mystic (Blessed Anna-Maria Taigi)*, ed. Douglas Newton. Glasgow, Scotland: Sands & Co. Ltd., 1952.

Blunt, Hugh F., LLD. *Witnesses to the Eucharist*. Manchester, NH: The Magnificat Press, 1929.

Bosco, John. *The Life of Dominic Savio*. St. Louis, MO: B. Herder, 1915.

Bowman, Leonard J. *A Retreat With St. Bonaventure*. Rockport, MA: Element, Inc., 1993.

Brown, Michael H. *Secrets of the Eucharist*. Milford, OH: Faith Publishing Company, 1996.

Buehrle, Marie Cecilia. *Kateri of The Mohawks*. Milwaukee, WI: The Bruce Publishing Company, 1954.

Cantalamessa, Raniero. *The Eucharist Our Sanctification*, trans. Frances Lonergan Villa. Collegeville, MN: The Liturgical Press, 1993. Copyright 1993 by The Order of St. Benedict, Inc. Used with permission.

Carter, Edward, SJ. *Tell My People: Messages From Jesus And Mary*. Ft. Mitchell, KY: Shepherds of Christ Publications, 1994.

Carretto, Carlo. *The God Who Comes*, trans. Rose Mary Hancock. Maryknoll, NY: Orbis Books, 1974

Carroll, Warren H. *The Founding of Christendom,* Vol. 1. Front Royal, VA: Christendom Press, 1985.

Chervin, Ronda De Sola. *Prayers of the Women Mystics*. Ann Arbor, MI: Servant Publications, 1992.

Chiavarino, Joseph L. *The Greatest Treasure*, trans. Maestre Pie Venerini. New York, NY: Society Of St. Paul, 1952.

Cizek, Walter J., SJ, with Daniel Flaherty, SJ. *He Leadeth Me*. New York: Copyright 1973 by Walter J. Cizek.

Clarke, A. M. *The Life of St. Francis Borgia*. New York, NY: Benziger Brothers, 1913.

Corcoran, M. J., OSA. *Our Own St. Rita: A Life of the Saint of the Impossible*. New York, NY: Benziger Brothers, 1919.

Cruz, Joan Carroll. *Eucharistic Miracles*. Rockford, IL: Tan Books and Publishers, Inc., 1987.

Currie, David B. *Born Fundamentalist, Born Again Catholic.* San Francisco, CA: Ignatius Press, 1996. Copyright 1996 Ignatius Press, San Francisco. Used with permission.

DeGrandis, Robert, SSJ, with Linda Schubert. *Healing Through The Mass.* Mineola, NY: Resurrection Press, 1992.

_____. *Praying for Miracles . . . A Workbook Approach.* Copyright 1990 Rev. Robert DeGrandis, SSJ.

DeMaria, Mother Saverio, MSC. *Mother Frances Xavier Cabrini,* ed. Rose Basile Green. Chicago, IL: Missionary Sisters of the Sacred Heart of Jesus, 1984.

De Montfort, Louis. *True Devotion to the Blessed Virgin.* Bay Shore, NY: Montfort Publications, 9th printing, 1996.

Dempsey, Rev. Martin. *Champion of the Blessed Sacrament: Saint Peter Julian Eymard.* New York, NY: Eymard League, Blessed Sacrament Fathers.

Devlin, Patricia. *The Light of Love: "My Angel Shall Go Before Thee."* Santa Barbara, CA: Queenship Publishing Company, 1995.

DiOrio, Ralph A., with Donald Gropman. *The Man Beneath The Gift: The Story of My Life.* New York, NY: Quill, 1981.

Dirvin, Joseph I., CM. *Saint Catherine Labouré of the Miraculous Medal.* Rockford IL: Tan Books and Publishers, Inc., 1984.

Doheny, Msgr. William J., CSC. *Selected Writings of St. Teresa of Avila.* Milwaukee, WI: The Bruce Publishing Company, 1950.

Dorcy, Mary Jean, OP. *Saint Dominic.* St. Louis, MO: B. Herder Book Co., 1959.

Dulles, Avery, SJ. *A Testimonial To Grace.* Kansas City, MO: Sheed & Ward, 1996. Reprinted with permission of Sheed and Ward, 115 E. Armour Blvd., Kansas City, MO 64111. (800) 333-7373.

Edmund, Fr., CP. *Hunter of Souls: A Study of the Life and Spirit of Saint Paul of the Cross.* Westminster, MD: The Newman Bookshop, 1947.

Egan, Harvey D., SJ. *Ignatius Loyola the Mystic.* Wilmington, DE: Michael Glazier, Inc., 1987.

Eudes, John. *The Sacred Heart of Jesus*, trans. Richard Flower, OSB. New York: P. J. Kenedy & Sons, 1946.

Faricy, Robert, SJ, and Lucy Rooney, SND. *The Contemplative Way of Prayer.* Santa Barbara, CA: Queenship Publishing, 1986.

Gaudoin-Parker, Michael L. *Heart in Pilgrimage.* Staten Island, NY: Alba House, 1994.

Garza, Janie. *I Am Your Mother Come From Heaven To Love You: Heavenly Messages for the Family.* Plano, TX: Z'Atelier Publications, 1994.

Gausseron, Nicole. *The Little Notebook.* San Francisco, CA: Harper San Francisco, 1995.

George, Eileen. *Beacon of God's Love: Her Teaching.* Millbury, MA: Meet the Father Ministry, Inc., 1990.

_____. *Conversations in Heaven.* Millbury, MA: Meet the Father Ministry, Inc., 1992

Germanus, Fr., CP. *The Life of Gemma Galgani: The Story of a Lay-Passionist Written by Her Confessor.* Pittsburgh, PA: St. Gemma Publications, 1992.

Gheon, Henri. *The Secret Of The Cure D'Ars*, trans. F. J. Sheed. New York, NY: Longmans, Green and Co., 1929.

Gobbi, Fr. Stefano. *To the Priests: Our Lady's Beloved Sons.* St. Francis, Maine: National Headquarters of the Marian Movement of Priests, 1991.

Groeschel, Fr. Benedict J., CFR, and James Monti. *In the Presence of Our Lord: The History, Theology, & Psychology of Eucharistic Devotion.* Huntington, IN: Our Sunday Visitor Publishing Division, 1997.

Guitton, Andre. *Peter Julian Eymard: Apostle of the Eucharist*, trans. Conrad Goulet. Ponteranica: *Centro Eucharistico*, 1996.

Habig, Marion A., OFM. *Everyman's Saint: Life, Cult, and Virtues of St. Anthony of Padua.* Paterson, NJ: St. Anthony's Guild, 1954.

Haffert, John M. *Sign of Her Heart.* Preface by Fulton J. Sheen. Washington, NJ: Ave Maria Institute, 1971.

Hamon, A. *Vie de la Bienheureuse Marguerite-Marie.* Paris: Gabriel Beauchesne & Cie, 1908.

Hardon, John A., SJ. *Retreat With The Lord.* Copyright 1993 by John A. Hardon, SJ. Ann Arbor, MI: Servant Publications. Used with permission.

Hebert, Albert J., SM. *Michael The Archangel: "Life" and Apparitions to Date.* P.O. Box 309, Paulina, LA 70763. 1996.

Hertling, Ludwig, SJ, and Englebert Kirschbaum, SJ. *The Roman Catacombs and Their Martyrs,* trans. M. Joseph Costelloe, SJ. Milwaukee, WI: The Bruce Publishing Company, 1956.

Hofer, John, CSSR. *St. Clement Maria Hofbauer: A Biography,* trans. John B. Haas, CSSR. New York: Frederick Pustet Co., 1926.

Hyatt, Thomas R. *Come To Me: Forgiveness, Inner Healing and Deliverance Through Confession.* Copyright Thomas R. Hyatt, 1993.

I Am Your Jesus Of Mercy, Vol. V. Santa Barbara, CA: Queenship Publishing Company, 1996.

Jenco, Lawrence Martin, OSM. *Bound to Forgive.* Notre Dame, IN: Ave Maria Press Inc., 1995. Used with permission.

Jeremy, Sr. Mary, OP. *Scholars and Mystics.* Chicago, IL: Henry Regnery Company, 1962.

Jorgensen, Johannes. *Saint Bridget Of Sweden,* Volume II, trans. Ingeborg Lund. London, England: Longmans Green & Co.

Kelly, Matthew. *A Call to Joy.* New York, N.Y: Harper San Francisco, 1997.

_____ *Words From God.* 17 Orient St. Batemans Bay, N.S.W. 2536, Australia.

Kelley, Bennet, CP. *Spiritual Direction According to St. Paul of the Cross.* Staten Island, NY: Alba House, 1993.

Keppler, Paul. *The Poor Souls in Purgatory.* St. Louis: Herder, 1927.

Kerns, Vincent, ed. *The Autobiography of St. Margaret Mary.* London: Darton, Longman & Todd., 1976

Keyes, Frances Parkinson. *Three Ways of Love.* Boston, MA: Daughters of St. Paul, 1963.

Kosicki, Rev. George W., CSB. *Intercession: Moving Mountains by Living Eucharistically.* Milford, OH: Faith Publishing Company, 1996.

Kowalska, Faustina M., *Divine Mercy in My Soul.* Copyright 1987 Congregation of Marians, Stockbridge, MA 01263. Reprinted with permission.

Leggatt, L.M., trans. *A Nineteenth Century Miracle: The Brothers Ratisbonne and the Congregation of Notre Dame De Sion.* London, England: Burns Oates & Washbourne Ltd., 1922.

Leseur, Elisabeth. *My Spirit Rejoices.* Manchester, NH: Sophia Institute Press, 1996.

Linn, Matthew, SJ, and Dennis Linn. *Healing Life's Hurts: Healing Memories through Five Stages of Forgiveness.* New York, NY: Paulist Press, 1978.

Lucia, Martin, SSCC. *Rosary Meditations from Mother Teresa of Calcutta.* Mt. Clemens, MI: Apostolate of Perpetual Adoration, 1984.

Madrid, Patrick. *Surprised By Truth.* San Diego: Basilica Press, 1994.

McColgan, Michael. *Open Your Hearts: Messages from Our Lord Jesus and His Blessed Mother.* Santa Barbara, CA: Queenship Publishing Company, 1995.

McCormick, John N., CSSR, and John A. Treinen, CSSR. *What Is the Mass?* Liguori, MO: Liguorian Pamphlets, 1957.

McCurry, Fr. James, OFM CONV. *Kolbe Novena in Honor of the Immaculate Conception.* Libertyville, IL: Marytown Press, 1988.

McKenna, Briege, OSC, with Henry Libersat. *Miracles Do Happen.* Copyright 1987 by Briege McKenna, OSC. Ann Arbor, MI: Servant Publications. Used with permission.

McMahon, John T. *Live the Mass.* Sydney: Pellegrini & Co. Pty. Ltd., 1946.

Menendez, Sr. Josefa. *The Way of Divine Love.* Rockford, IL: Tan Books and Publishers, 1981.

Merton, Thomas. *The Living Bread.* Copyright 1955 Abbey of Our Lady of Gethsemane. Copyright renewed 1984 by the Trustees of the Thomas Merton Legacy Trust. Reprinted by permission of Farrar, Straus & Giroux, Inc.

Meschler, Maurice, SJ. *Life of St. Aloysius Gonzaga*, trans. by a Benedictine of the Perpetual Adoration. St. Louis, MO: B. Herder, 1911.

Moorman, John R. H. *The Spirituality of St. Francis of Assisi: Richest of Poor Men.* Huntington, IN: Our Sunday Visitor, Inc.

Neumann, John, CSSR. *The Autobiography of St. John Neumann,* trans. Alfred C. Rush, CSSR. Boston, MA: St. Paul Books & Media, 1977.

Newman, John Henry Cardinal. *Loss and Gain: The Story of a Convert.* New York: Longmans, Green, & Co., 1896.

Nouwen, Henri J. M. *Can You Drink the Cup?* Notre Dame, IN: Ave Maria. 1996. Used with permission.

O'Brien, Bartholomew J. *The Cure of Ars: Patron Saint of Parish Priests.* Rockford, IL: Tan Books And Publishers, 1987.

O'Connell, Matthew J., trans. *The Eucharist of the Early Christians.* New York, NY: Pueblo Publishing Company, 1978.

Osburn, Charlie, with Fred Lilly. *The Charlie Osburn Story: "You Gotta Give It All to Jesus."* Pensacola, FL: Good News Ministries. Copyright 1986 Charlie Osburn and Fred Lilly.

O'Sullivan, Paul, OP. *The Wonders of the Mass.* Rockford, IL: Tan Books & Publishers, Inc. 1993.

_____. *Saint Philomena The Wonder-Worker.* Rockford, IL: Tan Books and Publishers, Inc., 1993.

Parsons, Heather. *Father Peter Rookey: Man of Miracles.* Dublin, Ireland: Robert Andrew Press, 1994. (20180 Governors Highway, Olympia Fields, IL 60461-1067).

Pastrovicchi, Angelo, OMC. *Saint Joseph of Copertino.* Rockford, IL: Tan Books and Publishers, Inc. 1980.

Paul II, Pope John. *Gift and Mystery: On the Fiftieth Anniversary of My Priestly Ordination.* New York, NY: Doubleday, 1996.

Peers, E. Allison. *The Autobiography of St. Teresa of Avila.* Kansas City, MO. 64141: Sheed and Ward, 115 East Armour Blvd. P.O. Box 419492.

Pennington, M. Basil, OSCO. *Thomas Merton, Brother Monk: The Quest for True Freedom.* San Francisco, CA: Harper & Row, Publishers, 1987.

Perrin, Ste. Marie. *St. Colette and Her Reform,* trans. Mrs. Conor Maguire and ed. George O'Neill, SJ. St. Louis, MO: B. Herder Book Co. 1924.

Petrisko, Thomas W. *The Sorrow, The Sacrifice, and The Triumph.* New York, NY: Touchstone, 1995.

Peyret, Rev. Raymond. *The Cross and the Joy.* Staten Island, NY: Alba House, 1983.

Philipon, M. M., OP, ed. *Conchita, A Mother's Spiritual Diary*, trans. Aloysius J. Owen, SJ. Staten Island, NY: The Society of St. Paul, 1978.

I Am Your Jesus of Mercy, Vol 5. Santa Barbara, CA: Queenship Publishing Company, 1996.

Ramirez, Msgr. Josefino. *Letters to a Brother Priest.* Plattsburgh, NY: Missionaries of the Blessed Sacrament.

Ratisbonne, M. L'Abbe. *The Life and Times of St. Bernard.* New York, NY: D. & J. Sadlier & Co.

Reyna, Msgr. William. *Eucharistic Reflections,* adap. by Winfrid Herbst, SDS, and trans. Ottilie Boediker. Westminster, MD: The Newman Press, 1957.

Roberts, Fr. Kenneth. *You Better Believe It.* Our Sunday Visitor, 1977.

Rosage, David E. *The Bread of Life: Scripture Readings and Reflections to Prepare for the Eucharist.* Ann Arbor, MI: Servant Books, 1979.

Ruffin, Bernard C. *Padre Pio: The True Story.* Huntington, IN: Our Sunday Visitor Publishing Division, 1991.

Schreck, Alan. *Catholic and Christian.* Copyright 1984 by Alan Schreck. Servant Publications, Box 8617, Ann Arbor, MI 48107. Used with permission.

Schug, John A., CAP. *Padre Pio.* Chicago, IL: Franciscan Herald Press, 1983.

Scott, Martin, SJ. *Isaac Jogues: Missioner and Martyr.* New York, NY: P. J. Kenedy & Sons, 1927.

Shea, John Gilmary. *Perils of the Ocean and Wilderness.* Boston, MA: Patrick Donahoe, 1857.

Sheen, Fulton J. *Treasure in Clay: The Autobiography of Fulton J. Sheen.* San Francisco: Ignatius Press, 1980. Reprinted 1993.

_____. *Calvary and the Mass.* Glenview, IL: Coalition in Support of Ecclesia Dei, 1996.

Spaulding, Fr. Jack. *Hope for the Journey.* Santa Barbara, CA: Queenship Publishing Company, 1995.

Stein, Edith. *Essays on Women,* trans. Freda Mary Oben. Washington, D.C.: I.C.S. Publications, 1987.

Stramara, Daniel F., OSB. *Driven by the Spirit.* Pecos, NM: Dove Publications, 1992.

Suarez, Federico. *The Sacrifice of the Altar.* New Rochelle, NY: Scepter Press, 1990.

Tartre, Raymond A., SSS. *The Eucharist Today.* New York, NY: P. J. Kenedy and Sons, 1967.

Terelya, Josyp. *In the Kingdom of the Spirit.* Pueblo, CO: Abba House, 1995.

Tesniere, Albert, sss. *Blessed Peter Julian Eymard: The Priest of the Eucharist,* trans. from the French. New York, NY: Fathers of the Blessed Sacrament, 1936.

The Guardian Angels: Our Heavenly Companions. Rockford, IL: Tan Books and Publishers, 1996.

The Mercy Foundation. Film Documentary, *Living Presence.* P.O. Box 383, Mundelein, IL 60060. Toll Free 888-286-3728.

Thibaut, Dom Raymund. *Abbot Columba Marmion: A Master of the Spiritual Life,* trans. Mother Mary St. Thomas. St. Louis, MO: B. Herder Book Co., 1942.

Thomas, Fr., CMF. *Saint Anthony Mary Claret: A Sketch of His Life and Works.* Chicago, IL: Claretianum, 1950.

Treece, Patricia. *Nothing Short of a Miracle: The Healing Power of the Saints.* New York, NY: Image Books, Doubleday, 1988.

_____. *A Man for Others.* Huntington, IN: Our Sunday Visitor Publishing, 1982.

Trochu, Francis. *Saint Bernadette Soubirous,* trans. John Joyce, sj. New York, NY: Pantheon Books Inc., 1957.

Trosclair, Margaret M. *Father Peter Mary Rookey, osm: Do You Believe that Jesus Can Heal You?* Marrero, LA: Mary's Helpers Publishing Company, 1996.

Uminski, Sigmund H. *No Greater Love: A Story of Saint Stanislaus Kostka.* New York, NY: The Polish Publication Society of America, 1969.

Von Balthasar, Hans Urs. *First Glance at Adrienne von Speyr.* Copyright 1981 Ignatius Press, San Francisco. Used with permission.

Von Speyr, Adrienne. *John: The Discourses of Controversy: Meditations of John 6-12,* trans. Brian McNeil, crv. San Francisco, CA: Ignatius Press, 1993.

Winkworth, Margaret, ed. *Gertrude of Helfta: The Herald of Divine Love.* Mahwah, NJ: Paulist Press, 1993.

Wallace, Susan Helen. *Matt Talbot: His Struggle and His Victory over Alcoholism*. Boston, MA: Pauline Books & Media, 1992.

Waugh, Evelyn. *Edmund Campion*. New York, NY: Sheed & Ward Inc., 1935.

White, Charles. *Mother Seton: Mother of Many Daughters*. Garden City, NY: Doubleday & Co Inc., 1949.

Magazines, Pamphlets and Newspapers

Blache, Claudia. "I Thought I Had Always Believed in the Real Presence." *Perpetual Eucharistic Adoration Newsletter*, Vol 8, No. 1, March 1995, Los Angeles, CA.

Burke, Ray. "Knock and the Eucharist." *The Irish Family*, Friday, February 17, 1995.

D'Arcy, Bishop John M. "The Eucharist: A Response." Diocese of Fort Wayne, South Bend, June 13, 1993. Feast of Corpus Christi

Danylak, Bishop Roman. "Eucharistic Miracle in Korea Reveals Sacred Heart of the Divine Victim." *Heart of the Harvest*, Abba House Publications. 519 W. 11th St. Pueblo, CO 81003.

Doran, Bishop Thomas G. "Jesus is Really Present Because He Loves Us." *The Observer*, Rockford, IL, October 4, 1996.

Forrest, Fr. Tom, CSSR. "The Eucharist and Evangelization." *The Vine*, Catholic Charismatic Renewal Services of Chicago. Blue Island, IL, March, 1996.

Gallio, Daniel. "The Spirit Makes Progress: Development of the Sacred Liturgy to 225 AD." *Immaculata*, Conventual Franciscan Friars of Marytown, Libertyville, IL, Jan/Feb 1996.

Hinnebush, Paul, OP. "The Eucharist as Evangelization." *Homiletic & Pastoral Review*, January 1995.

Kosicki, Fr. George, CSB. "Why I Spend so Many Hours in Eucharistic Adoration: A Day with Fr. George Kosicki, CSB." *Friends of Mercy*, Association of Marian Helpers, Stockbridge, MA 01263.

Kowalska, Faustina M. "My Life from Birth to Death on the Cross will be the Rule for You. Live According to What You See." *Perpetual Eucharistic Adoration Newsletter*, Vol 5, No. 2, October 1992, Los Angeles, CA.

Krewer, Elaine. "Hahn, 'Soak' in Scripture, Sacrament." *The Catholic Post*, Peoria, IL. Vol. LXVIV, No. 25. Sunday, June 28, 1992.

McCarrick, Archbishop Theodore. "The Eucharist: The Center of Our Lives." *Our Sunday Visitor*, January 1, 1995.

McNamara, Joseph. "The Eucharist and the Chastisement: An Interview with Father Gerard McGinnity." *Signs of the Times*, April/May/June 1994.

Myers, Bishop John. "Mother Teresa on Eucharistic Adoration" and "The Eucharist, Sacrifice of Love." *Immaculata: Special Issue, Eucharistic Adoration*, Conventual Franciscan Friars of Marytown. Libertyville, IL.

O'Leary, James O., SJ. "Freedom!" *Company*, 3441 N. Ashland Ave., Chicago, IL 60657.

Odell, Catherine M. "Missionary for Eucharistic Adoration." *Columbia*, August 1995.

Swearingen, Carrie. "The Healing of the Healer." *Immaculata*, Conventual Franciscan Friars of Marytown. Libertyville, IL. March/April 1997.

Tomes, Bro. Bill. "Notes from Brother Bill." *Brothers and Sisters of Love*, P.O. Box 430, Evanston, IL 60204. New Years, 1996

Wood, Charles. "People Praying for Priests." *Catholic Digest*, University of St. Thomas. Des Moines, IA. September 1996.